SARTRE

Peter Caws

The George Washington University

Routledge & Kegan Paul
London, Boston, Melbourne and Henley

First published in 1979
by Routledge & Kegan Paul plc
39 Store Street, London WC1E 7DD,
9 Park Street, Boston, Mass. 02108, USA,
464 St Kilda Road, Melbourne, Victoria 3004, Australia and
Broadway House, Newtown Road,
Henley-on-Thames, Oxon RG9 1EN

First published, with additional notes, as a
paperback in 1984

Photoset in Intertype Garamond,
printed in Great Britain by
Unwin Bros, Gresham Press, Surrey.

British Library Cataloguing in Publication Data
Caws, Peter
Sartre. (The arguments of the philosophers).
1. Sartre, Jean Paul
I. Series
194   B2430.S34   79-40105
ISBN 0-7102-0233-4

To
Mary Ann, Hilary
and Matthew

Contents

Acknowledgments

The dedication of this book acknowledges my greatest human debt, but it acknowledges an intellectual debt as well, especially to Mary Ann Caws, whose enthusiasm for the life of the mind and whose exigent standards with respect to its products have sustained and purged the work.

I am grateful to the Research Foundation of the City University of New York for a Faculty Research Award during the tenure of which I began writing, and to several helpers - Frances Cutler, Ruth Davis, and Frederica Goldsmith, but especially Dharie Vanbimol, whose labours were Herculean - for turning the writing into a finished typescript. My thanks also to Giuliana Carugati for locating many of the published English versions of passages I had cited in my own translation, and to Hugh Silverman for coming to the rescue with some texts which were otherwise unavailable when they were needed.

My debt to students and colleagues - particularly to an insistent group of undergraduates at the University of Kansas, now more than twenty years ago, with whom I first read Sartre seriously - is too extensive to be detailed, but I wish to acknowledge with special thanks the careful reading of the early chapters of the book by Jonathan Moreno.

Finally I must thank the following publishers for permission to cite extended passages from works to which they hold the copyright: The Philosophical Library and Methuen (*Being and Nothingness*), George Braziller (*Saint Genet*), Alfred A. Knopf and Methuen (*Search for a Method*), and New Left Books (*Critique of Dialectical Reason*).

Peter Caws

Notes and Abbreviations

Because this book has been written over a period of time in which there was intense activity in the translation of Sartre's works, many of the citations which in the first draft had to be given in my own versions have in the final text been able to be rephrased to bring them into line with available English versions. In general I have used the available translations even when I found them stylistically infelicitous, and have kept my own only in those cases in which the translator has actually misunderstood the original. It would have been tedious to explain in every case the reasons for dissatisfaction, however, and I have discussed the shortcomings of the translations only when they make a serious difference to the sense of the passage in question.

References are provided in the text, rather than in notes, by names of authors or, in the case of works by Sartre or Simone de Beauvoir, by abbreviations of titles. I have adopted the following conventions: if the abbreviation is in Roman type, then the work is in English; if in Italic type, then it is in French. If the page number is in Roman type, I have just cited or referred to what is on the page in question; if in Italic type then the passage is quoted in my own translation. (The class of references with Roman abbreviations and Italic page numbers is therefore null.) A list of abbreviations used in the references is given below. References to works cited in passing, for which the provision of an abbreviation would have been pointless, are to bibliographical entries in the usual way, but in these cases also my own translations are indicated by italics. In the list below, the abbreviation of the English title is given along with that of the French one, and vice versa, whenever there is a difference and there has been occasion to refer to both versions.

List of Abbreviations

Works in English:

ASJ	*Anti-Semite and Jew (RQJ)*
B	*Baudelaire*
BEM	*Between Existentialism and Marxism*
BN	*Being and Nothingness (EN)*
CA	*The Condemned of Altona*
CP	*The Communists and Peace*
CDR	*Critique of Dialectical Reason (CRD)*
DGL	*The Devil and the Good Lord*
E	*Existentialism*
EA	*Essays in Aesthetics*
EAM	*The Ethics of Ambiguity* (de Beauvoir)
EMO	*The Emotions (ETE)*
FC	*Force of Circumstance* (de Beauvoir)
IM	*Imagination*
INT	'Intentionality'
LPE	*Literary and Philosophical Essays*
L/S	*Life/Situations*
N	*Nausea*
NYT	*New York Times* interview
PI	*Playboy* interview
PL	*Politics and Literature*
POL	*The Prime of Life* (de Beauvoir) *(FA)*
PSI	*The Psychology of Imagination (IE)*
RW	'The Responsibility of the Writer'
SBH	*Sartre by Himself*
SG	*Saint Genet*
SIT	*Situations*
SM	*Search for a Method*
SS	*The Spectre of Stalin*
TE	*The Transcendence of the Ego*
WA	*The Wall*
WIL	*What is Literature?*
WO	*The Words (MO)*
WS	*The Writings of Jean-Paul Sartre* (Contat and Rybalka) *(ES)*

Works in French:

CRD	*Critique de la raison dialectique* (CDR)
EN	*L'Être et le Néant* (BN)

ES   *Les Écrits de Sartre* (Contat and Rybalka) (WS)
ETE   *Esquisse d'une théorie des émotions* (EMO)
FA   *La Force de l'âge* (de Beauvoir) (POL)
IE   *L'Imaginaire* (PSI)
IF   *L'Idiot de la famille* (vols 1 and 2; vol. 3 appears as *IF 3*)
IN   *L'Imagination*
MO   *Les Mots* (WO)
RQJ   *Réflexions sur la question juive* (ASJ)
S   *Situations* (*S I* to *S X*; these correspond to various different titles in English, since they have been translated piecemeal if at all)
TE   *La Transcendance de l'Ego*

Note to second printing: Two significant posthumous works (both Paris, Gallimard, 1983) have appeared. They are:

CDG   *Les Carnets de la drôle de guerre*
CM   *Cahiers pour une morale*

I

Introduction

This book is a reading of Jean-Paul Sartre's philosophical writings. Its aim is to present and criticize the arguments found in those writings, which constitute Sartre's claim to attention from other philosophers. *A* reading: while the arguments I present here are those that have impressed themselves upon me in working my way, sometimes quickly and sometimes slowly, sometimes with delight and sometimes in despair, through Sartre's monumental corpus – about 10,000 pages of it, not counting the fiction and the theatre – I cannot claim that they reflect Sartre's own intentions adequately, or that many of them could not be successfully refuted by other arguments drawn from the same corpus. But still a *reading,* that is to say the result of a careful perusal of those pages, and of reflection on them over a period of years, so that at the same time I do not think that an entirely alternative account of Sartre's philosophical views could reasonably be given.

If by 'argument' is understood a sequence of propositions, beginning from premises laid down with some plausible warrant and proceeding by way of intermediate steps, each accompanied by a justifying reason, to a conclusion firmly established, the discovery of arguments in Sartre's work is not always easy. In the early academic writings (from *The Transcendence of the Ego* to the first chapters of *Being and Nothingness*) he is, it is true, relatively careful and conventional, working within the traditional context of professional philosophy in France; but these works form only a small part of his extraordinary output as a writer, and the arguments in them are not those on which his philosophical reputation most obviously rests. That reputation is mixed: Sartre is admired for his range and insight and relevance, castigated for his looseness and verbosity. On the one hand he has made contributions of the first importance to existential ontology and the Marxist theory of the collective; on the other a great deal of his writing proves on inspection to be merely opinionated, and to make demands on the reader's patience and on the world's supply of paper that can only be called extravagant.

Sartre's philosophy presents itself, not only in its style but in the mode of development of its content, as a series of finished assertions, with little apparent concern for the alternatives and objections usually found in philosophical texts. Much of it is argumentative if not argued, in that it consists of statements, often metaphorical and sometimes outrageous, that cry out for clarification or questioning or contradiction – but these, especially in the later work, are piled upon one another in such profusion that the task of arranging them so as to make possible even the beginning of a counter-argument is a daunting one. Sartre's attitude to the world has been described by Simone de Beauvoir as resting on 'unshakable certainty' (POL 35), and the combination of this with an almost total fluency of language makes for texts that simply overwhelm, rather than convincing on the grounds of reason. But this as it stands is no criticism: to say of an argument that it is dogmatic, insufficiently reasoned, metaphorical, long-winded or arrogant is not to say that it is invalid. The problem is to disentangle it and bring it to light. The first task of this book, then, is to reconstruct the major arguments of Sartre's philosophy in such a way that lucid criticism can be brought to bear on them.

It is important to note at the outset that Sartre's philosophical work has been done in an intellectual and political context the commonplaces of which it presupposes. As they are set down, therefore, many of his arguments are enthymematic, and the missing premisses need to be supplied. Many of them, again, can be clearly understood, and some can be clearly formulated, only in the light of special conditions which may have to be sought elsewhere, in fiction or journalism belonging to the same period. But the period may be very short: although there is a discoverable body of Sartrian doctrine with the kind of stability under change that is characteristic of philosophical systems, the sheer speed with which Sartre seems to have lived from day to day produces surprising fluctuations. Projects are abandoned or metamorphosed, convictions changed or adapted: 'we created our own attitudes, theories, and ideas', says Simone de Beauvoir of herself and Sartre; 'we refused to be tied down to any one of them, preferring to live in a state of permanent revolution' (POL 287). A second and more difficult task, then, is to assemble the arguments into a coherent philosophical structure strong enough to sustain these vagaries. Taking all the works together does make possible the articulation of such a structure, broader in range and more integrally consistent than Sartre's philosophy is often supposed to be. It is commonly said that there are two Sartres, the early existentialist and the later Marxist (just as it is commonly said that there are two Marxes, the early humanist and the later historical materialist), but internal evidence does not bear out the hypothesis of a radical change in philosophical project. At the same time the structure has diachronic as well as synchronic features, so that some more or less sequential exposition is inevitable. I give in the first chapter an overview of Sartre's work and of his intellectual development as they appear from the perspective of a philosophical interest.

There are two other senses of 'argument' which are appropriate to this preliminary discussion: its polemical sense and its dialectical sense. Sartre is always getting into arguments, and when he is at his best the withering and incisive brilliance of his attack recalls Marx's annihilation of some of his own contemporaries. Good examples of this are to be found in his treatment of Lukács in 1949 and of Lévi-Strauss in 1965, both dealt with in chapter IX below. Such attacks are usually forms of defence, and they demolish conclusions rather than establishing them, but they are nevertheless often informative about Sartre's own position. They occur mainly, however, in the occasional writings. In the main philosophical works the notion of argument most consistently exemplified is the dialectical one that is to be found in Plato, when Socrates speaks of 'following the argument where it leads'; it is not known what conclusion will emerge, or even whether one will, but from point to point in the dialogue one turn of inquiry necessitates another, and perhaps in the end the participants just get tired and go home. Most of Sartre's major works peter out in this way: beginning from a relatively concise question and a series of tightly-argued paragraphs, the subdivisions of the work become longer and longer, the digressions more and more substantial, until the whole is concluded with the promise of a second volume, which characteristically fails to appear. It is remarkable, however, how often some other work, not the expected sequel, takes up the thread, not to be sure of the argument as it was left, but of a related one, modified by the addition of premisses or the supervention of conditions easily recovered from other sources of information. A single example will suffice here: at the end of *Being and Nothingness* Sartre promised a work on existential morality; seven years later he abandoned the project – but in the meantime he had written *Anti-Semite and Jew*, and shortly afterwards published *Saint Genet, Actor and Martyr*; these works contain just the elements of such a morality, while avoiding the abstractions whose inevitability in a more theoretical work led him to give up his intention of writing one.

The structure of the major works as just described – from a tightly organized beginning to a verbose and unstructured ending, abruptly cut off – may be plausibly understood as a natural consequence of Sartre's dual allegiance to philosophy and literature: he starts out as a philosopher, with the best of intentions to be lucid and rigorous, but the writer gradually takes over, the distance from conception to expression is progressively reduced, critical restraint yields to enthusiasm, and the whole enterprise gathers momentum. With the stimulus of drugs and political excitement, the very activity of writing occasionally takes on heroic proportions. At the height of the Algerian war and the production of the *Critique of Dialectical Reason*, says Simone de Beauvoir,

> it was not a case of writing as he ordinarily did, pausing to think and make corrections, tearing up a page, starting again; for hours at a stretch he raced across sheet after sheet without rereading them, as though absorbed by ideas that his pen, even at that speed, couldn't keep up with. (FC 385)

In view of the product, this account is entirely believable, and in this particular case even Sartre himself admitted, later, that the argument might have been made more compact (PL 117), but presumably no editor dared intrude; indeed it sometimes seems as if pages must have been dispatched one at a time by runner from the Café Flore to the composing room of the Imprimerie Floch at Mayenne, without passing under any watchful eye at Gallimard.

In these circumstances it would be unreasonable to expect consistency throughout, and only too easy to raise the sort of critical objection that exact minds habitually level at excitable ones. Under such criticism almost any part of the Sartrian edifice might seem vulnerable. And yet the edifice is impressive not only for the consistent quality of its parts as sheer writing – for in spite of its bulk and the rate of its production Sartre's work is, from the point of view of style, a sustained *tour de force* – but also for the sometimes dazzling conceptual intricacy that it displays, for the purposeful articulation of its major components (in spite of their individual incompleteness), and for the firm and probably irrevocable way in which it has settled into the landscape of contemporary philosophy. Sartre's radical engagement with the problems of the modern world preserves a surprising degree of relevance in spite of changing philosophical fashion (indeed it may well be that the historical moment of the greatest relevance of the *Critique of Dialectical Reason* is yet to come).

Sartre's work has been the subject of an enormous amount of exposition and criticism; it may be asked what, apart from the formal exigencies of a publisher's series, justifies still another book. This one can hope, perhaps, to make two contributions. The first is precisely to see Sartre's work as an essentially completed whole, at any rate as far as its philosophical standing is concerned. The still unfinished works will never be finished; if the argument is to continue, it will have to be taken up by others. As to unpublished materials, the forthcoming Pléiade edition may contain literary surprises but it seems less probable that it will contain philosophical ones; between the last volumes of *Situations* and the indispensable appendix to the Contat and Rybalka bibliography (WS 2) the main lacunae in the published corpus have been filled, and unless the notebooks lost between 1930 and 1940 should come to light, or Sartre's health and interests take a joint turn for the better and back to philosophy ('as for philosophy', he said at the time of the publication of the *Critique of Dialectical Reason*, 'I will do no more than make brief mental notes about it, for my own purposes' (BEM 9)), there seems less risk now than formerly in making a comprehensive assessment.

Second, this book may provide a perspective on Sartre's work not easily accessible to those who have a prima-facie sympathy with it – or, conversely, it may provide a means of access for those who do not have such a sympathy. The alleged split between Anglo-Saxon and European philosophical interests would not have become the cliché it has if it had not contained a germ of truth; in fact philosophical traditions and preoccupations have histories much too complicated to be summed up in any such easy formula, but there is a structure behind the formula that may clarify Sartre's relation to parts of the philosophical world more familiar to English-speaking readers. Given that the philosopher is an individual person inhabiting a world that is both natural and social, it follows immediately that there are three large and virtually independent sets of problems to the solution of which he or she may attach importance, each of these sets containing difficulties so profound and so fraught with implications that a philosopher preoccupied with one of them might be pardoned for forgetting, or for not having noticed in the first place, that the others existed. One set consists of problems having to do with the knower's relation to the natural world conceived of as independently given; here will be found perception construed as the basis for empirical knowledge, truth, universals, laws of nature, induction and the rest, and language in so far as this appears as a neutral medium for conveying truths about the world. This is familiar territory, from Locke to Russell and Carnap, and it provides comfortable accommodation for logic and mathematics too as aspects of a Platonically objective order. A second set, having almost no point of intersection with the first, consists of problems having to do with the knower's status as an individual person; here will be found Cartesian doubt (and certainty), subjectivity, consciousness, intentionality, egocentric predicaments and existential dread, and so on. These things may be considered by enthusiasts of the former set to be false problems, surds, inaccessible to anything philosophy has decent criteria for, but to their own partisans they are likely to be matters of overwhelming and immediate moment, beside which curiosity about nature or anything not infused with human subjectivity seems insensitive if not irresponsible.

Phenomenalism belongs to the first of these domains, phenomenology to the second: an ideological gulf reduced to an accident of terminology. These two doctrines represent limiting cases – the examination of the 'immediately given', on the one hand as objective and independent, on the other as relative to consciousness, but in either case as an irreducible ground of certainty, to go beyond which entails philosophical risk. But practically we cannot discover or take our stand upon this ground of certainty without having already incurred the risk, for the entertaining of philosophical propositions and the making of philosophical assertions presuppose our involvement in and reliance upon a society and a language. The third set of problems, then, consists of those that deal with the knower's relation to other knowers, the agent's to other agents: here are found ethics and politics, culture, language construed as a contingent feature of social interaction, cultural and linguistic products such as myth, literature, kinship structures and the rest. Philosophers in the other two problematic domains may feel that the content of this one strays outside philosophy altogether, and if they deal with it at all they tend to do so on their own terms, as the complex behaviour of organized matter on the one hand, the creative interplay of subjectivities on the other, approaches mutually criticized as 'positivist' or 'impressionistic'.

Now if we characterize these three traditional sets of philosophical problems, for the sake of simplicity in reference, as 'objective', 'subjective', and 'collective', we may say of Sartre that he begins in the subjective tradition and moves toward the collective, but that he is completely indifferent to the objective. According to Simone de Beauvoir 'he flatly refused to believe in science', going so far as to maintain 'that microbes and other animalculae invisible to the naked eye simply didn't exist at all' (POL 39). For a writer wholly nurtured in the objective tradition to undertake the very reading, let alone the exposition, of Sartre, especially in view of the latter's punishing long-windedness, requires explanation. The reason for it is a conviction that, whatever ideal unity one might wish for, philosophy must contain a multiplicity of virtually autonomous problematic domains – at least the three I have sketched, for the reasons given, and no doubt at a deeper level of analysis others as well – and that the dismissal of one problematic as unphilosophical in favour of another supposed to embody the essence of philosophy is itself an anti-philosophical act: the domains are complementary, and it is of the greatest importance that workers in each should have some appreciation of what goes on in the others. It is however a reassuring indication of the unity of philosophy that this appreciation can generally be achieved, if one goes about it in the right spirit, in terms intelligible to and compatible with the outlook of one's own domain. There would be no point in trying to make of Sartre an analytic philosopher (although he has his moments of linguistic rigour), but there are grounds on which the two types can meet. The indispensable condition for such a meeting is that one of them should understand what the other is up to, and how he can have come to think his problematic important when (as it seems to us) it obviously overlooks the most critical problems. This requires, as a minimum, a willingness to respect the other's enterprise, and to get clear what he actually said and not what polemical critics say he said. I hope in this book to have made it easier for some readers unacquainted with Sartre to satisfy these conditions.

One final note about the critics: it will be noticed as the book proceeds that I have paid very little attention to the secondary literature. My excuse, if one is needed, is that the series for which this work is intended is called 'The Arguments of the Philosophers' and not 'The Arguments about the Philosophers'; for the latter a quite different approach would have been required, and it would have been impossible within the limits of the book to deal with more than a fraction of the material. Some of the expositions and commentaries through which Sartre has become familiar to those who have been unable or unwilling to read him at first hand, or who having done so felt the need of interpretation, are works of great distinction and importance in their own right. A few are gross oversimplifications if not outright betrayals. But to assess praise or blame here would be invidious even if there were time or room for it.

Note to second printing: Sartre's death in March 1980 removed the remote possibility envisaged above that further works might still be undertaken. However the available philosophical corpus has been extended by about a thousand pages with the publication of the surviving wartime notebooks and the working notes for the first *Morale*. This material does not require any major revision of the views put forward in this book, but it is rich and some notice of it is taken at the end of the next chapter.

I

A Conspectus of Sartre's Writings

It will be useful to begin with a general view of Sartre's output, from start to finish, if only to provide a series of points of reference with respect to which the arguments developed later can be located. For Sartre is, always and above all, a writer; by his own account his vocation as such was explicitly established in infancy, and his self-conscious being consisted, as the title of his autobiography indicates, of words. At the other end of his career the monumental study of Flaubert opens with a question: 'What can we know of a man, today?' whose implicit identification of 'man' with 'writer' is characteristic. Not that this makes him any less a philosopher: philosophy was forced upon him, partly because his ambition to be a novelist and professor of literature led through the philosophical requirements of the École Normale Supérieure, partly by the intrinsic interest of what he found in Bergson and in phenomenology (PI 70). But his properly philosophical writings constitute cuts into a long and almost unbroken syntagma that includes other segments: fiction, criticism, theatre, reportage, political manifestos, editorials; and the whole could not have been produced by a single individual if the mode of its production had not been more or less continuous, rapid, and immediate. The coherence of this *oeuvre* is to be found in the man himself, in his intellectual development and his changing situation. In what follows I shall give some details of minor texts that are unlikely to be alluded to again in the body of the book but shall merely indicate, without elaboration, the occurrence of topics (contingency, bad faith, and so on) which will occupy a major share of attention later on.

Sartre's earliest publications date from 1923, when he was still only seventeen; they consist of a short story and some fragments of a novel, and are worth noting both for the maturity of their style and for their indication of what were to become well-known concerns: the subjective experience of the world in the form of a sickness, the bad faith of mediocrity, the identification of life with writing and the emptiness of official recognition, the contrast between the world as imagined and the world as experienced. In the very first text, 'The Angel of Morbidity', he speaks of 'the nausea, the disgust, of journey's end', and dismisses the hero, who escapes like a coward when his perverse attempt to seduce a consumptive girl leads to a messy attack of the disease, in a final sarcastic sentence: 'he never wrote a thing again and at the age of fifty-five was awarded the Legion of Honor, the indisputable mark of "Bourgeoisie" ' (WS 2:4, 8). These texts antedate Sartre's university studies in philosophy, in the course of which he appears to have acquired 'his idea of contingency and of consciousness as a void in being' (WS 1:6). The first philosophical text to have survived follows in 1927; it is the English version of an article on 'The Theory of the State in Modern French Thought' that appeared in a tri-lingual university review, and again anticipates familiar themes, notably the reduction of the individual (the *moi transcendental* or 'transcendental me') to a role or a function, the tendency of realist methods to conceal idealist ends and to slight existential realities.

Literary and philosophical modes meet for the first time in a fragment, 'The Legend of Truth', published by Nizan in the journal *Bifur* in 1931. We know from Simone de Beauvoir that Sartre at an early stage opposed the concrete reality of being to any attempt to bring it under universal categories:

he went to unheard-of extremes in his total rejection of universals. To him general laws and concepts and all such abstractions were nothing but hot air: people, he maintained, all agreed to accept them because they effectively masked a reality which men found alarming. (POL 30)

It is clear that Sartre misunderstood the role of these categories in science at any rate, but at the time it was a principle of consistency that led him to cast his attack upon them in the form of a legend; to quote Simone de Beauvoir again:

since he placed no faith in universals or generalizations, he denied himself the right even of formulating this repudiation in generalized terms. He had to replace proposition by demonstration [*au lieu de dire, il lui fallait montrer*]. He admired those myths to which Plato, for similar reasons, had had recourse, and did not blush to imitate them. (POL 41)

'The Legend of Truth' as published was part of a larger work whose intention appears to have been to show the inadequacy both of science and ideology as collective enterprises of belief, and to affirm the necessity of individual judgment on the part of exceptional men: artists, writers, and

9

philosophers. The published fragment deals with the levelling effect of scientific and philosophic agreement, in a tone like that of a muted and more reasonable Nietzsche. The need for a truth that can be agreed upon arises out of commerce – nomadic peoples required 'beautiful beliefs', agricultural societies were satisfied with consistent appearances – so that the apparently eternal exactitude of truth is in fact a late cultural invention. Its drawback is that it arrests and distorts (there is an unmistakable echo of Bergson here): 'The earth's slight tremor, when plotted in red ink, is already no longer the same' (WS 2:50). But, worse, it removes altogether the possibility of certain forms of understanding. In the city of merchants a new maxim is published – 'A thing cannot be itself and something other than itself at the same time and in the same respect.' 'By the time the merchants had become familiar with this new law', says Sartre, 'all the roads which could have led toward the past and a historical explanation had been blocked' (WS 2:42). Modern science and philosophy were born among machines and are applicable only to machines; they are adequate neither for the authenticity of individual experience nor for the complexity of human society in its historical development.

In the note that accompanied the publication of this text Nizan described Sartre in these terms: 'Young philosopher. Is preparing a book on destructive philosophy.' This book never appeared. Sartre went off to begin his career as a teacher at Le Havre, the model for Bouville in *Nausea*, a work which he began at about this time as a 'pamphlet on contingency'. But the course of his philosophical development, whatever it was during the years 1931-3, was irreversibly changed by his discovery of phenomenology and his year's residence in Berlin from 1933 to 1934, during which he 'read Husserl, Scheler, Heidegger and Jaspers for the first time' (SM 38). The writings so far taken account of constitute in a sense Sartre's philosophical prehistory; there is a gap of five years between 'The Legend of Truth' and the succeeding publications, but these when they appear belong to the corpus of his mature work. *Imagination* was his first book, and in the same year (1936) 'The Transcendence of the Ego' was published in *Les Recherches philosophiques*. Sartre had worked on the problem of the imagination for his *diplôme d'études supérieures* under the direction of Henri Delacroix, and the early part of *Imagination* no doubt represents the fruit of these researches, but the main interest of the work lies in its resolution of the problems posed by classical conceptions of the image in terms derived from Husserl's theory of intentionality. He is no mere follower of Husserl, however, and in 'The Transcendence of the Ego' criticizes Husserl's transcendental ego in favour of a theory, in some respects not unlike that of Ryle in *The Concept of Mind*, of the self as an object in the world among other objects, to be discovered in much the same way as other selves.

The relation of that contingent self to the world and the justification of its presence there form the problematic of *Nausea* (1938). The second draft of the 'pamphlet on contingency' had been completed in Berlin, but the influence of phenomenological studies on it is not obvious; the final draft was called 'Melancholia' after Dürer's woodcut of that name. (The publisher, Gallimard, chose the eventual title.) These details are relevant because *Nausea* is the existentialist novel *par excellence* and its visceral title had a great deal to do with the public image of the philosophical movement that was to follow. In the following year appeared *The Wall*, a collection of short stories that represent in 'my opinion the peak of Sartre's achievement as a writer of fiction and deal in a more polished form with some now familiar themes as well as introducing new ones: authentic evil in 'Erostratus', the inauthenticity of the ruling class, and anti-semitism, in 'The Childhood of a Leader'. This last is a brilliant study of the infection of existential immediacy, the account of which in the young Lucien has clearly autobiographical elements, by the 'ideas of the dominant class', to borrow a phrase from Marx. Although he was tempted on more than one occasion, at about this period, to join the Communist Party, there is no evidence that Sartre had been much influenced by Marx, and he himself has disclaimed any interest in Marxism up to that time (PI 70). He had, rather, arrived independently at many conclusions of which Marx, if not his inheritors, would have approved.

At the same time Sartre continued to work on phenomenology; a note of January 1939 in *La Nouvelle Revue française*, entitled 'Intentionality: a Fundamental Idea of Husserl's Phenomenology', is of almost Lacedaemonian brevity, one of the most economical and lucid philosophical texts he ever wrote; in the same year *The Emotions*, another fragment, this time of a large projected work on psychology, offers a Husserlian solution to a problem set by James. A phenomenological approach also marks *The Psychology of Imagination* (1940), although this contains a good deal of the rejected second part of *Imagination* that seems on internal evidence to have been written before the year in Berlin. It is the last of what may be called the 'academic' works, in which Sartre deals with relatively restricted topics in a relatively conventional way. Thereafter all the major works will be monumental and original, written more freely and with more force, and less concerned, on the philosophical side, with the exigencies of professional style. Two such works, one literary and one philosophical, were in progress at this time: the long novel *Roads to Freedom*, and *Being and Nothingness*. In the latter is to be seen conspicuously the influence of Heidegger, to whom Sartre refers occasionally in earlier works although he seems not to have studied him in depth until he gave his seminar on the subject to a group of priests, in a prison camp where Heidegger was the only philosopher the Germans would allow him to read (PI 70).

The concept that dominates Sartre's writing during the period of the

German occupation of France is that of freedom, but his involvement with it was already of long standing – the project for *Roads to Freedom* dates from 1938. Two plays written and staged during the occupation, *The Flies* and *No Exit*, deal with different aspects of it, political and interpersonal. The immediate political force of *The Flies* was lost under its classical disguise, but there is no doubt that the war stimulated a development of Sartre's thought about freedom in the direction of active participation in political affairs.

> His new morality was based on the notion of 'genuineness' ...
> [which] required every man to shoulder the responsibility of his
> situation in life; and the only way in which he could do so was to
> transcend that situation by engaging upon some course of action.
> Any other attitude was mere escapist pretense, a masquerade based
> upon insincerity. (POL 342)

'Insincerity' here is a translation of '*mauvaise foi*', a crucial term for Sartre sometimes rendered as 'self-deception' but best left simply as 'bad faith', an inadequate but the least misleading equivalent. The concept was Sartre's answer to the Freudian unconscious, all of whose properties he believed he could account for in its terms; *Being and Nothingness* can most plausibly be read as a competitor of psychoanalysis, an alternative view of the status in the world of the 'existing individual', to use Kierkegaard's expression. It brings together into systematic form the sum of Sartre's philosophical preoccupations up to that point, but leaves dangling at the end the problem of moral action towards which those preoccupations have been obviously leading.

The moral side of existentialism – a term introduced in 1943 by Gabriel Marcel (WS 1:12) – is dealt with at a popular level in a lecture delivered by Sartre at the Club Maintenant on 28 October 1945, published in the following year as *Existentialism is a Humanism*. (A brilliant burlesque of this public occasion is to be found in Boris Vian's account, in *L'Écume des jours*, XXVIII, of a lecture by Jean-Sol Partre, author of a work on electric signs called *La Lettre et le néon*.) This was intended as a defence of existentialism against charges of defeatism, sordidness, anti-humanism and the like, and it is a model of straightforward clarity. It is also 'the only work Sartre has largely rejected' (WS 1:133), but his rejection is not binding on the reader who finds its arguments convincing. In fact most of them hold up admirably once Sartre's premises are granted, and his discontent presumably springs from the fact that the premises themselves are not argued for at any length, appearing rather as a ready-made body of doctrine than as the outcome of long philosophical reflection. This was the period of existentialism as a vogue and the beginning of Sartre's notoriety, a period when he occupied an almost wholly independent position philosophically and politically. Apart from some attempts during the occupation to come to terms with the communists he had not engaged in organized politics; he now found himself the moving spirit in a group that rejected the bourgeois condition of pre-war France and looked forward to a new social order, but he was critical both of the inequalities inherent in American free enterprise and of the repressions inherent in Stalinist communism. Sartre had visited the United States as a journalist in 1945, bringing back decided opinions about alienation, race relations and the like. He had projected but abandoned a series of 'sketches on America' (FC 76); an echo of this project is perhaps to be found in the short play *The Respectful Prostitute*, in which a white prostitute is the crucial witness in the coming trial of a black who is accused of raping her. In the original version she agreed, under pressure from the son of a Southern Senator, to testify against the black; but in the version shown in the Soviet Union and elsewhere Sartre rewrote the ending and had her refuse to testify, on the grounds that the breakdown in class solidarity represented by her siding with the oppressors would comfort capitalism and discourage the revolution.

This adaptability of art to didactic politics aroused a certain amount of cynicism in Sartre's critics, but it is not inconsistent with his own view, at this time, of the responsibility of the writer. The group alluded to above founded in 1945, under Sartre's leadership, the review *Les Temps modernes*, whose opening statement begins: 'All writers of bourgeois origin have experienced the temptation to irresponsibility: for a century now it has been the tradition in literary careers' (S II·9). The ambitions of *Les Temps modernes* were to contribute to the changing of post-war society, to defend the rights of the person, and at the same time to keep up literary standards. This conception of writing as committed, as making a real difference in the world, becomes central for Sartre in the years immediately after the war; in 1946 he delivered an address on 'The Responsibility of the Writer' for the founding of UNESCO, and in 1947, in *Les Temps modernes*, he published *What is Literature?*, which took up in a more systematic way the questions of what it is to be a writer, why anyone should write, and for whom. This work ends with a discussion of 'the situation of the writer in 1947', which has often been considered to date the whole irremediably; in one sense it does, of course, but in another it is the condition for the applicability of the theory of literature that is being put forward, to 1947 or to any other time, since Sartre's concept of situation requires a specific personal and historical reference on pain of irrelevant abstraction. The question of what it is to be a writer *in general* is an empty one. Similarly, philosophical questions posed out of any historical context can only produce pious futilities.

The danger in such an attitude is its elevation of the parochial to world-historical status, a move which has always been easy for the French but which in Sartre acquires the respectability of a philosophical principle. It is important to understand what he takes this principle to involve. Simone de Beauvoir interprets it in biographical terms, as a disillusionment with literature induced by popular success: 'Literature had shed its sacred character, so be it; henceforth he would posit the absolute in the ephemeral; imprisoned in his own epoch, he would choose that epoch against eternity, consenting to perish entirely along with it' (FC 40-1). But this does not do justice to the philosophical issue. One of the most important of Sartre's concepts, to the realization of which, it would not be implausible to say, his career has been devoted, is his version of the Hegelian 'concrete universal', the particular, local, historical episode, played out by a particular person or persons, which captures and embodies a universal truth – which constitutes, indeed, the only possible way in which such a truth could be apprehended. For there are only men, and things, and real relations between them (*cf.* SM 77); philosophical abstractions are useful only to the extent that they throw light on these realities or, to adopt a moral point of view, ameliorate them. Philosophy has traditionally been the domain of necessity, but its point of application lies in contingency. (We might say that this has always been true, but that its truth has been concealed by the fact that the contingency in question was precisely that of the philosopher's personal apprehension of necessity.) And it is for this reason that Sartre has turned so often to the theatre, the very paradigm of the ephemeral; for him the theatre is philosophical, and philosophy is dramatic, because both are concerned with man *in action* (BEM 12). But their modalities remain distinct. *No Exit* was not a restatement of *Being and Nothingness*; it was not philosophy in theatrical form, but theatre formed by philosophy, which the audience could appreciate as theatre without looking for a philosophical message in it (BEM 10).

To return to the chronology: in keeping with these convictions Sartre directed his attention, at about this time, to a number of topical problems – the Stalinist distortion of Marxism, for example ('Materialism and Revolution'), and anti-semitism as a paradigm of bad faith, a topic already touched upon in the conclusion of 'The Childhood of a Leader' (*Anti-Semite and Jew* – both works from 1946). But the most interesting form of contingency remains the human individual self, especially the writer; and Sartre published in 1947 the first of his extended studies of literary figures, *Baudelaire*. Baudelaire, for Sartre, is an example of the man who makes an 'original choice' of the contingency he happens to be born into, rather than of a new project; the study concentrates, therefore, on his relations with his mother and step-father, the French courts that condemned *Les Fleurs du mal*, and so on. It says hardly anything about Baudelaire's poetry, being intended originally as an introduction to his confessional writings. It is among the more speculative and less brilliant of Sartre's works, but hardly merited, even so, the outraged scorn it aroused on the part of poets and critics, for some of whom it constituted, as Pierre Reverdy put it, Sartre's own suicide. This reaction can be interpreted as vindicating Sartre's view of the artificially sacred character of literature, but it can also be seen as pointing to a limitation in his own conception of it.

At the end of *Being and Nothingness* Sartre had announced a work on existential morality as a project for the near future. This *Morale* never appeared, for a complex series of reasons. Immediately after the war, and for several years, Sartre was preoccupied with political matters and with the public career of existentialism, so that much of his output was in the form of lectures and occasional publications. Then his fascination for individuals 'in situation' – Baudelaire, Mallarmé, Genet – seems to have taken precedence over more purely philosophical concerns. When political activity decreased it was because political theory was a growing preoccupation, and in an interview published in 1960 Sartre describes a search, during the previous fifteen years, for 'the political foundations of anthropology' (BEM 9). Part of this search involved re-thinking the whole question of social reality from a Marxist point of view; Sartre's definitive abandonment of the *Morale* came in 1950, along with an intensive period of reading in history and economics and a re-reading of Marx, because of a conviction that

> 'the moral attitude appears when technical and social conditions
> render positive forms of conduct impossible. Ethics is a collection of
> idealistic tricks intended to enable us to live the life imposed on us
> by the poverty of our resources and the insufficiency of our
> techniques'. (FC 199 – Simone de Beauvoir is here quoting an
> unpublished note of Sartre's own.)

And meanwhile, in any case, Simone de Beauvoir had published *The Ethics of Ambiguity*, a work which sprang precisely from an attempt to 'base a morality on *Being and Nothingness*', which she thought possible 'if one converted the vain desire to be into an assumption of existence' (FC 67). (In 1964-5 Sartre took up again a project for a *Morale*, this time using as a point of departure the *Critique of Dialectical Reason*, in connection with a colloquium on 'Morals and Society' organized in Rome by the Gramsci Institute. It is reported that in 1969 he considered himself to have worked out completely a system of dialectical ethics, which needed only to be written up for publication (WS 1:449)).

A great deal of what would no doubt have gone into the *Morale* is in fact to be found, as I have indicated, in *Saint Genet, Actor and Martyr*, published in 1952. This includes a long meditation on the problem of Good and Evil (a problem that is dealt with on the level of ambiguity in practice in the play *The Devil and the Good Lord* of the previous year) and on the respective roles of the criminal and the saint in keeping up the appearances of bourgeois morality. There are echoes of these problems in the later play *The Condemned of Altona* (1959), which however refers also, among other things, to the practical situation of French soldiers who had been involved in torture in Algeria. (Torture and persecution form a recurrent theme in Sartre's works addressed more or less explicitly to the French people – *The Victors* of 1946 refers back to the activities of collaborators during the occupation.) The Algerian problem as well as the Soviet invasion of Hungary in 1956 were matters of concern in the late 1950s; the latter was the occasion of Sartre's break with the French Communist Party, 'regretfully, but completely' (FC 360). Since the occupation he had had an uneven but on the whole sympathetic relationship with the Party, on the grounds that if a choice had to be made between capitalism and communism, communism was the only acceptable alternative, since no other viable road to socialism seemed to present itself. In *The Communists and Peace* of 1952-4 he had come to its defence against the rabid anti-communism of the epoch; in *The Spectre of Stalin* of 1956-7 he lamented that after Hungary the French Left found itself once more having to refuse both Soviet repression and Western colonialist adventurism (as represented by the Anglo-French Suez episode), even though the Soviet Union remained the only embodiment, bloody and self-destructive as it might be, of authentic socialism (SS 61). But while he broke with the Party (of which, it should be recalled, he had never been a member) he did not give up hope for it, resolving to help in its further de-Stalinization (SS 108).

The Communists and Peace was the first product of Sartre's re-examination of Marxism; it contains not only a vivid and detailed criticism of Party policies, but also a great deal of theoretical reflection on the notion of the collective and the idea of class. The mature working-out of these preoccupations, and the formulation of a radically dialectical view of history – albeit history of a somewhat local kind, namely social and political developments in France since the revolution, with special reference, at the end, to Algeria – are to be found in the *Critique of Dialectical Reason* (1960), which had been preceded by an attempt in *Search for a Method* to resolve the apparent antinomy between existential freedom and uniqueness on the one hand, and Marxist–historical collectivity and determination on the other. The method yielded by this inquiry had been intended since 1956 for use on the case of Flaubert, to whose life Sartre turned attention seriously in the intervals of writing his own (*The Words*, 1963) and thereafter more or less continuously; two volumes of *L'Idiot de la famille* appeared in 1970 and a third in 1972. It would be fair to say that Flaubert has dominated Sartre's last twenty years and that his presence is to be reckoned with from the latter's childhood when he first read *Madame Bovary* (WO. 55-6). The deeper reasons for this affinity are beyond the scope of the present study, but it is relevant for our purposes to note the status of Sartre's later philosophy as stimulated by non-philosophical interests and constituting a series of digressions from them, originating in his own image as 'written hernias' which occur when 'one is writing works which are non-philosophical, while still ruminating on philosophy' (BEM 10). Philosophical ideas proliferated for him 'like a generalized cancer' and were likely to be put into whatever he happened to be writing, until he was able to organize them into a properly philosophical work and so get them out of his system. The *Critique*, to extend (as Sartre does) this somewhat distasteful clinical imagery, is thus represented as a necessary purge which will enable *L'Idiot de la famille* to dispense with a truss (BEM 9, 11).

The new dialectical *Morale* referred to above, the second volume of the *Critique*, and the fourth volume of the Flaubert ⫫ an extended *explication de texte* of *Madame Bovary* – represent Sartre's major unfinished projects. The many occasional texts of the last decades include some striking philosophical clarifications, especially in an interview with Pierre Verstraeten on 'The Writer and his Language' in 1965, another with a group at the Sorbonne on anthropology in 1966, and more recently the 'Self-Portrait at Seventy' with Michel Contat (1975), as well as a remarkable dramatic attack on psychoanalysis in 'The Man with a Tape-recorder' (BEM 199 ff.). In the last fifteen years Sartre's refusal of the Nobel Prize in 1964, his participation in the Russell War Crimes Tribunal from 1967, his reaction to the events of May 1968, and his involvement with the leftist publication *La Cause du peuple* from 1970 on, have demonstrated in sometimes unexpected ways what the French would call the 'actuality' of his philosophy. I have in mind here less his overt political action – for example his support of Maoist and other groups on the radical left just because of the violence of their opposition to the established order – than the ready applicability of the categories of his later thought to real, although usually short-lived, features of social organization at a time of practical if not overt imperialism and of incipient revolution. The fact that the imperialism is not overthrown, that the revolution is never more than incipient, is evidence more of the character of collective being, poised, like individual being, always on the brink of its own future, than of the error of Sartre's analysis.

Philosophical thought itself, after all, partakes of temporality in just this way. Any philosophy worth the name – and in Sartre's view it is a rarity – must be 'simultaneously a totalization of knowledge, a method, a regulative Idea, an effective weapon, and a community of language' (SM 6); it is thus a collective and historical activity, to be transcended when the appropriate conditions arise. And Wittgenstein's remark about his own work in the *Tractatus* – that 'anyone who understands my propositions eventually recognizes them as nonsensical, when he has used them as steps – to climb up beyond them. (He must, so to speak, throw away the ladder after he has climbed up it.)' (Wittgenstein 1961: 151) – is echoed independently by Sartre in a far more general sense when he says (PL 110-11) that philosophy is 'designed to cancel itself out' and that it is continually destroyed and reborn. Also any given philosophical project may

17

come to an end, indeed at the end of life it must. 'I have decided', says Sartre, 'that I have said everything I had to say' – but he reminds us in the same place that coming to an end is not the same as finishing, for 'no man who undertakes a work of literature or philosophy ever finishes' (L/S 20).

Note to second printing: Les Carnets de la drôle de guerre (Notebooks from the Phony War) and *Cahiers pour une morale (Notes for a Treatise on Morals)*, the latter written in 1947–8, constitute Sartre's posthumous *oeuvre* to date. However the early notes are the more relevant to morality, which tends to be occluded in the later ones by history, politics, and metaphysics. In the wartime notebooks Sartre is in pursuit of a personal notion of authenticity, and refuses consciousness as a refuge, an ivory tower, not now because it is an inconsistent notion but because it is, for him, an inauthentic one (*CDG* 393–7). In the notes for the *Morale* he is much preoccupied with conceptual puzzles left over from *Being and Nothingness,* as well as developing his awakened notion of history.

What is striking in the reflections on history is that they are as yet unaffected by the compulsive Marxism of the *Critique,* that they represent anticipatory criticisms of the positions taken there and approach the more mature conclusions of the third volume of the *Idiot.* But it is clear why the project of the *Morale* had to be left in suspense while Sartre struggled with the problem of history: morality according to him depends on history, it can only come into being at the end of history (*CM* 149). Another reason is Sartre's obvious ambivalence about what morality is: we learn not only that it is correlative to history but that it is for him indistinguishable from metaphysics (*CDG* 106), that it is a project of salvation (*CDG* 107), that it is a system of ends (*CDG* 136), that it is a permanent conversion (*CM* 12), that it is 'the goal one gives oneself when there is no goal' (*CM 110*).

Both books contain extended passages of typical conceptual and stylistic brilliance that are worth the effort of disentangling from the rest and enrich (without essentially modifying) the totality of Sartre's work. It seems worth drawing special attention to the explicit reflections on the influence of Heidegger (*CDG* 224), to long and thoughtful essays on violence (*CM* 178ff.) and on action as creation (*CM* 524ff.), and to a poignant self-analysis of the writer who could not manage to be a poet and yet discovered 'with amazed stupor that I had precisely created with my prose the beautiful object ... I vainly demanded of poetry' (*CDG* 381, *391*) – an early text that it seems appropriate to read, with the benefits of hindsight, in conjunction with the remarks on pp. 25–7 below.

II

Language and its Uses:
Literature and Philosophy

That philosophy is chiefly a linguistic activity has come to be generally recognized in this century. Whether or not the realities it deals with are taken to transcend language, the facts that its arguments are always conducted in some language, and that the structure and history of that language will have an effect on those arguments, seem inescapable. The consequences of this view for the philosopher's conception of his own activity have commanded less attention. He may think of himself as a thinker, but his thought will be barren (apart from any private benefits it may confer) if he is not also a talker or a writer. For the most part this goes without saying: talking and writing are natural activities and no great fuss need be made about them. The question is worth raising, however, as to the relation between thought and its verbal expression – whether the latter is, utilitarian considerations apart, merely a transcription of the former, or whether the former can be said to have an antecedent and independent status at all. Socrates was a talker; does it make sense to speak of Socratic thought, apart from what we suppose actually to have been said by Socrates together with what follows from it? Is what a philosopher writes (e.g., the *Tractatus*) to be regarded in a different light from what his listeners remember him to have said (e.g., most of Wittgenstein published later than the *Investigations*)?

The point of these reflections, in the present context, derives precisely from Sartre's status as a writer, always and above all. This need not detract from his status as a philosopher: 'writer' is generic, 'philosopher' specific; writing is a mode of being, philosophy a mode of action. But putting things in this order does suggest a relation between thought and language quite different from that which is characteristic of most English-speaking philosophers. We observed at the beginning of the last chapter a tendency to assume that to be a man and to be a writer are more or less equivalent conditions, and evidences of this specialized perspective on the world are

19

to be found throughout. As a small but significant example, Sartre recounts in *The Words* how the complaints of his grandfather about royalties opened his eyes to 'the exploitation of man by man' (WO 27), so that even the roots of his Marxist sensibilities can be placed in a literary context. It is natural enough that the first half of the only major autobiographical text should be called 'Reading', its second half 'Writing'; that, in Sartre's universe, is enough for a life.

To a philosopher thus formed and sustained by it, language might be expected to be an object of special theoretical concern. But Sartre is not a philosopher of language in any of the senses in which that appellation has come to be understood in contemporary philosophy. To begin with, he has not the slightest interest in technical linguistics, and given his views of the scientific enterprise in general it would be unreasonable to expect this. His attitude to science has something in common with that of Sherlock Holmes to the Copernican theory: it is irrelevant to his purpose, it can only get in the way – worse, it puts everything in just the wrong light. So it comes as no surprise to find him, in an essay on Brice Parain's *Recherches sur la nature et les fonctions du langage*, dismissing linguistics with a certain scorn. The linguist deals with an anonymous language:

> words are thrown on the table, killed and cooked, like dead fish. In short, the linguist studies language when nobody is speaking it. Dead words, dead concepts: the word 'freedom' as it is fished out of a text, not this word living, intoxicating, irritating, mortal, as it resounds today in angry or enthusiastic speech. Parain, for his part, cares about language 'as it is spoken'. (S I:178)

This rhetoric is immoderate – the linguist might reply that to under-stand language when nobody is speaking it is essential if we are to understand how it works when somebody is doing so. But Sartre is less concerned with how *it* works than with the speaker's situation, and from this perspective the changes that have taken place in linguistics do not improve matters much. The distinction between deep and surface struc-tures and the consequent possibility of a slippage between them does, it is true, bring under the scope of linguistic analysis a phenomenon that Sartre goes on to describe: 'Words drink our thought before we have time to recognize it. We have a vague intention, we clarify it by means of words and suddenly we find ourselves saying something quite different from what we meant' (LPE 143). But this remark, while it corresponds neatly to his view of action in a more general sense, is in fact intended less to throw light on the nature of language than to support Parain's view of lying, which the latter thinks impossible: 'There are no liars. There are only the oppressed who manage with language as best they can' (ibid.). This connection between morality and language is typical of Sartre's attitude; it may be worth further attention from linguists.

In the second place, Sartre's interests are characteristically ontological or ethical (later political) rather than epistemological or logical, and this also distinguishes his concerns about language from those of many other contemporary philosophers. For the existentalist, language poses a special difficulty because it is essentially a collective entity – the idea of a private language, suitable for a radically individual subject, makes no sense. In the early Sartre this can only be left as an unresolved ambiguity. He expresses it through the person of the misanthropic hero of 'Erostratus':

> Words for example: I wanted *my own* words. But the ones I used
> have dragged through I don't know how many consciences; they
> arrange themselves in my head by virtue of the habits I have picked
> up from the others and it is not without repugnance that I use them
> in writing to you. (WA 49)

But it was the natural exteriority of language rather than its social character that first impressed itself upon Sartre, and this leaves the existential subject unchallenged. Looking back on his childhood he admits to an early confusion of words with things, so that men in the park and animals in the zoo seemed less real than their counterparts in the books of his grandfather's library (WO 31-2), and the thing-like qualities of words remain important for him, at any rate as far as their literary use is concerned. This exteriority of language is a mode of constitution of the world before it is a mode of production of the individual. Sartre describes the soliloquies of Genet's early wanderings:

> Who is speaking? Nobody. Or rather, language itself. And what is
> language when it speaks to itself if not the world with its suns, its
> breezes, its marble steps and its flower gardens, *the world producing itself
> in the verbal attribute?* (SG 303)

The thing-like character of words, however, is ambiguous; from their role as standing for, in the sense of *replacing*, objects, Sartre rapidly moves on to their being natural objects in their own right, and thence to their standing for other objects in the sense of *referring* to them. It is as natural objects in their own right that the creative writer first uses them, as constituents of a magical domain. 'You create words, or rather you create combinations of words, just as a child might build a sandcastle – for the beauty of the thing itself, not in order to show it off' (PL 81). Even in this use, of course, words have their meanings, but the meanings 'impregnate them like a soul' (RW 58) – words are as it were naturally *significant* objects, capable of natural relations among themselves which have nothing to do with the establishment of any system of rational ideas. But – and this is important for an understanding of Sartre's career as a writer – it proves impossible to cling for ever to the innocence of word-play on this level. The word in itself drops out of the field of attention, we see through it to the thing or the idea it designates. Language becomes a relationship not only between us and the world, but also between each of us and the others. Now all theories of language have to account for this sign-relation, which is sometimes taken to inhere in the structure of language itself; for Sartre, however, the constitution of a sign as such springs from the person as signifier. The signifying relation is dealt with in *Being and Nothingness* first in connection with the special involvement with the Other that is represented by the phenomenon of love.

This phenomenon is considered under the modality of seduction, which represents, for Sartre, the attempt to persuade another person to recognize oneself as 'a fulness of being'; it is a more agreeable form of Hegel's 'fight to the death for pure prestige' in the dialectic of the Master and the Slave (Kojève 1969: 7). The enterprise of the seducer is to bring the loved one to see him as signifying at once his own existential depth and his setting in and power over the world. He proposes himself as such an object for the other: but 'this proposal could not be sufficient in itself; it is only a besieging of the Other. It cannot take on value as fact without the consent of the Other's freedom' (BN 372). This is the difference, as Sartre points out, between his case and Hegel's, since the Master does not care about the Slave's freedom (a mistake on his part, because the Slave's merely slavish recognition does him no good).

The proposition by the other of the signifying object, won by the self as signifier, may be thought to presuppose language; Sartre is prepared to go one better and say that it *is* language.

> For while psychological and historical problems exist with regard to the existence, the learning and the use of a *particular* language, there is no special problem concerning what is called the discovery or invention of language. Language is not a phenomenon added on to being-for-others. It *is* originally being-for-others; that is, it is the fact that a subjectivity experiences itself as an object for the Other. In a universe of pure objects language could under no circumstance have been 'invented' since it presupposes an original relation to another subject. (ibid.)

He goes on to cite approvingly the Heideggerian formula 'I am what I say': I *am* language because my acts and projects once exteriorized have 'a meaning which escapes me and which I experience'. This is consistent both with his conception of himself in *The Words* and with the critique of subjectivity in *The Transcendence of the Ego*.

Now we may be ready enough to concede that 'the signifying movement – inasmuch as language is at once an immediate attitude of each person in relation to all and a human product – is itself a project' (SM 172), without being convinced that the problem of the invention of *language* is thereby solved. The affinity of Sartre's position with that of

Husserl in the *Cartesian Meditations* is striking: what confers reality on me as a subject in a world along with others, as distinct from a subject solipsistically imprisoned, is for Husserl the experience of 'a *universal superaddition of sense to my primordial world* ... ; the other Ego makes constitutionally possible a new infinite domain of what is "other" ' (Husserl 1960: 107). What is lacking in Sartre is a *carrier* for this sense; the sense is given in the recognition of the other, but the language is not. The problem of the invention of language is not just the problem of the emergence of sense, it is also the problem of the availability of a structure capable of being invested with this sense. It has been suggested that in the convergence of a structure of sense with one of sound, language can 'come into being all at once' (Lévi-Strauss 1966: xlvii). If so, the independent character of this sound structure is all-important; it is this that has been studied by phonologists and, in its later association with the structure of sense, by grammarians, and it is this side of the matter that Sartre for the most part ignores. He does, it is true, compare language in one place to 'a sort of vast electronic system: you push certain buttons and you can get certain results' (PL 77-8); but he does not inquire into the structure of the system as such. But once again this is not a matter for surprise. For Sartre's views of significance in the wider sense, and of meaning, stress the situation of the user of language rather than the structure of what he uses. In consequence his interpretation of some key terms of linguistics differs from the interpretation of the same terms by linguists themselves. The pair signifier/signified (*signifiant/signifié*) is a case in point.

We have already seen that for Sartre the subject himself is the true signifier; the signified, naturally enough, will be the object (PL 86). Linguists have found such a view inadequate because it leads to ambiguities, the same object being capable of appearing under different descriptions or concepts, and the same subject capable of expressing himself in a variety of ways; since Saussure the essential sign-relation has been between a concept as the signified and an idealized sound-element as the signifier, a more modest but surer connection. But Sartre's interest in the matter is on a different scale, as it were, or along a different dimension. He defines 'signification' as 'a conventional relationship which makes a present object the substitute of an absent object', hence as not able to belong to a thing but needing to be 'conferred upon [it] from without by a signifying intention', in order to contrast it with 'meaning' as 'the participation of the being of a present reality in the being of other realities, whether present or absent, visible or invisible, and, eventually, in the universe' (SG 304). (It is worth noting here that he gives elsewhere a quite different definition of 'signification' as 'the logical entity constituted by words, the meaning of a sentence' (PL 86), which suggests a general caution to be observed, in dealing with Sartre's thought, against placing too much confidence in the consistency of his vocabulary – the rule that language is to be caught alive in a situation applies to his own philosophical discourse.) The contrast is illustrated as follows: 'The siglum "XVII" *signifies* a certain century, but in museums that entire period clings like a veil, like a spider's web, to the curls of a wig, escapes in whiffs from a sedan chair' (SG 304). So it is not words that have meaning, but things themselves – but once again cultural things, elements of the practico-inert. We are surrounded by things that are meaningful for us, whose 'transcendence has fallen into immanence,' i.e., which permeate our human world rather than belonging to an objective natural world.

Things have meaning, persons signify; language, in all this, is a tool men have devised to bring themselves into relation with one another and with things, a tool which has its own objectivity in the world of things, so that languages too can have meanings, although not the meanings linguists mean by the term. Nobody can doubt that 'French', which *signifies* a certain language, 'clings' to a literature, a cuisine, a style of life and thought, just as Sartre's 'XVII' clung to the wig and the sedan chair. But leaving aside that kind of difference between languages, the function of words within a language is to bring the individual into the universal.

> Words belong to everybody; they are man himself as universal
> subject. If I say that I am unhappy, anyone will understand me, for
> anyone could have said and will be able to say that he is unhappy,
> and consequently, insofar as I am *understood*, I am anyone. (SG 43-4)

We encounter here, not for the first time and certainly not for the last, the root dilemma of Sartre's philosophy: the antinomy of the individual and the collective. As in 'Erostratus', and under a different modality in 'The Legend of Truth', the use of a common vehicle has a levelling effect, a thrust towards anonymity; but there is no alternative, without it one would be nothing. The individual must therefore be constructed on the other side of the universal, as it were; being 'just anybody' (*n'importe qui*, to use Sartre's later formula) and using a language common to everybody, it nevertheless speaks or writes itself as unique. 'If he speaks', says Sartre of Genet, 'it is in order to hear himself *as Another*; when he writes, it is in order to read himself' (SG 427).

Once again Sartre implicitly identifies man and writer; even for men who do not write, their insertion into the world is an inscription, taking the form of language. In the vocabulary of more recent French philosophy this might be generalized to the making of some trace in the world, altering things, no matter how slightly, in a significant way. But Sartre would not agree that any abstract structure of language can have a determining force in this matter, and would certainly reject the structuralist formula 'I am *written*', in spite of his early conviction that language came to him from elsewhere (*cf.* 'It talks in my head', WO 218). For him the writer is free, and the exigencies of language are there as a challenge

to be overcome. To be sure, words have their own history and interrelations; and this historical and structural fixity has seemed to some people
to give language the upper hand, so that we can no longer say what we
want to say but are bound to say what it wants us to say. Sartre is rightly
scornful of this view. To those who would complain that language is
always inadequate for our purposes, that we are imprisoned in it, and so
on, he replies that these conditions are just what makes language
interesting, that the writer is indebted to them for the challenge and the
opportunity they present: 'That's his job. That is what we call style. . . .
The writer . . . ought to make this contradiction the very stuff of his
writing' (PL 87-8).

For Sartre there are three kinds of writing. On one side stands poetry,
in which words are used as natural objects – or if not wholly natural, then
practico-inert, that is to say existing alongside natural objects and at first
glance indistinguishable from them, since to the unreflective person
growing up in the modern world nature and culture present themselves as
an undivided whole; nature is cultural, with its farms, country lanes,
avenues of trees, and culture is natural, with its immemorial customs, its
language belonging to the soil, and its music to the elements. In poetry
language is opaque. On the other side stands prose, in which words are
used as conventional signs and are therefore transparent – what we hear or
read is the content of what is said or written and we do not attend to the
words as such. But there are two kinds of prose, literary and philosophical,
the former still coloured by the thing-like nature of words, the latter in
principle purified of it. If a literary writer describes a table, he does it in
such a way

> that that combination of words constitutes a kind of reproduction or
> bodying-forth of the table, so that the table is as it were incarnate in
> the words. . . . When I am writing what is known as literary prose,
> then, that aspect is always present; otherwise there would be no
> point in writing in that language. On the other hand, the most
> difficult thing about philosophical communication is that it is purely
> a question of communication and nothing else. When I wrote *Being
> and Nothingness* it was uniquely in order to communicate by means of
> symbols. (PL 82-3)

The object of literary prose is to bring author and reader together to the
experience of the universal singular or the concrete universal (PL 96); the
episode, the event of the literary work is particular and unique, like any
concrete moment at an actual place, but its detachment from real space and
time, its shared character (with many readers, perhaps), its paradigmatic
quality lend it universality. If there is sufficient community of language
and experience this place of the universal singular 'is where really the
deepest part of literary communication can take place' (ibid.). Such

communication is not conceptual; if it is to succeed the participants must have an understanding of their desires and of their history, the inner and the outer components of existential situation, but the essential feature of literature is that these enter it concretely and not abstractly. Philosophy, on the other hand, is wholly conceptual.

> As I see it the point of philosophy – which is neither that of anthropology nor that of any kind of science of man, nor is it even that of history – is to come as close as possible, by means of conceptual approximation, to the level of the concrete universal as given us in prose. (PL 108)

Here it is precisely not a matter of appealing to a community of lived experience, to the particularities of history and desire, to suggestive turns of language.

> If I forget my self for a moment and use a literary turn of phrase in a philosophical work I always feel slightly that I am pulling a fast one on my reader; it is a breach of trust. I once wrote the sentence – remembered because of its literary aspect – *'L'homme est une passion inutile'* ('Man is a useless passion'). A case of breach of trust. I ought to have put that in strictly philosophical terms. In *A Critique of Dialectical Reason* I do not think I was guilty of breach of trust at all. There are two very different things at issue here. In the realm of literature this kind of thing does not constitute breach of trust because the reader is forewarned. (PL 96)

The philosophical writer has a responsibility, in other words, not to slip in misleading literary expressions or allusions that may trip the unwary reader, whose proper expectation is of lucid concepts conveyed in transparent language; by parity of argument, a reader who looks for philosophical content in a literary work is put on his guard. It is hard to tell whether Sartre or his readers have committed the greater offence against this pair of principles, but he at least recognizes the danger.

> One thing I should point out is that after all I write in so many different languages that things pass from one to another; I write the language of prose, I write the language of philosophy, I write the language of theatre, and so on. (PL 123)

All these languages, as Sartre uses them, have this in common, that they can deal in their different ways with the themes he finds significant: anguish, commitment, self-deception, authenticity, choice, freedom and the rest. The fact that he does cover this territory in all these modes, turning aside (as we saw in the previous chapter) from literature and literary studies to philosophy when conceptual problems call for resolution, explains why in this book I have not found it necessary to deal explicitly with the non-philosophical writings. But Sartre does not write in the language of poetry. The reader of poetry is put on his guard even more explicitly than the reader of literary prose; poetry is pure colour, like the work of a painter, and it is unreasonable to look in it primarily for any kind of communication. There would be no sense, then, in expecting philosophy to approximate conceptually what is conveyed in poetry. It is striking that even in his essays on art and artists Sartre is less interested in the works of art as such than in the concepts they seem to express or in the social or psychological circumstances of their production: in his long essay on Tintoretto, for example ('The Prisoner of Venice', SIT 9 ff.), it is the moral and commercial structure of sixteenth-century Venice that occupies the foreground, and in the end the painter is identified with the city itself; in the surviving fragment of the lost essay on Mallarmé (cf. WS 2: 281) anarchy, suicide and chance receive more attention than does poetry. 'The Mobiles of Calder' (EA 123 ff.) is perhaps an exception to this rule, but only because Calder's work has for Sartre the form of a concept. This apparent indifference to the 'literary' qualities of literature may account in part for the misunderstanding that has surrounded the essay on Baudelaire. I shall return to this point in chapter VIII.

In prose what comes into play is not the word's status as an object but its relation to other objects, among them the object it names; the writer by his manipulation of the word changes the world, and he does this by *uncovering* things in the world and hence transforming them from the innocence of immediacy to the consciousness of mediation. This may have the effect of enriching our lives by objectifying what would otherwise be transient pleasures ('ever since he has been *telling* about his masturbation and intercourse Genet has known happiness' (SG 557)), but its more characteristic effect in Sartre is to add to the burden of our responsibilities. Things passed over in silence are not seen for what they are, we may continue to do them or condone them blindly (whether wilfully or from ignorance), but once it is named the agent must take cognizance of the act – it is delivered to him, as it were: ' "This is what you're doing now; come to grips with it." The deed, thus named, loses its innocence' (RW 169). Actions become responsibilities only when they are named, and the writer's own responsibility is to name them. This being the case, his silence also becomes an act.

> If therefore a writer has chosen to be silent on one aspect of the world, we have the right to ask him: why have you spoken of this rather than that? And since you speak in order to make a change, since there is no other way you can speak, why do you want to change this rather than that? Why do you want to alter the way postage stamps are made rather than the way in which Jews are treated in an antisemitic country? (RW 170)

What requires to be named at any given time is determined by history at that time; in 1946, the year from which these citations are taken, it is the need for liberty, the danger of violence – for responsibility will become culpability if 'in fifty years it may be said of us: "They saw the greatest world catastrophe coming and they kept silent" ' (RW 186). The writer's responsibility is not eternal and abstract, it is immediate and specific. He must 'give his thoughts without respite, day in, day out, to the problem of the end and the means; or, again, the problem of the relationship of ethics and politics' (RW 185).

This view is taken by Sartre to apply to philosophy as well as to other prose writing, even though as we have seen the business of philosophy is conceptual approximation rather than concrete representation. Not that the classical idea of philosophy as belonging to a transcendent domain, above the generation and corruption of the everyday world, is unintelligible to him – it is just that he judges it to be self-indulgent and irresponsible when human liberty is at stake, as it continually is. Our attitude to the literary and philosophical classics themselves is to be scrutinized in the light of this imperative. In *What is Literature?* he denies the possibility of innocence not only to writing but also to reading. The difficulty is, of course, that the values people in fact require in literature are aesthetic or stylistic ones, in philosophy logical or systematic ones; they are not looking for political relevance but for intellectual stimulation. Sartre recognizes this, and he does not wish to deny the possibility or value of aesthetic or logical excellence, but he considers it a betrayal of the classical authors if that is all we see in their works, and he considers contemporary authors who put such considerations first to have betrayed themselves. Pascal and Giraudoux provide the terms of a devastating comparison: Pascal, *committed* (to attacking the Jesuits), produces, first as the fruit of that commitment and only secondly out of a concern for style, the *Provincial Letters*; Giraudoux on the other hand reverses these priorities: ' "the only concern is finding the style; the idea comes afterwards"; but he was wrong. The idea did not come' (WIL 20). The trouble with the aesthetic or the merely intellectual is that they may appeal, not to liberty, but to pleasure. It is comfortable and amusing and even in its way rewarding to sit in the library, analyzing old arguments, admiring their order and rigour or explaining their psychological motivations; and yet these arguments were forged in commitment, they had when constructed an immediate force which the critic belittles by the neutrality of his criticism.

> Rousseau, the father of the French Revolution, and Gobineau, the
> father of racism, both sent us messages. And the critic considers them
> with equal sympathy. If they were alive, he would have to choose
> between the two, to love one and hate the other. But what brings

them together, above all, is that they are both profoundly and deliciously wrong, and in the same way: they are dead. (WIL 25-6)

Language and the products of language are, in other words, serious matters, and Sartre gives absolute priority to their intersection with the historical and political realities of the moment. Their importance lies partly in the fact that they constitute man as what he historically is in each moment. In this Sartre maintains a consistent attitude from *What is Literature?* to the *Critique of Dialectical Reason*, and it no doubt explains the absence of fiction in his later writing, since of all forms except poetry fiction lends itself most readily to the self-indulgence of the maker of sand-castles.

Language as the practical relation of one man to another is *praxis* . . . for an individual to- discover his isolation, his alienation, for him to suffer from silence or, for that matter, to become integrated into some collective undertaking, his relation to others, as manifested in and by the materiality of language, must constitute him in his own reality. (CDR 99)

The inscription of language into a more general theory of praxis belongs in a later chapter, but it is worth noting here that the reciprocal relation between language and history set forth in the *Critique* becomes in the last phase of radical involvement a ground not merely for the changing of history by language, but for the changing of language as a means to the changing of history. In a late interview Sartre sees the philosopher's task as the creation of a language, for the explanation of political realities, that will be intelligible to everyone. Philosophical language is good only for communication among philosophers – it is useless for answering the 'real questions' posed, albeit naively, by children or workers; what we need is 'a language that is honest, by which I mean we have to use words which are not loaded with a past' (NYT 116). And the only valid form of writing is now the political tract: 'in a capitalist country the straight press doesn't really count, so why write for it?' (ibid. 118).

This represents an apparently definitive commitment to the most radical class doctrine; the responsibility of the writer is now narrowly constricted by political considerations – it is no longer a question of unremitting reflection on the relation of ends and means, but of the active support of any means to the revolutionary end ('even if I don't always agree with their ideological position' (ibid.)). There can be no doubt, of course, that many philosophical ideas, even difficult ones, are capable of expression in simple language, in words 'not loaded with a past' – or, since every word in every language is so loaded, in words used in such a way that it does not matter if one is unaware of their past, or has forgotten it. But one would suppose that only the ahistorical parts of philosophy could be so

29

expressed, the parts that belong to what I called in the Introduction the 'objective domain'. Man would be constituted by these words as a timeless observer but not as a historical agent. It is true that, as Sartre complains, the language of orthodox communism is by now as encrusted with historical weight as the language of philosophy, that it 'is clear only to the initiated', but his own language, even at its most simple, suffers the same drawback, although the history in question may be somewhat shorter. An allusion to a strike at Flins is in its way as arcane as an allusion to Fichte. And again, an ephemeral language cannot constitute a historical man if history·is not itself to be ephemeral.

The problem of language, then, is for Sartre the problem of its use rather than its structure, of the manner in which it changes the world rather than the manner in which it expresses meanings – or rather the manner in which it changes the appearance of the world and hence our conduct in it. 'A language' becomes a form of life; in one of the first texts to make specific reference to the *concept* of language, '*Aminadab* or the Fantastic Considered as a Language', a review of a Kafka-like work by Maurice Blanchot, dating from 1943, Sartre seems not far from the position of Wittgenstein at about the same time, though he expresses himself very differently. The truths caught in the language of the fantastic 'will lose their colour and their life once they are out of the water' (LPE 73) – translated into another language, say Heidegger's, they seem banal, but once one enters their proper domain, the domain of Hoffmann, Poe, Lewis Carroll, and the surrealists, they shine 'with a strange brilliance'. Something of the same sort might be said for Sartre's own philosophical language; one has to be prepared to enter the domain, and to resist the impulse to paraphrase what one finds there into the vocabulary of another tradition, of another form of philosophical life.

III

Image, Emotion,
and Intentionality

Sartre, then, is a man of words but not a philosopher of language. The professional categories into which his work fits are rather ontology and philosophical anthropology, with excursions into ethics and the philosophy of history. And among these ontology is dominant. The development of his thought can without too much distortion be represented as an ontological ascent from consciousness to history, by way of the self, the other, and the group, and the chapters which follow can best be viewed as tracing that ascent.

The early philosophical works, however, emerge as much from the writer's interests as from the philosopher's. Sylvie Le Bon asserts that *The Transcendence of the Ego* is 'Sartre's very first work' (*TE* 7), but in fact the first problem on which his mature philosophical attention was engaged was that of the imagination – an obvious topic for a literary type constrained to follow philosophical studies. For the status of the imaginary is a classical problem both in literature and philosophy, and the standard doctrine – which is that the imaginary is a degraded form of the real – is obviously false and thus makes an easy target; also the writer has a professional stake in the possibility of a world lived in the imagination.

Whether the strategic decision to approach the problem of the imagination from the point of view of consciousness dates from the university exercise on which *Imagination* (1936) is based (*cf.* WS 6), it is hard to say; the argument of the book begins with criticisms of the views of Descartes, Spinoza, and Leibniz, but these are preceded by a short introduction in which the Hegelian categories of 'in-itself' (*en soi*) and 'for-itself' (*pour soi*) are neatly set forth as they arise from an examination of my relation, as consciousness, to a given thing in the world – say a sheet of white paper – as object. (Although Sartre claims not to have known Hegel's work well until after the war he admits to having 'assimilated many things' from him by 1939 (L/S 127).) The categories of being-in-itself

(*Ansichseins*) and being-for-itself (*Fürsichseins*) are introduced in the Preface
to the *Phenomenology of Spirit*. For Hegel 'everything turns on grasping and
expressing the True, not only as *Substance*, but equally as *Subject*' (Hegel
1977: 10); roughly speaking the in-itself corresponds to the former and the
for-itself to the latter. The qualities of the sheet of paper do not depend
on me, they present themselves to me, they are 'for-me' (*pour moi*) but at
the same time they are inert, and inertia is the defining characteristic of the
in-itself. The in-itself has no spontaneity, neither mine nor that of others.
But the thing-like character of the in-itself cannot be shared by my
consciousness, whose mode of being is self-awareness; consciousness is in
the first instance for-me – but that amounts to saying that it is for-itself.
'For consciousness, to exist is to be conscious of its existence. It appears
as a pure spontaneity, confronting a world of things which is sheer
inertness' (IM 2). This presuppositionless and inexplicable confrontation of
consciousness and world is a fundamental and constant element in Sartre's
philosophy; it is his *cogito*, his Archimedean fixed point, and he never
abandons it.

If I turn my head away from the sheet of paper it ceases to be for-me
without thereby, I suppose, ceasing to be in-itself. The problem of the
imagination arises when I reflect that nevertheless, without looking back
at it, I can call up at will the appearance of the sheet of paper – not *a* sheet
of paper but that self-identical one in its essence, understanding 'essence'
to comprise both structure and individuation. The imagined sheet of paper
and the real one have identity of essence but not identity of existence –
the image is not in-itself, 'it does not assert itself as a limit to my
spontaneity' (IM 2-3). And according to Sartre I am never deceived by the
image into confusing it with the real thing. We might represent the
situation in the terminology of his introduction as follows: the thing
unperceived is in-itself but not for-me; perceived it is in-itself and for-me;
in image it is for-me but not in-itself. The claim that one cannot be
mistaken in this matter may be too strong, but at any rate we are not
likely to be confused about the modes of existence involved. And yet
traditional views have almost all given the image the status of a thing, a
thing copied after the original or a lesser version of it, and it is this
reification of the image that has constituted their error.

The classical position is that imagination and sensation are two species
of the same genus, but that the latter is more vivid and more immediate.
The image, like the idea produced in perception, is in Spinoza for example
an affection of the body; but it stands to the idea, says Leibniz, as opacity
to clarity. The image serves as a representation of the object in the absence
of immediate perception; this view is common to empiricism and rationalism, their difference residing in the empiricist belief, and the rationalist
denial, that thought itself consists of images. (Leibniz occupies an
intermediate position: for him thought and image are interpenetrating

domains.) Terminology is not stable here – for what Locke and the associationists called 'ideas' are just images in this sense, at any rate when they are detached from perception; and similarly for 'weak perceptions' in Hume. Putting all this into the context of French philosophical history makes Taine the representative of associationism and of positivism in general. Taine is a mechanist, whose method commences with the analysis of complexes into their elements. It is to be noted for future reference that Sartre calls this 'regressive analysis', a standard expression in French logical terminology for arguments from effects to their causes or from wholes to their parts. But when Taine comes to the synthetic stage of his method all he can do is to reassemble the parts by 'simple recomposition'. The result is a fragmented domain of thought-images without any principle of unity, no underlying or transcending spirit.

It is characteristic of Sartre to point out that the mid-nineteenth-century reaction against Taine, which paved the way for Ribot's 'creative imagination', sprang from the fact that associationist doctrines were *politically* unacceptable under the Second Empire, when it seemed important to fight against the anarchism and atheism that had so nearly brought civilization to ruin. Taine's dry positivism seemed to leave no room for spiritual (i.e., patriotic) values. Even if in fact introspective analysis reveals nothing but a complex of images, 'there had to be something else: a thought which at every moment organizes and trancends the image' (IM 26). The Academy of Moral and Political Sciences accordingly offered, in 1882, a prize for the re-establishment of the doctrines that associationism tended to subvert. But in spite of reactionary insistence on an autonomous subjectivity lying behind and synthesizing the activity of the imagination, the status of the image itself remained that of a mental object provoked by sensation and constituting an echo of it. Ribot's 'psychology of synthesis', which improved on Taine's simple recomposition by introducing evolutionary and functional considerations, makes no difference to this basic conception; and as Sartre goes on to show in a long and cutting criticism of Bergson, even the latter's complicated (and inconsistent) scheme, in spite of its claim to be a philosophical revolution, leaves the image in the same unsatisfactory state – in Bergson's own words 'almost matter in that it may still be seen and almost mind in that it cannot be touched' (quoted IM 57).

The Würzburg psychologists (Binet, Bühler, *et al.*) escape, in Sartre's view, from these confusions only to retreat to the Cartesian position, namely that thought is independent of imagery, that the latter in fact gets in the way. Their contribution is to see that thought requires no intermediary in order to appear to itself, that 'thinking and to know that one is thinking are all one' (IM 67). But Binet falls into contradiction when, in puzzling over the manner of this awareness in particular cases, he concludes that thought must in fact be unconscious, requiring images again in order to be brought into consciousness. The upshot of this critical review of traditional positions is that no new solution is possible as long as the starting-point in the classical conception of the image itself, as something *in* consciousness, obeying its own proper laws, remains unchanged. A wholly different approach is needed. If the image is assimilated to perception, there will be trouble when we want to separate them again, and such complications do not do justice to the clarity with which, in fact, we spontaneously distinguish them. Making images inert destroys the spontaneity of any thought that depends on them, reducing it to a play of associations; it takes a courageous philosopher like Hume to adopt this view openly, and others who see no way out of it but cannot accept its consequences are a prey to hopeless inconsistencies. The one philosopher to whom Sartre gives credit for having scotched the image is Alain, but he succeeds only at the price of negating it altogether; for him all images are simply false perceptions (as when in fright we mistake a tree for a man), and consequently the image cannot play the role in thought which, Descartes to the contrary notwithstanding, it seems quite clear that it does play.

What Sartre takes himself to have established in the main body of *Imagination* is, first, the indubitable psychic reality of the image, and, second, the impossibility of accounting for it as a sensible content of consciousness. The clue to a solution of the problem of the image lies in a rethinking of the nature of consciousness itself. If images are the carriers of thought, and words the carriers of meaning, we are tempted to ask what lies behind the images or under the words that might give substance to thought and meaning.

> But it is clear that there is *nothing* under the words, behind the
> images, because there can be nothing there. We call spontaneous an
> existence which determines its own existence by itself. In other
> words, to exist spontaneously is to exist for itself and by itself [*pour
> soi et par soi*]. Then a single reality deserves to be called spontaneous:
> namely consciousness. For it, in effect, to exist and to be conscious of
> existing are one and the same. In other words, the great ontological
> law of consciousness is the following: *the only mode of existence for a
> consciousness is to have the consciousness that it exists.* (IN 125-6)

Consciousness thus appears for Sartre as a presuppositionless, absolute given, to which the image appears – and it appears, not in the first instance as a thing, but precisely as an appearance. But then things also appear in the first instance as appearances. The location of the problem shifts, therefore, from the *content* of consciousness to its *object*.

The solution of the problem, or at least the direction for its solution, lies in Husserl, whom Sartre introduces almost as a *deus ex machina* in a short final chapter. From Husserl's dictum that every consciousness is *consciousness of* something Sartre draws a parallel assertion that every image is an *image of* something – that the image is in fact a vehicle for intentionality, in a mediated relation between a consciousness and its object as opposed to the immediate relation which is the grasping of the object in perception. The image is not the thing, nor is it in any way thing-like – rather it refers to the thing or stands for it in an experience that is structurally similar to, but ontologically distinct from, the experience of the thing itself. Sartre quotes at length the passage from the *Ideas* in which Husserl talks of a flute-playing centaur, which concludes:

> Naturally the centaur itself is not mental, it exists neither in the soul, nor in consciousness, nor anywhere else, it is in fact 'nothing,' mere 'imagination'; or, to be more precise, the living experience of imagination is the imagining *of* a centaur. To this extent, indeed, 'the centaur as meant,' the centaur as fancied, belongs to the experience itself as lived. But we must also beware of confusing this lived experience of imagination with that in the experience which is imagined, *qua* object imagined. (Husserl 1931: 91)

> This is a key passage. The nonexistence of the centaur or of the chimera does not entitle us to reduce them to mere psychic functions. No doubt on the occasion of these nonexistents there are real psychic formations. ... Husserl restored to the centaur, in the very heart of its 'unreality,' its transcendence. Irreality [*néant*], if you please: but by that very token it is not in consciousness. (IM 134)

The image is not a thing, a constitutive element of consciousness, it is one of the ways in which consciousness 'intends' the thing. This view immediately clears up a confusion about those other things called 'images', namely paintings, photographs, and the like; they cannot be 'in' consciousness as the classical doctrine of the image required, but nothing prevents their being used by consciousness as a mediation of its intentional relation to what they represent, just as purely mental images are used. And yet this case is not quite so simple – for we can still spontaneously tell the difference between the photograph and *its* image. Further analysis of the intentional structures involved in perceiving and imagining is required in order to justify the ease and clarity with which, as Sartre insisted at the beginning of the book, we distinguish between them in practice. And it is on this problematic note that *Imagination* ends. The solution is to be found, we feel, in Husserl, but Sartre has not yet found it.

Husserl's concept of intentionality is the subject of a separate text, 'Intentionality: A Fundamental Idea of Husserl's Phenomenology', in which Sartre moves decisively beyond the interpretation given in *Imagination*. This text begins with a sardonic attack on what Sartre calls the 'alimentary' or 'digestive' philosophy of the French academic tradition, which assimilates experience *into* consciousness. 'We have all read

Brunschvicg, Lalande and Meyerson, we have all believed that Spidery Mind trapped things in its web, covered them with a white spit, and slowly swallowed them, reducing them to its own substance' (INT 4). For Husserl, on the contrary, things are not of the same nature as consciousness, they cannot be assimilated by consciousness but remain where they are, over against it, in their concrete individuality. This is no Bergsonian realism – things do not have prior and independent existence: 'Consciousness, and the world are given at one stroke: essentially external to consciousness, the world is nevertheless essentially relative to consciousness' (ibid.). The only image (in the sense of metaphor) that Husserl can find for the fact of consciousness is 'perhaps the quick, obscure image of a burst'. (The term *'éclatement'*, which means 'explosion' or 'rupture' or in general any violent or blinding movement tending to burst or shatter, has no single equivalent in English capable of neutralizing an occasional absurdity of expression.) This bursting forth of consciousness into the world makes it impossible that anything should be *in* consciousness – consciousness has no interior, it is as it were out in the world. I cite the following passage at length because of its power and its crucial relevance to the existential themes of Sartre's later work:

> Imagine for a moment a connected series of bursts which tear us out of ourselves, which do not even allow to an 'ourselves' the leisure of composing ourselves behind them, but which instead throw us beyond them into the dry dust of the world, on to the plain earth, amidst things. Imagine us thus rejected and abandoned by our own nature in an indifferent, hostile, and restive world – you will then grasp the profound meaning of the discovery which Husserl expresses in his famous phrase 'All consciousness is consciousness of something.' No more is necessary to dispose of the effeminate philosophy of immanence, where everything happens by compromise, by protoplasmic transformations, by a tepid cellular chemistry. The philosophy of transcendence throws us on to the highway, in the midst of dangers, under a dazzling light.
>
> Being, says Heidegger, is being-in-the-world. One must understand this 'being-in' as movement. To be is to fly out into the world, to spring from the nothingness of the world and of consciousness in order suddenly to burst out as consciousness-in-the-world. When consciousness tries to recoup itself, to coincide with itself once and for all, closeted off all warm and cosy, it destroys itself. This necessity for consciousness to exist as consciousness of something other than itself Husserl calls 'intentionality'. (INT 5)

(The term translated here as 'effeminate' is *'douillette'*, which lends an anti-clerical overtone to the text, since it means not only 'coddled' and 'cosy' but is also the name of a sort of quilted soutane worn by priests in winter.) The self-transcendence of consciousness applies not only to knowledge of things but also to other modes of our relation to the world: fear, hate, love – or, to put it differently, things themselves take on the aspect of sympathy or horror. There is no longer, therefore, a separation between emotion as interior, the world of things as exterior: we are delivered from the myth of an 'inner life',

> since everything is finally outside, everything, even ourselves. Outside, in the world, among others. It is not in some hiding-place that we will discover ourselves: it is on the road, in the town, in the midst of the crowd, a thing among things, a man among men. (INT 6)

The echo of this passage to be found a decade later in the following text will concern us in the next chapter, but it seems worth juxtaposing them: 'For the mind is not even a metaphorical "place." On the contrary, the chessboard, the platform, the scholar's desk, the judge's bench, the lorry-driver's seat, the studio and the football field are among its places' (Ryle 1949: 51). Ryle's concern with the mind and the misconceptions people have had about it is matched by Sartre's with the being, whatever it is, which was formerly thought to have the power of ingestion but is now seen as thrown out into the world by the *éclatement* of consciousness. He completed at about this time a work of philosophical psychology, *La Psyché*, of which however only a fragment was published (as *The Emotions: Outline of a Theory*), raising the question as to the very possibility of a unified science of 'man', an entity which after all we do not understand as well as we thought, and which indeed may, as a knowable entity, the object of a science, not exist at all. The sciences of nature, as he points out, have come to limit themselves to the accumulation of experimental results, and to the interpretation of those results in terms of the conditions of possibility of further phenomenal experience rather than in terms of knowledge of an objective world. And if natural science has abandoned 'world', perhaps social science should abandon 'man', these two notions being, in Heidegger for example, complementary and inseparable.

Here Sartre anticipates a theme of great importance in later commentary on the human sciences and their epistemological status. Foucault, for example, concludes *The Order of Things* by saying that 'man is an invention of recent date. And perhaps one nearing its end' (Foucault 1970: 387), and at about the same time Lacan in his *Écrits* writes 'There is no science of man, because the man of science does not exist, but only its subject' (*Lacan 1966: 859*). But even if psychology is considered nothing more than the study of human behaviour, the question of what counts as behaviour requires an analysis of the interaction between agent and world, subject and situation, and on the side of the subject a further distinction has to be made between mere bodily reactions, behaviour properly speaking, and the states of consciousness that accompany them. We are therefore compelled to ascend to the source of subjectivity, to transcendental consciousness. Once again Husserl is invoked to correct the deficiencies of traditional psychology. The fault of the psychologist is to deal with the psychic state as though it simply existed as such, without signifying anything; the virtue of phenomenology is to realize that all human phenomena are significative.

So Sartre proposes an experiment in phenomenological psychology – to deal with emotions as phenomena in a domain of significance. He begins with the observation of William James, that emotional states always have marked psychological components, and from James's view that the accompanying state of consciousness must simply be the consciousness *of* the psychological changes that take place. Janet's criticism of this was that it 'overlooked the psychic component', which he attempted to supply by interpreting the physiological disturbance as displacing or avoiding some other form of behaviour. But this notion is radically ambiguous, as Sartre shows in recounting the story of a patient of Janet's who comes to tell him of her secret obsessions but is too embarrassed to do so. '*Then* she sobs. But does she sob *because* she cannot say anything? ... Or does she sob precisely *in order not to say anything?*' Janet sees little difference between the cases;

> but in reality these two theories are separated by an abyss. The first, in effect, is purely mechanistic. ... The second, on the contrary, really brings us something new. ... If we reintroduce finality here, we can understand that emotional behaviour is not a disorder at all. It is an organized system of means aiming at an end. And this system is *called* upon to mask, substitute for, and reject behaviour that one cannot or does not want to maintain. (EMO 31-2)

But even this account is unsatisfactory; the function of emotion is clear, but in itself it remains unintelligible. We have to look for the *significance* of the particular form that an emotion takes, and here psychoanalysis enters the picture. But psychoanalysis has its own difficulties:

> Psychoanalytic interpretation conceives the conscious phenomenon as the symbolic realization of a desire repressed by the censor. Let us note that for consciousness this desire *is not implied in its symbolic realization.* In so far as it exists by and in our consciousness it is uniquely what it announces itself to be: emotion, desire for sleep, theft, fear of laurel-trees, etc. If it were otherwise and if we had some consciousness, *even implicit,* of our true desire, we would be in *bad faith** and the psychoanalyst does not see it that way. The result is

*Sartre himself italicizes the expressions I have marked with an asterisk – 'mauvaise foi', 'signifié', 'signifiant' – as though aware that he is using relatively novel terms of some importance; in this and the following citations, which I have given at length, the English translation does not do justice to this terminology.

that the significance of our conscious behaviour is wholly exterior to that behaviour itself, or, if you prefer, the *signified** is wholly cut off from the *signifier**. (*ETE 35*)

The conscious event, then, acquires the status of a thing, causally determined by something other than itself, and this Sartre finds incompatible with the very concept of consciousness in the tradition of the *cogito*:

> to constitute consciousness as a thing in relation to the signified, is to admit that consciousness constitutes itself as signification without being conscious of the signification that it constitutes. There is a flagrant contradiction in this, unless one thinks of consciousness as an existing thing of the same type as a stone or a tarpaulin. But in this case it is necessary to renounce the Cartesian *cogito* altogether, and make of consciousness a secondary and passive phenomenon. (*ETE 36*)

That, thinks Sartre, is too much even for psychoanalysis, which covertly admits a comprehension of the symbol by consciousness under the form of an analogy; the symbol, as symbol *of* the suppressed, is constitutive of consciousness:

> In this case, there is nothing behind it and the relation between symbol, symbolized and symbolization is an intra-structural connection in consciousness. But if we add that consciousness symbolizes under the causal pressure of a transcendent fact, the repressed desire, we fall back into the theory discussed above which makes the relation between signified and signifier a causal one. The profound contradiction of all psychoanalysis is to present *at the same time* a causal relation and a relation of comprehension between the phenomena that it studies. (*ETE 37*)

The basic mistake in all this, as Sartre sees it, is the implicit assumption that people are aware of *having* their emotions, when in fact it would be truer to say that their emotions *are* modes of awareness of the world. If the emotion-ridden consciousness is conscious of itself this can only be in what he calls the 'non-positional mode', i.e., not positing itself as an object of consciousness (and thus separated from itself, set over against itself) but being aware of itself in some other way. The trouble is that we tend, along with psychoanalysis, to think that if we are not conscious of something in the usual way, holding or having it held out to us as an object, we must be unconscious of it. But action is characteristically unreflective, and yet it would be quite wrong to consign it to the domain of the unconscious. When Sartre writes, for example, he is not conscious of doing so – he thinks, not about writing, but about the words. And yet 'the act of writing is not at all unconscious. It is a present structure of my consciousness. Only, it is not conscious *of* itself' (EMO 54). Later on, in *Being and Nothingness*, this non-self-conscious consciousness will be called the 'pre-reflective cogito'. My relation to my own actions is quite different from my relation to those of others; what they will do next can only be for me a matter of probable conjecture, what I will do next can be, under suitable circumstances, a matter of certain intention – I feel the exigences of the enterprises I undertake, the necessity of their realization. 'Action constitutes a class of certain objects in a probable world' (EMO 55), an existential reality 'non-thetically' conscious of itself. ('Non-thetic' and 'non-positional' are essentially equivalent expressions, differing only in their classical roots.)

The exigences of my own actions are, however, not spun out of my subjectivity. They appear as features of the world, or rather as features of my interaction with the world. Now the world is *difficult*: its difficulty is given as 'the noematical correlative of our activity whether undertaken or only conceived' (EMO 58). And because this difficulty, this urgency of the world is sometimes too much for us, the confrontation of consciousness and world becomes intolerable; consciousness as it were intuitively changes its own modality so as to escape, not from itself, but from its situation. This change in modality is what we recognize as an emotion. An emotion is 'a transformation of the world'; in an emotional state 'it is the body which, directed by consciousness, changes its relation with the world in order that the world may change its qualities' (EMO 58, 61). But this is not a game, or, if it is, it is one in which we really believe. There are false emotions (pretended joy at a gift to which we are really indifferent) but they are short-lived and require to be sustained; true emotions impose themselves, and the qualities they project upon the world are experienced as veridical.

Sartre is not wholly consistent at this juncture: if the body is '*directed* by consciousness' to induce a change on the world then it cannot be said without qualification, as he does, that an emotion is 'suffered' (*subie*). But the essential point is that the world becomes new under the influence of emotion, and the agency of this novelty is the body, on the one hand part of the world and on the other 'the lived' of consciousness without mediation. '*Le vécu*' is a category of great importance for Sartre; the closest approximation to it in current English would be 'lived experience', but that would be misleading because experience is always thought of as someone's experience, whereas '*le vécu*' is impersonal, or rather we might say pre-personal. It is not reflective. When subject to emotion, therefore, consciousness lives a world which it has created but in which it believes: it lives a *magical* world. In falling into a magical world, consciousness falls into a trap – usually, although not always, one that it has set for itself. Sometimes, it is true, we react with immediate horror or delight to features of the world that we have not had time to work up into objects of emotion, and at such times things will seem to have an objectively magical

40

aspect. But these cases will turn out to belong to a particular existential structure of the world which is characteristically magical, and of which the paradigm is our perception of other people. Here emerges another crucial preoccupation of Sartre's, the ontological status of other consciousnesses; our encounters with others, if genuine, will typically be marked by emotion – 'man is always a sorcerer for man and the social world is first at all magical' (*ETE 58*).

The domain of significance within which the phenomena of emotion are encountered, then, is a domain defined by consciousness and world conjointly. Consciousness is the reality of the human, world its *facticity*, that is, the boundary conditions imposed upon it. The phenomenal content of experience can be analysed in either direction, from consciousness to world or from world to consciousness; the latter is another form of regressive analysis. 'The various disciplines of phenomenological psychology are *regressive*, and yet the term of their regression is *for them* a pure ideal. Those of pure phenomenology are, on the contrary, progressive' (EMO 94). 'For them', because while consciousness cannot ever be reached through scientific inquiry, it is fully aware of itself as the starting-point of pure phenomenological description. The latter however will yield only inexplicable content – an emotion, but why this emotion rather than some other? – in the absence of determining conditions provided by empirical investigation. At this stage Sartre does not see how the two methodological moments – phenomenological progression and psychological regression – can be brought together.

The status of the 'world' component of this pairing of consciousness and world remains problematic. If it can be magically changed by consciousness under the influence of emotion, what are we to say of its real nature? The turn that Sartre's work takes after *The Emotions* inverts this problem: what sort of unreal world might consciousness project if not bound by facticity? or how might it escape the limitations of the real world? *The Psychology of Imagination* sets out to describe the function of consciousness that Sartre calle '*irréalisante*', a term not easily translatable, since while it means 'making unreal' it does not mean even that in its ordinary English sense – it is not only a question of rendering unreal something otherwise real, but also of 'realizing' something new and unreal, the imaginary as the noematic correlate of the imagination. In a note at the beginning of the book Sartre remarks on a slight change in the meaning he wishes to attach to the term 'consciousness': its usual use is too passive, apparently indicating something that simply experiences various 'states'; 'we shall use the term "consciousness",' says Sartre, 'not to designate the monad and the ensemble of its pyschic structures, but to name each of these structures in its concrete particularity' (*IE 11*). This has the effect at once of neutralizing the problem of the substantial and continuous subject – since the particularity of each episode of consciousness can be dealt with independently of other episodes belonging to the same subjective history – and of permitting a symmetrical and dynamic relation between the terms called above 'consciousness' and 'world' rather than a one-sided one in which an active world impresses itself on a passive consciousness after the manner of the empiricists.

The initially impersonal character of consciousness echoes *The Transcendence of the Ego* (see chapter IV). But its active character throws into sharp focus a chronic difficulty in Sartre's thought. It was in the second and unpublished part of *Imagination* (i.e., precisely the first draft of *The Psychology of Imagination*) that Sartre, according to Simone de Beauvoir, 'crystallized the first key concepts of his philosophy: the conscious mind as *tabula rasa,* and its capacity for annihilation (*néantisation*)' (POL 168). The difficulty is to reconcile in any intelligible way the emptiness and the power. A power of annihilation would seem, of course, to be just the kind of power emptiness would have, but it is hard to see how it could be wielded, how something not merely empty and otherwise substantial (after the manner of a hollow vessel) but identified as it later came to be with Nothingness itself, could take the kind of initiative that consciousness must take in Sartre's account of the imaginary. This is a new form of an old problem, which crops up elsewhere as mind/body, freedom/determinism and the like. The nearest thing to a solution in Sartre will come in *Being and Nothingness,* but the problem itself becomes clearer in the course of *The Psychology of Imagination.*

The first part of the book is a new phenomenology of the image, and it is entitled 'The Certain' because according to Sartre what is given in reflection is certain although any explanatory hypothesis about it can only be probable. (The second part is called 'The Probable', and it is interesting to note that this arrangement echoes the original plan for the work of which 'The Legend of Truth' was a fragment.) No justification is offered for this conviction, which seems debatable even on the grounds of the distinction already made in *The Emotions* between the unreflective consciousness of action (and, by parity of argument, of experience) and the reflection which takes conscious account of it. (Nor is any argument given to support the claim that the essence of the image 'is the same for everyone' (PSI 4) – in spite of the later existentialist claim that there can be no presumption of a human nature, Sartre implicitly assumes, not only in his phenomenology but also in his ethics, a practical identity of constitution between men.) What this certainty of reflection delivers to us is a series of propositions: that the image is a consciousness (in the revised sense); that it is incapable of giving new information; that it is 'positional' but in certain specified ways; that it is spontaneous; and that it is never part of a more inclusive consciousness but is *sui generis*. The modes in which the image is positional, or thetic, are important for Sartre: it posits its object, he says, either as non-existent or as absent or as elsewhere, the last two cases being distinguished presumably by the emphasis in the one case on the here where the object *is not,* in the other on the *not-here* where it is. In all three cases the operative modality is negation. In this the image differs from the concept – I may have the concept of my absent friend in his present circumstances, and this may be wholly positive, but 'It is of the very nature of my image [of Pierre] not to touch him or see him, a way he has *of not being* at such a distance, in such a position' (PSI 17-18). In other words 'the "imaging" consciousness posits its object as a nothing-ness' (*IE 23*). (The English translation, at PSI 14, renders the term *'imageante'* as 'imaginative'; I have preferred in this and the next few citations not to use it.)

Sartre proceeds to offer a whole series of specific analyses of concrete images: photographs, portraits, imitations, signs, faces seen in flames, stains on walls, boulders in human shape, figures seen in coffee-grounds or in crystal balls, and so on. He makes rather heavy weather of some of these; a good example is his treatment of imitation, in which it is a question of a music-hall actress who 'does an imitation' of Maurice Chevalier. In such a case we say 'that's him all right' or 'it doesn't come off' – what is going on in our consciousness? Sartre resorts to some dubious conjectures: 'When I see Maurice Chevalier, this perception involves a certain affective reaction. This projects on to Maurice Chevalier's face a certain indefinable quality that we could call its "sense"' (*IE 45*); the imitation awakens this affective reaction in us, the actress seems to be possessed: 'Maurice Chevalier, absent, chooses in order to manifest himself the body of a woman' (ibid.). Here as in many other examples it seems hardly necessary to invoke an *image* at all, since Sartre admits conceptual knowledge, memory, and the rest – we *recognize* Maurice Chevalier in the imitation, and what makes it entertaining is the simultaneous knowledge that the actress is not Maurice Chevalier; the effect depends on cognition rather than on imagery. But the point of Sartre's catalogue has been to lead to the conclusion that the snapshots and blotches and imitators, up to and including 'mental images' in the more usual sense, play a special role in relation to the object of the image – they 'stand for' it as its *analogon.*

> The imagination seizes upon present objects in order to make
> contact, through them, with absent ones and ... the imaginary act
> produces, by one and the same movement, a "presentification" of the
> absent and an "absentification" of the present; I have given the name
> *analogon* to a present object which is a prey to an absence. (SG 347)

In the case of the mental image, however, the content of the image is known only through its being the analogon of the object whose image it is – Sartre seems to conclude that, unlike photographs and boulders, it does not in addition have its own independent properties (PSI 77).

The consciousness that is the image of an object cannot be equated with knowledge of the object. Knowledge, Sartre agrees, is consciousness of relations, at any rate when it is knowledge in a 'pure' or 'free' state, and this means that it is empty of sensible content, since in it things are thought as terms of relations only. It is Husserl's view that the function of the image is to fill out the emptiness of cognitive consciousness, but Sartre finds this view shocking (*IE 81*); the image, as a consciousness in its own right and *sui generis*, cannot be called on to supplement another consciousness. Nevertheless there is a continuity between them: pure knowledge sometimes aims at what can *also* be known as sensible, so that there is a form of cognitive consciousness which seeks to transcend itself and become an 'imaging' consciousness. Something similar happens in reading, itself an independent consciousness and again *sui generis*, in which however the mode of knowledge of what is read varies in the degree of its tendency to move towards an image. Consider, says Sartre, the two expressions 'the association of Parisian apartment-house owners' and 'he rushed down the apartment-house stairs' – in the former 'apartment-house' enters into our knowledge abstractly, in the latter it enters *as an object*. Not yet an *imagined* object, but one that might legitimately be transformed into an imagined object. The distinction here could also, of course, be made in the manner of linguistic analysis: in the second case, but not in the first, it would be legitimate to ask 'Which apartment-house?' or 'How many steps?' But if we accept the setting of Sartre's treatment of the subject it seems quite reasonable to admit the obvious introspective fact that words in some uses but not in others assume as it were the force of incipient images. Also, as he points out, the very orthographic configuration of a word, or its sound, may come to represent for us the sensible qualities for which it stands; the word '*belle*' in French, for example, represents or enacts the role of 'this *something* which is a beautiful young woman' (PSI 95), and this phenomenon, says Sartre, is commoner than we might think. This might have formed the starting-point of a theory of poetic language more acceptable to critics than the essay on Baudelaire, but as far as I know the argument is not developed anywhere else in Sartre's work.

While knowledge as a consciousness has to be distinguished from the image, the latter does have a cognitive component; its 'profound structure', says Sartre, is a mixture of cognition and affect. He seems to suggest that the cognition comes from the apparent presence or proximity of the object imagined, the affect from its real absence or distance, as in memory or nostalgia. (The object is not to be thought of as always imagined under a visual aspect; the image can also be kinaesthetic or even verbal.) But the cognitive status of the image suffers an absolute limitation in comparison with that of perception: it cannot be resorted to either for new knowledge of the object, or even for the confirmation of old knowledge. I cannot, says Sartre, quoting an informal experiment performed by Alain, count the columns on my image of the Pantheon. I may be able, with conceptual helps, to reconstruct this kind of information, but the object as imagined is not even a quasi-perceptual object. And this is because whereas in perception 'everything presents itself as being what it is' (PSI 129), the image does not necessarily obey either the principle of individuation or that of identity.

Sartre's theory of the image persists, therefore, in regarding it as an autonomous category of experience and of psychic activity, a consciousness *sui generis*. Its role in our psychic life is comparable in structure and importance to the role of what we ordinarily call thought. Theories which make the image the unique vehicle of thought are clearly wrong – reflective, conceptual thought can certainly dispense with it. But it can and does serve as the vehicle for a certain class of thoughts, namely those that are unreflectively concerned with sensible contents (in the broadest sense). This form of thought is also properly called conceptual; 'in fact,' says Sartre, 'there are not *some* concepts and *some* images, but there are two *modes* in which the concept can *appear*: as pure thought in the reflective domain and, in the unreflective domain, as image' (*IE 148*); the English translation has 'there are no concepts and no images' (PSI 162). Image and thought are related as species to genus (PSI 174); image and perception, on the other hand, are the 'two main irreducible attitudes of consciousness' (PSI 171) – perception is the starting-point for images and provides their material, as it were, but images properly speaking 'can arise only at the cost of the annihilation of perceptual consciousness' (PSI 174). As far as that goes the same must surely be said for the concept itself, although Sartre does not at this point say it; and it might also be said that the power of annihilation is mutual – it is quite impossible to have full perceptual awareness of an object and *at the same time* to form clearly either the concept or the image of that object.

The last major section of *The Psychology of Imagination* is entitled 'The Imaginary Life', and it begins, as *The Emotions* ends, with magic: the power of imagination is a magical power. It is capable of summoning to consciousness what is lacking in perception, and Sartre makes much of a 'defined lack' – if I conjure up the image of Pierre, it is because it is just *he* who is not here; I perceive his absence directly and it 'constitutes the essential structure of my image' (PSI 180). The object summoned is thus *unreal*, but that does not mean that it does not exist. It exists precisely *as* unreal, as emptiness, as the reflection of the feeling that projects it – so definitely, indeed, that that feeling can by a kind of positive feedback work itself up to a physical and therefore quite real manifestation, such as nausea. Memory can have a similar effect, what was really present to me yesterday being unreally present today. And Sartre extends his analysis to the experience of imagined pain, in the case of a psychasthenic patient who imagines that he has cancer; here the analysis becomes somewhat stretched, since Sartre feels obliged to say that the patient does not 'really suffer' although the pain is 'unreally there'. The theory will not permit the patient to perceive the imagined pain, at any rate as long as the spontaneous distinction between perception and imagination holds up, but by now the conditions being described begin to border on the pathological and it seems plausible that one pathological symptom might precisely be the breaking down of that distinction.

But Sartre proceeds to underline afresh the dualism of perception and imagination, assigning to each a whole set of accompanying feelings, respectively 'true' and 'imaginary'. He now admits, however, that the imaginary *feelings* are not necessarily unreal, it is just that they are aroused only by imaginary objects (perhaps the patient felt the pain after all). These two kinds of feeling correspond in fact to two distinct personalities:

> the imaginary self with its tendencies and desires – and the real self.
> There are imaginary sadists and masochists, persons of violent
> imagination. At each moment our imaginary self breaks in pieces and
> disappears at contact with reality, yielding its place to the real self.
> For the real and the imaginary cannot co-exist by their very nature.
> (PSI 210)

The dominance of the real derives from its novelty, its unexpectedness, which mark it unmistakably because according to Sartre the imaginary cannot possibly have these properties. It is easy to see why: consciousness can be surprised by the world but it cannot be allowed to surprise itself on pain of the contradiction already discussed above (*cf.* the citation from *The Emotions*, EMO 46); hence the content of the imaginary must always be known in advance. This gives it a comforting certainty, and accounts for the pathology of schizophrenia, for example, in which the unreal is *lived*. Imagination takes over the schizophrenic's world altogether – and yet he knows all the time that this world is unreal (PSI 213).

The ground for these assertions is once more the non-positional awareness that is the keystone of Sartre's theory of consciousness.

> The spontaneity of consciousness ... is identical with the
> consciousness of that spontaneity. ... Here we must fall back on the
> distinction made by Descartes: it is possible to speak or to breathe
> without being aware of doing so. But I cannot *think* that I am speaking
> without *knowing that I think that I am speaking.* (PSI 218)

This is said against Lagache, who tries to explain hallucinations of perception by what amount to excuses in terms of influences, absent-mindedness and the like, with the Freudian unconscious no doubt hovering nearby as the excuse *par excellence*. Sartre will allow consciousness no excuse. It knows perfectly well the difference between the real and the imaginary, and can only be culpably deceiving itself if it pretends not to. This knowledge extends to dreams as well, paradigm cases of the imaginary; Descartes was wrong in maintaining that we might be tricked into thinking that reality is a dream, or vice versa, the dream being, not a counterfeit of reality, but a sort of story about it, which we follow avidly without falling (any more than we would in reading a novel) into a confusion of the two. We cannot, says Sartre, dream *possibilities*, nor can we *foresee* in dreams (a remark not contradicted by the obvious fact that we can dream *of foreseeing* some event or other), and these limitations mark the imaginary world 'as a world without freedom: nor is it determined, it is the opposite of freedom, it is fatal' (PSI 246).

In summary: the imaginary is posited, but under a different modality from the object grasped as real on the basis of a perception which carries its own warrant. The latter is posited as the noematic correlate of a cognition that one might call constituted, contextual, and affirming, in opposition to Sartre's characterization of the 'imaginative act' as constitutive, isolating, and annihilating (PSI 263). Imagination is to be distinguished, again, from memory and anticipation, themselves modes of grasping the real either as past or as future. But its annihilating power is *specific*.

> For an image is not purely and simply the *world-negated*, it is always *the world negated from a certain point of view*, namely, the one that permits the positing of the absence or the non-existence of the object presented 'as an image'. (PSI 268)

The point of departure for the imagination, therefore, is always a specific relationship of consciousness to the real, perceptual world, and it requires this real world as a constant background. Now the content of perceptual consciousness is always specific (we might say, to adapt the passage just quoted, that such consciousness is not the world affirmed, purely and simply, it is always the world affirmed from a certain point of view). At this juncture Sartre introduces another term of cardinal importance for his later writings: 'the different immediate ways of apprehending the real as a world' are to be called, he says, *situations* (PSI 268). The production of a particular image then corresponds to and is determined by consciousness in situation.

It now appears, therefore, that the positing of the image is an exercise precisely of the freedom of consciousness to transcend the situation in which it finds itself. The imaginary world is not a world of freedom – but the real world is, and one product of that freedom is the imaginary world. The unreal that constitutes it is then *doubly* annihilating – it negates the world in relation to the self, but also the self in relation to the world. And this clarifies in passing the status of art as imaginary, since art is one of the forms of unreality that consciousness can choose to produce. The work of art (the words, the painted surface, the sounds) serves as *analogon* for a non-existent object in the domain of the imaginary, capable of lifting us out of ourselves and our situation. (The exercise of the imagination as paradigmatic of freedom no doubt provides a clue to the long association of art and liberty.) That is why, says Sartre, 'the real is never beautiful', and why 'it is stupid to confuse the moral with the aesthetic' (PSI 281), because the activities of the Good take place in the real world and are subject to 'the basic absurdity of existence'. If by chance we should find a real object beautiful, that is because it serves as the *analogon* for itself.

Imagination as an escape from absurdity and from contingence: the theme is a repeated one in Sartre's literary works. Eve, for example, in 'The Room', is advised by her father M. Darbedat not to try to 'live uniquely by the imagination' in refusing to believe that her husband Pierre is insane; that, says M. Darbedat, is 'beyond human strength'. But Eve's tragedy is that Pierre has actually succeeded in living uniquely by the imagination – he calls her 'Agathe' and is visited by flying statues – and that she cannot join him in his unreal world (WA 49). M. Darbedat's world, in which his sick wife holds her breath while eating an obsequious square of Turkish Delight in order not to get powdered sugar on her book, is absurd, but Pierre's, however sinister, is not. The imagination can serve not only to replace this world with another but to 'fictionalize' this one so that its contingencies become necessary: thus Jean Genet '*in reality* ... steals because he is a thief ...; *in the imaginary*, he steals in order to become a thief. .. He becomes an actor' (SG 350). An otherwise vicious reality is rendered tolerable if it can be construed as imaginary, even if what really transpires is in no way changed: 'The coins that *really* drop into his hand drop into a fake hand: the hoodlum is playing the role of a prince who is playing the role of a hoodlum' (SG 357). Or the imagination can be a weapon against an unacceptable situation in a world held in contempt; Sartre describes how the young Flaubert and his fellow-students in Rouen, in revolt against the ascendancy of the bour-geoisie (they themselves, however, taking an aristocratic stance as revolu-tionaries of the right), chose to '*waste* their time deliberately in imagining the impossible and to devour themselves by the dream not because they did not realize its futility but in order to provoke the world and their own selves to mutual destruction' (*IF 1:419*).

Imagination then gives access, as we have seen, to the '*irréel*', which is more like an alternative reality than the absence of reality. But its power is derivative: it depends on consciousness and on the world, which could not be negated if their prior existence were not assured. Sartre's work on these secondary, even pathological aspects of conscious activity leads inevitably, therefore, to the confrontation of consciousness as a primary and existential mode of being, to the elucidation of the so far unchallenged assumption of its status as absolutely given without presupposition. This is the philosophical task adumbrated in *The Transcendence of the Ego* and brought to its conclusion in *Being and Nothingness*.

If I have devoted a disproportionate amount of attention to the early works, and to problems which in the light of the great ontological and political questions of the better-known Sartre seem minor, it is because in his treatment of the minor problems nearly all the categories invoked later have been worked out. They can be seen more clearly in the comparatively modest and obscure writings than in the more portentous context of the major works. The in-itself and the for-itself (and the by-itself, a crucial term curiously neglected by critics of Sartre – *cf.* the citation above from *IN 125-6*), the nothingness of consciousness apart from its world, its exteriority, the non-positional mode of self-awareness, bad faith, the *vécu*, the Other, facticity, the regressive and progressive methods, the negating or 'nihilating' relation that holds between at least one form of consciousness and its world, the status of consciousness as freedom – all this typically Sartrian philosophical apparatus turns out to be in working order before *Being and Nothingness,* the work with which many expositions of Sartre's philosophy begin.

IV

Consciousness
and Subjectivity

The imagination, as we have seen, is one way – and often a pathological one – of bringing the contingency of the world under control. This contingency is encountered as absurd; we are, in the language of the essay on intentionality quoted above, 'rejected, abandoned by our very nature in an indifferent, hostile and intractable world' (*S I:31*). But it is not yet clear who we are, who it is that exercises the power of nihilation of which consciousness disposes, one of whose manifestations is the image of the absent object, posited as a negation of that absence. Whose consciousness, in fact, is it? In the first instance surely *mine*: these words are my words, these images my images. But 'there is nothing under the words, behind the images' (*IN 125*) – nothing *interior*, 'for finally everything is outside, everything, even including ourselves' (*S I:32*). The 'me', therefore, cannot be a concrete, substantial *subject*, occupying a place in the world over against the concrete, substantial objects that it encounters in perception or posits in imagination. Subjectivity, whatever it may turn out to involve, cannot mean the living of a private life; whatever may be true of me cannot be secretly true, nor can I know it as it were from the inside.

These convictions of Sartre's, reminiscent as they are of Wittgenstein and Ryle (or rather anticipatory, since they precede by a good decade the propositions of the *Philosophical Investigations* and *The Concept of Mind*), are held polemically: the whole tradition of French, that is of Christian, philosophy has been to attach not only substance but eternal significance to subjectivity – I am my interiority, my immortality; my fate is for me the dominant concern; I can be saved or lost; the world by comparison has no importance. But this view requires the warrant of some metaphysical or theological absolute, in the absence of which I am as contingent as the world is. The reduction of subjectivity to empty consciousness and the attribution of all psychic properties to an exteriorized self seems to be another strategy, not this time pathological, for the neutralization of contingency. As long as we think of the subject as substantial its emergence into whatever situation happens to obtain seems unaccountable - it is *de trop* in the world, a condition that Sartre finds intolerable: 'I wished I were dead or that I were needed by the whole world' (WO 166). If however it can be represented as the presence of consciousness to situation, without the attribution of substance, then it will no longer have to be accounted for as if it were something unexpectedly come across in the world. Consciousness may indeed come across something unexpected in the self regularly associated with the situations to which it is present, but this will be a bit of the world it learns, not something extraneous to the world.

Getting all this clear requires some lucidity about an otherwise confused set of terms - 'I', 'me', 'self', 'Ego', 'subject', 'consciousness'. Sartre's use of them is not always lucid, but he puzzles over their interrelations in *The Transcendence of the Ego*, which deals in particular with the status of the 'me' or the 'Ego' as opposed to 'consciousness'. The fact that Latin *'ego'* is the grammatical subject 'I' should not be allowed to confuse - *the* Ego has something of the standing given it by Freud as a psychic entity. (And yet this ambiguity is the source of some confusion for Sartre.) Although 'the I' and 'the me' ring oddly in English I shall ignore this fact in what follows as Sartre does the analogous oddity in French.

The Transcendence of the Ego was published in the same year as *Imagination*, although the bulk of the latter work had been written considerably earlier. It sets itself against the view that the Ego is an 'inhabitant' of consciousness - a formal principle of unification of experience or a material centre of desire or action. Its thesis is, rather, that the Ego 'is outside, *in the world*. It is a being of the world, like the ego of another' (TE 31). This thesis, if sustained, would represent an escape from the Cartesian egocentric predicament, from the thorny metaphysical problem of the isolation of the subject, whose solution would provide the key to so many other problems - perception, mind and body, freedom and the rest. For an interior structure of the subject–object relation would constitute a link between the two sides of Descartes's dualism, which otherwise confront one another as mutually external.

One is not obliged, of course, to accept the problematic in these terms at all. The classic dismissal of it is Ryle's sarcasm about the Ghost in the Machine. Sartre's conclusion, as has been indicated, has something in common with Ryle's, but his motives are a good deal more colourful. 'He always had a horror of "the inner life": it was radically suppressed as soon as the existence of consciousness was made to depend on a perpetual transcending of itself towards an object' (*FA 194*). This 'perpetual transcending', as we have seen, is Husserlian intentionality, but the problem - as Husserl himself admits in the *Cartesian Meditations* - is Descartes's. Husserl does not see his way out of the predicament, or at any rate his strategies for escape seem contrived, because he begins, according to Sartre, from a 'transcendental Ego' as substantial. The title of *The Transcendence of the Ego* is intended as a corrective to that view; the purpose of the work is to displace the Ego, as it were, from the hither to the further side of consciousness. It may therefore be as well to get clear at the outset what Husserl's view is.

The *Cartesian Meditations* start, just as their classical precursors did, from a search for indubitable or apodictic certainty, and like them arrive quickly at an '*ego cogito*'. But whereas for Descartes the *cogito* was a minimal point of certainty, an Archimedean fulcrum on which the reality of the rest of the world could be pivoted (through deduction after the argument for the existence of God), Husserl gives it a quite different status.

> It must by no means be accepted as a matter of course that, with an
> apodictic pure ego, we have rescued a little *tag-end of the world*, as the
> sole unquestionable part of it for the philosophizing Ego. ... This
> Ego, with his Ego-life, who necessarily remains for me, by virtue of
> [the] *epoché*, is not a piece of the world ... (Husserl 1960: 24-5)

In this Husserl is closer to Descartes's insight than the latter's own deductive strategy allowed him to remain; for although he argues for the radical separation, indeed the incommensurability, of the *res cogitans* and the *res extensa,* as thinking and unextended on the one hand, unthinking and extended on the other, Descartes begs the question of the subject's participation in the *res extensa* by his argument for the veridical character of perception as guaranteed by God. For Husserl, World and Ego are non-overlapping categories. The world as objective is phenomenologically unreal, it is *transcendent* with respect to phenomena, it can be included in the contemplation of the subject only *as* unreal.

> If this 'transcendence,' which consists in being non-really included, is
> part of the intrinsic sense of the world, then, by way of contrast, the
> Ego himself, who bears within him the world as an accepted sense
> and who, in turn, is necessarily presupposed by this sense, is
> legitimately called *transcendental*, in the phenomenological sense.
> (ibid. 26)

The Ego is not in the objective world, but the important thing to see is that he is not in the phenomenological world either, rather he 'bears it within him'. It seems unlikely that Sartre understood this, since he appears to attribute to Husserl a view of the substantiality of the Ego not as a *category* of substance (as in Descartes's opposition between thinking substance and extended substance) but as a substantial *inhabitant* of the conscious world, which inverts Husserl's position, placing the Ego in the world rather than the world in the Ego.

Sartre begins his argument with an attack on what he considers a mistaken interpretation of Kant, which consists precisely in giving substance to the transcendental, although Kant did not mean it to have this status. Kant says in the *Critique of Pure Reason* that 'the I think *must be able* to accompany all our representations', he does not say that it *does* accompany them all; 'transcendental consciousness is for him only the set of conditions necessary to the existence of an empirical consciousness', so that to hypostatize it is to turn a *de jure* judgment into a *de facto* one. People who ask themselves what a transcendental consciousness can be are driven back to the idea of an unconscious, not at all a Kantian notion. The question of fact is nevertheless a reasonable one, even if Kant did not intend it to be asked. Sartre rephrases it: 'is the *I* that we encounter in our consciousness made possible by the synthetic unity of our representations, or is it the *I* which in fact unites the representations to each other?' (TE 34). And a science of fact is available to answer it, namely phenomenology. Phenomenology discovers a constitutive consciousness, corresponding to Kant's transcendental consciousness, and this consciousness recognizes a physical and psycho-physical me, which however is transcendent and hence must fall under the phenomenological *epoché*. But, Sartre thinks, there is no need for this consciousness also to embody an I: the physical and psycho-physical me is enough for purposes of individuation, even if it has to be bracketed. It follows from this view that the transcendental, like the *vécu*, is impersonal (or 'pre-personal'), without an I; the I will emerge only 'at the level of humanity' (TE 36) and will be nothing more than the active aspect of the me; consciousness as such will not require a personality at all.

The transcendental Ego, therefore, is for Sartre an unnecessary duplication of the Ego with which we become acquainted in consciousness. Husserl's argument for it is represented as invoking it not only for the purpose of individuation but also as providing a necessary principle of unification, a function which however Sartre thinks can be simply fulfilled by intentionality itself, provided consciousness has suitable objects to intend – transcendent ones like mathematical truths, for example, or even its own previous states, which 'by a play of "transversal" intentionalities' provide a ground of unification for a consciousness that has nothing but its own continuity to save it from a 'solipsism of the present moment', to use an expression of Santayana's. But these objects do not require a domain of subjective representation, as it were, in which to be contained – rather they are *aimed at*. Not only is the transcendental Ego, arrived at as a formal exigency of the structure of consciousness, useless – what is worse, it is destructive: in the ordinary way we are transparently, non-positionally and non-reflectively conscious of our consciousness; to introduce the I is to make that transparency opaque.

Consciousness is loaded down; consciousness has lost that character

which rendered it the absolute existent *by virtue of non-existence.* . . .
All the results of phenomenology begin to crumble if the *I* is not, by
the same title as the world, a relative existent: that is to say, an
object *for* consciousness. (TE 42)

As we have seen, the notion of the non-positional character of consciousness as immediate means simply that consciousness is not its own
object, is not intended, not placed *there* over against itself. This does not
mean that consciousness is not aware of itself, only that in the first
instance it is not reflexive. The factual *cogito* of Descartes goes beyond the
Kantian unity of apperception, since the latter is a formal condition of
thinking, while the former involves always an actual episode of thought
(*cf.* Descartes in the second *Meditation*: 'I am, I exist, is necessarily true
each time that I pronounce it or that I mentally conceive it'). But it goes
further than the case warrants, Sartre would say, if it assumes (as Husserl
does) that the I that pronounces or conceives is the same I that is or exists.
The former is non-positional; the latter is positional, and its affirmation by
the former is what we call reflexive. If I wish to apprehend (as opposed
to *being*) the non-positional and unreflected consciousness involved in the
conception of anything (not only of the *cogito*), I can only do it through
the memory; and memory yields up again the content of experience but
no unreflected I to experience it. At best the remembering I enters into a
sort of complicity with the former consciousness, noticing it alongside, as
it were, while directing attention to its revitalized objects.

This last conclusion emerges from an analysis of a remembered
experience of reading:

> while I was reading, there was consciousness *of* the book, *of* the
> heroes of the novel, but the *I* was not inhabiting this consciousness.
> It was only consciousness of the object and non-positional
> consciousness of itself . . . there was no *I* in the unreflected
> consciousness. (TE 46-7)

In fact memory has contributed nothing essential here: the present non-
positional awareness of awareness occupies the same vantage-point as the
past one, the only difference being that its objects are now remembered
rather than present (better: they are present in imagination rather than in
perception). The question whether there *was* an unreflected I is equivalent
to the question whether there *is* one. It is true that if asked to say what
I am doing (counting, for example), I am no longer doing that when I
am answering the question – my attention is drawn from what I am doing
to the formulation of it, and when formulated it is to that extent no
longer immediately present. It went by without reflection, it is 'not-
reflected-on in my immediate past' (BN liii). But the affirmation of an

unreflected I as the subject of this unreflected activity is a question less of memory than of understanding; one might, thus averted, come to experience the transcendental Ego in the moment.

That would be to think two things at once; the intentional content and the intending consciousness. But this can pose no difficulty for Sartre, in view of his insistence on the necessary accompaniment of every act of consciousness with a state of unreflective self-awareness. 'Self-awareness' is the natural thing to say in English; it introduces, however, the supposition that the object of this unreflective awareness is the self, i.e., the Ego, and this is precisely what Sartre wants to question. The thrust of his argument is to break the identification of consciousness with self. Now we might wish to grant that consciousness, when it first comes to awareness of itself, does not yet know whose consciousness it is, without wishing to draw the conclusion that it is not yet anybody's consciousness; and we might wish to maintain that even if, at first, this unreflective consciousness is not the consciousness of self, it might subsequently become so. If this should come about, the self might be as fully an object of its own awareness as any other object could be, and yet not come thereby to be located in the world like those other objects, maintaining rather its status as a necessary condition of the world (understood in the Husserlian sense as 'containing' the world) and thus as transcendental.

In his struggle with this problem Husserl seems to have understood the difficulty that principally concerns Sartre, namely that the Ego must be more than our momentary experience of it, if it is to have the stability required in order for us to enter the world as persons with histories, to endure through time. We are familiar with objects that have this kind of stable entry into the world, and it is characteristic of them that we experience them only one aspect at a time; indeed (unless one adopts some version of Russell's aspect theory, according to which the object *is* just the sum of its aspects) there will always be infinitely many aspects of the object never perceived. Objects in this sense are really transcendent. Consciousness, on the contrary, sees itself entire, with no suggestion that it might be turned, as it were, so as to bring new facets into view. It is not that kind of object at all. How then can it acquire the necessary stability and duration? Husserl's solution is to suggest that the *cogito* has its own special form of transcendence (which he calls 'transcendence in immanence' (Husserl 1931:173)) different from that of objects. Having transcendence for purposes of temporal continuity would not, for him, destroy the status of the *cogito* as transcendental. This, Sartre thinks, is to beg the question: *All* transcendence should fall under the *epoché*. It is nonsense, he thinks, to assert, as Husserl does, that a transcendental consciousness identifiable as an Ego could survive a reduction properly carried out.

But this may be less a genuine problem than a weakness of the pure phenomenological method. According to Sartre's view, there could, strictly speaking, not be said to be any philosopher left to philosophize after the *epoché* – nobody to carry on the inquiry. And yet the inquiry proceeds, not in the confused and bewildered way that ought presumably to be characteristic of a new-born consciousness without presuppositions, but making use of the full arsenal of logic and language. It is disingenuous, then, to pretend, as Sartre does, that the *cogito* can mean only that *there is* consciousness, not that *I have* it. It may have been Descartes's good sense, and not an oversight on his part, that he did not retreat all the way to pre-personal and subjectless thought in his version of the *cogito,* and it may be Husserl's good sense similarly to insist on the integrity of the transcendental Ego. For if we carry reduction as far as Sartre wants to carry it there really will be no way out of the predicament, not now because there is no route of escape, but because there is nobody to take it. Husserl's genius was to see the bankruptcy of any strategy involving the progressive whittling away of a tag-end of the world into nothingness, and to turn the whole problem inside out so that the transcendental Ego becomes the condition of the existence of the world not in a merely formal but in a full metaphysical sense.

Sartre's claim, then, that the I is 'always, even when conceived abstractly, an infinite contraction of the material Me' (TE 54), misses the mark. (In the original French version of *The Transcendence of the Ego*, Sartre has a habit of capitalizing the categories 'Ego', 'Je', 'Moi', which has not been imitated by the translators except in the obvious case of 'I'. Since he obviously meant to do this I have taken the liberty of restoring the capitalization in citing from the translation, which is perfectly adequate in other respects.) But there is still the material Me to be reckoned with. Here Sartre's criticism of the usual strategy of relegating this Me to the unconscious is much more effective. The tables of the argument seem to be turned: whereas before the immediacy of the *cogito* was held not to be adequate to the transcending endurance of the I, now the postulation of an enduring and unconscious Me is held to go gratuitously beyond the immediacy of my emotional experience. The unconscious is often held to be the seat of desire, dissimulated in the familiar Freudian manner; here Sartre's old impatience comes to the fore – if I bring help to Pierre that is because I perceive immediately and without reflection his need of it, not because of something unfelt (because unconscious) in myself, which is invoked to explain how Pierre's sufferings are unbearable to me, so that my helping him is a means of relieving my own distress. Here too, however, Sartre wishes to place this immediacy on an impersonal or pre-personal level: Pierre's distress confronts me in the world as the colour of an inkstand confronts me; it belongs to the intentional correlate of the pre-personal *cogito*. That *I* am in a state of pity for Pierre appears to me only on reflection. The aspect of the I which so appears is passive, acted upon by Pierre's need, and is therefore to be distinguished from its other aspect which acts in the world, perceives, inquires, and so on. These aspects are what Sartre calls respectively the Me and the I.

> The I is the Ego as the unity of actions. The Me is the Ego as the unity of states and of qualities. The distinction that one makes between these two aspects of one and the same reality seems to us simply functional, not to say grammatical. (TE 60)

The Ego, with its correlative aspects of I and Me, therefore falls for Sartre between two unacceptable extremes: the momentary, transcendental, and impersonal field of consciousness on the one hand, and the inert and hidden weight of the unconscious on the other. Parallel to its transcendent unity of states and actions there is, Sartre admits, an immanent unity of reflected consciousness, 'the flux of consciousness constituting itself as the unity of itself' (TE 60) – it is just that this immanent unity is not that of the Ego. The Ego is derivative, it cannot be the ontological foundation of anything; ontological priority must go to whatever it is that has this immanent unity; this only can stand in the place of the '*être par soi*', of 'being-by-itself', the gratuitous and spontaneous origin at once of consciousness and of the world. This brings us back once again to the old problem: what is the ground of this spontaneity? Or whose spontaneity is it? One of the most difficult problems of phenomenology, says Sartre, is the distinction between *active* consciousness and merely spontaneous consciousness, and this is indeed a crucial problem for him in view of the ontological weight that is to be carried by spontaneity in relation to the moral weight that is to be carried by action. Oddly enough, however, he decides to skirt this problem altogether, remarking only that concerted action is necessarily transcendent, because it appeals to a world of things that goes beyond what is contingently present to consciousness at any given moment. The Ego is the 'pole' of such actions; and since these actions lend themselves to psychological analysis, the Ego is said to be 'on the psychic side' i.e., capable of being the object of scientific inquiry. It is in a way the world in which psychic objects and events are encountered: 'the Ego is to psychical objects what the World is to things' (TE 75).

Now clearly the Ego in this sense *must* be transcendent, because such a totality can only be experienced piecemeal. The risk here is that once the Ego is equated to a psychic world waiting to be explored – a world which may contain surprises, the laws of whose behaviour may not appear on its surface – it begins to look suspiciously like the Freudian Id. Sartre attempts to head off this difficulty by interpreting the correlative pair, Ego and World, after the manner of Heidegger, for whom under special circumstances World may uncover itself in the background or on the horizon of things; what is exceptional for World is, according to Sartre, habitual for Ego: 'the Ego, on the contrary, always appears at the horizon of states. Each state, each action is given as incapable of being separated from the

Ego without abstraction' (TE 75). But one cannot have it both ways: either the Ego is thus immediate in every conscious experience, albeit at the horizon, or it is transcendent in such a way as to escape the grasp of this immediacy; and if the latter is the case, as on Sartre's account it seems required to be, then we can have no guarantee that it does not contain depths and complexities of which we are not aware. In the latter case another Ego, more like the Freudian Ego, would be called for if those depths were to be explored. 'Where Id was, there Ego shall be': analytic lucidity is something won actively against the reluctance and dissimulation of the primitive self.

Sartre, however, refuses to accept this division, or rather attributes both sides of it to the Ego as its active and passive aspects. What in Freud would be represented as the Ego uncovering the structure of the Id, in Sartre might be represented as the I investigating the Me. The difficulty with this is that the Me as a unity of states finally vanishes if the states are peeled away, as it were, one by one, and if this happens the Ego vanishes with it, and yet the Ego is supposed to maintain these states by a sort of 'conservative spontaneity', a spontaneity which is not, however, to be confused with that of consciousness as such. This is very puzzling: the spontaneity of consciousness is clear enough – it is the by now familiar 'by-itself', the ontological category for which no explanation can be asked or given, the existential surd whose acceptance is necessary if there is to be a world, or any thought about the world, at all. But one such surd is surely enough, and credulity is strained if a transcendent Ego is also to be a ground of spontaneity. Things are made even more difficult by the fact that the Ego does not appear *except* at the horizon, when we are not looking at it but at something else; in such a moment the I (which, it must be remembered, is an aspect of the Ego), being wholly occupied with its object, whatever that may be, also vanishes, as we have already seen; 'it is quite simply an empty concept which is destined to remain empty' (TE 89). The Sartrian Ego has the elusiveness of a burst bubble, and the outcome of the analysis is an empty I, correlative to a Me reduced to nothingness, together maintaining a spontaneous unity of states and actions.

Before concluding that Sartre's book should in fact have been called 'The Evanescence of the Ego' we should be reminded of his intentions in undertaking this extraordinary argument. In fact the object of his inquiry is much less the Ego as such than the field of consciousness from which it arises: 'the transcendental field', he says at the beginning of the conclusion of *The Transcendence of the Ego*, 'purified of all ego-logical structure, recovers its primary transparency' (TE 93). It is a domain of *absolute* existence, and as such can be allowed no taint of the personal. At every moment it comes into being *ex nihilo* – nothing determines it to do so, nothing lies behind it, it is neither caused nor generated. The importance of this 'by-itself' cannot be exaggerated. The problem we are left with at the end of the book is *its* relationship to *us*. For however much we may wish to make contact with an impersonal ground of being, the conclusion seems inescapable that the 'by-itself' is already individuated when we first come in contact with it. Granted that the details of what we are (the structure of self, or of Ego, or of personality) are not accessible without reflection; still the sense of self, which on reflection shows itself as the Ego, is immediately present in our first spontaneous awareness – or at any rate in the first spontaneous awareness of which we are non-positionally aware. (Any awareness prior to this would for Sartre be a contradiction in terms; I introduce the qualification only because the notion of an evanescent or pre-personal by-itself is not in fact absurd – it would correspond to something like the 'solipsism of the present moment' referred to above, which Santayana attributes for example to animals – although it could play no part in the ontology of human subjectivity.)

The fundamental thesis of *The Transcendence of the Ego*, namely that 'transcendental consciousness is an impersonal spontaneity' (TE 98), cannot therefore be maintained without artificiality, and we are forced to conclude that Husserl is right when he insists that there is an aspect of the Ego that survives reduction. This may after all not be such an unwelcome result for Sartre; in a late interview he says of this work, 'I wrote it actually under the direct influence of Husserl; although I must confess that in it I take an anti-Husserl position. But that's because I'm argumentative by nature' (SBH 30). The achievement of the work is nevertheless considerable. The foundations of an ontology are securely laid, even if they turn out to be more closely tied to personal subjectivity than Sartre might have wished. There are echoes here of the controversy between Hegel and Kierkegaard: the former wished to found an ontological system absolutely and without presuppositions, the latter insisted that such a system would be incomplete in one crucial respect, namely that there would be no room in it for Hegel – but the only possible place for Hegel is at the very beginning, and, if he is put in there, the absolute and presuppositionless character of the system is irretrievably lost. The plight of ontology is that it wishes desperately to rid itself of the subject, but cannot do so. Sartre believes himself to have succeeded in effecting this purge. The subject–object duality, which according to him is a purely logical one, should

definitely disappear from philosophical preoccupations. The World has not created the Me; the Me has not created the World. These are two objects for absolute, impersonal consciousness, and it is by virtue of this consciousness that they are connected. This absolute consciousness, when it is purified of the I, no longer has anything of the *subject*. It is no longer a collection of representations. It is quite simply a first condition and an absolute source of existence. (TE 105-6)

But what can it mean to say that this primordial condition and absolute source of existence is a *consciousness*, if not that it is already individual, already the *specific* subject of whatever content it may have? How can I make the grammatical distinction between subject and object, for example, if I am not already a real subject, the object of whose attention is, for the moment, grammar? What can it mean to say of a consciousness that it is impersonal if I do not already have the concept of person, and if I already have it, in what sense is this impersonality to be understood? It cannot mean that I am in doubt as to *which* consciousness I am, my own or somebody else's; nor does it help to imagine a kind of generalized consciousness (the Hegelian Spirit becoming aware of itself).

If the phenomenological claim that every consciousness is a consciousness of something is admitted, and if Ego and World are correlative to one another, then it follows also that every consciousness is somebody's consciousness. The person whose consciousness it is need not be identifiable at first any more than the thing of which it is consciousness – both require clarification, and this is precisely what the activity of phenomenology provides. But an impersonal or pre-personal *consciousness* is as unthinkable as a non-objective or 'pre-objective' one, i.e., a consciousness having no object, or not yet having one. The object of consciousness need not, of course, be a separable thing, an entity with clearly marked boundaries able to be distinguished from everything else, in order to have the status of an object, and similarly the subject need not be a fully-defined person with all the attributes that subsequent analysis will reveal in order to be an individual subject. And so in spite of himself, and following in the steps of Kierkegaard, Sartre's ontology must be considered to have its point of departure in the existing individual.

This conclusion flies in the face of Sartre's most stubborn convictions – his 'horror of the inner life' has already been referred to, and a scepticism about subjectivity has persisted; in the late interview 'The Writer and his Language' he remarks 'as far as I am concerned there is no such thing as subjectivity; there are only internalization and exteriority' (PL 90). Is it reasonable, then, to insist on this personalization of the subject at the very commencement of the ontological interpretation of Sartre's system? Here it is worth recalling a classical distinction in philosophy, found as early as Aristotle, between what he called the 'order of being' and the 'order of demonstration': the argument may proceed either from what is ontologically prior, or from what is 'better known to us'. While it might be desirable or even necessary to begin from an impersonal starting-point if the enterprise were one of abstract understanding under the aspect of eternity, which would show how subjectivity might arise in a subjectless world by the interiorization of exteriority, it is surely impossible for Sartre to adopt or even to pretend to adopt such a Godlike stance – he is bound to pursue the argument existentially, starting from his own situation as perceiver, thinker, knower and agent. While, therefore, at the beginning of *Being and Nothingess*, he celebrates the overcoming of the distinction between interior and exterior in favour of a kind of phenomenalism (even citing the example of the sciences in a surprising appeal to something like the positivism of Ernst Mach) everything he says elsewhere testifies to his confident acceptance of his own vantage-point as a subject.

There was to be sure a time in our lives when we were not yet the subject, but that time has irrevocably gone by, and we can no more go back to an innocent starting-point than we can rise to a divine one.

> Many people have testified to the fact that, around the age of ten, they discovered their individuality with amazement or anguish. . . . A slight change in the landscape, an event, a fleeting thought, is enough to give rise to the reflective awareness which reveals our Ego to us. (SG 22)

Once this has happened it is too late to hope for a presuppositionless beginning to philosophy, but before it no philosophical reflection could have arisen. And for the most part we are convinced, as Descartes was, of the reality of the self as subject, whatever status we may accord to objects or other people. That is why Sartre describes Genet's condition as pathological:

> Genet is a child who has been convinced that he is, in his very depths, *Another than Self*. . . . He regards the existence of adults as more certain than his own and their testimony as truer than that of his consciousness. He affirms the priority of the object which he is to them over the subject which he is to himself. Therefore, without being clearly aware of it, he judges that the appearance (which he is to others) is the reality and that the reality (which he is to himself) is only appearance. He sacrifices his inner certainty to the principle of authority. He refuses to hear the voice of the *cogito*. (SG 35-6)

This 'voice of the *cogito*' cannot fall under the *epoché*; it accompanies philosophical discourse from the beginning. This is not to say, of course, that it corresponds to our usual perception of ourselves.

> For nobody may say the simple words: I am I. The best and freest of men may say: I exist. Which is already too much. For the others, I suggest that they use such formulas: 'I am Himself' or 'I am so and so *in person*'. (SG 83)

But that is another problem altogether. Authenticity may be hard to come by, but that does not make subjectivity any easier to escape.

V

Being and Negation

If, after all, I can and do live a private life as an existential subject, and if my subjective consciousness is (as it is) an absolute condition for the existence of a world, then I still have the problem of getting out of that privacy into the world thus rendered possible. Sartre's impersonal consciousness was intended to circumvent this difficulty, but as we have seen his strategy will not work. In the long history of the egocentric predicament the device that comes closest to providing a plausible way out is the one used by Husserl in the *Cartesian Meditations* when he argues that it is the significance we find in the world that persuades us of its externality; but significance presupposes other subjects, who must on this account be given at the same time as the world is. Sartre does not arrive at the Other until later. For the moment, then, I confront the phenomenological content of my consciousness alone. As material for the building of a world it is not, perhaps, very promising, but I do have certain powers in relation to it, and can already draw certain conclusions. I can conclude, first, that it is an appearance, and, second, that it is not identical with me (nor I with it – the grammatical distinction again). A logical and ontological relation of negation therefore holds between me and it, and this relation parallels the power I have, which, as we saw in the chapter on imagination, is a power of nihilation (*néantisation*). The affirmation of this power is at the same time an affirmation of my reality as against the world's appearance.

If the world in the first instance is an appearance, that inevitably suggests a reality of which it might be the appearance. This inevitability holds only for subjects to whom the opposition appearance/reality is already intelligible, so once again the pretence of philosophical innocence has to be abandoned. But Sartre's concern at the beginning of *Being and Nothingness* is to transcend all these old dualisms in favour of a new one, 'that of finite and infinite' (BN xlvii); it is not so much that the appearance is the appearance of *something else* as that we must look at the

appearance itself in a new way. Here Sartre moves beyond a phenomenology of consciousness and imagination, in which the object of
consciousness is nothing more than its intentional correlate, to a deeper
ontological level, in which appearance is to be taken as the appearance of
Being. He thus turns from Husserlian preoccupations to Heideggerian
ones. The appearance that I confront, the phenomenon, has a being of its
own, the 'being of the phenomenon'; is this, Sartre asks, equivalent to the
'phenomenon of being'? Clearly not, he replies – if there is a being whose
phenomenon this is, that being must itself be trans-phenomenal. This
conclusion involves an extraneous conviction, for Sartre might well have
stopped with the being of the phenomenon, contenting himself with the
phenomenalism to which he seemed to appeal in the opening section of
the book. But, given his antecedents – Hegel, Husserl, Heidegger –
nothing could be more implausible than such an abandonment of the
game before it even begins. The Quest for Being will not be satisfied with
anything as thin as a play of appearances. (And yet it is worth noting,
before plunging into the ontological depths, that it might have been
satisfied with this.)

The first step towards the establishment of trans-phenomenal being is to
authenticate the being of what appears in terms of the one species of being
about which we can really be certain, namely our own. The things I am
conscious of are not themselves in consciousness – consciousness intends
them, they belong in the world. We come to know them through
consciousness.

> The first procedure of a philosophy ought to be to expel things from
> consciousness and to re-establish its true connection with the world,
> to know that consciousness is a positional consciousness *of* the world
> ... the necessary and sufficient condition for a knowing consciousness
> to be knowledge *of* its object, is that it be consciousness of itself as
> being that knowledge. This is a necessary condition, for if my
> consciousness were not consciousness of being consciousness of the
> table, it would then be consciousness of that table without
> consciousness of being so. In other words, it would be a
> consciousness ignorant of itself, an unconscious – which is absurd.
> This is a sufficient condition, for my being conscious of being
> conscious of that table suffices in fact for me to be conscious of it.
> That is of course not sufficient to permit me to affirm that this table
> exists *in itself* – but rather that it exists *for me*. (BN li-lii)

There is an obvious flaw in this argument, which consists in the move
from 'consciousness ignorant of itself' to 'unconscious', when the strongest
conclusion the premises warrant would be 'unselfconscious'. But this flaw
does not affect the main point of the passage, which is to introduce the
'for-me' as the first category of being after the 'by-itself'.

We thus return to the starting-point of *Imagination*, this time however on a different quest. The 'for-me' is *phenomenal* – its being consists in the first instance in its being perceived: If we could be content with that, we would have a Berkeleyan idealism without God. But the formula *esse est percipi* fails, according to Sartre, because what is *merely* perceived is relative and passive, and these predicates could not apply to any form of being as such. To be relative or passive, he maintains, a thing would have to have some other kind of being, and *then* enter into relation or submit to action. Sartre's argument here is not altogether convincing, since intentionality provides a mechanism for the projection of a kind of relative being which precisely does not have this independent existence; if the world were imaginary, for instance, then it might well be a Berkeleyan world without substratum or transcendence. But Sartre insists that the phenomenon is the phenomenon of a being that transcends phenomena. The error of the phenomenalists, he says, was that 'having justifiably reduced the object to the connected series of its appearances, they believed they had reduced its being to the succession of its modes of being' (BN lx); the modes can be relative and passive, since these terms 'designate relations between a plurality of already existing beings', but they cannot do justice to the being of the object in itself.

That the object has such a trans-phenomenal being seems to be a matter of assertion rather than of inference; Sartre offers what he calls an 'ontological proof', but it involves a certain sleight of hand.

> As we have seen, consciousness is a real subjectivity and [sense] impression is a subjective plenitude. But this subjectivity can not go out of itself to posit a transcendent object in such a way as to endow it with a plenitude of impressions. If then we wish at any price to make the being of the phenomenon depend on consciousness, the object must be distinguished from consciousness not by its *presence* but by its *absence*, not by its plenitude, but by its nothingness. (BN lx)

What this means, apparently, is that if the object is a connected series of appearances, then on any given appearance most of it does not appear – or, in Sartre's own words, which are beginning to grow excited and repetitive as the exposition warms up,

> it is the impossibility in principle for an infinite number of terms of the series to exist at the same time before consciousness at the same time as the real absence of all these terms, except one, which is the foundation of objectivity. If they were present, these impressions – even infinitely many of them – would dissolve into the subjective, it is their absence which gives them objective being. Thus the being of the object is a pure non-being. It defines itself as a *lack*. (EN 28).

Now this non-being, this lack, appears as such only by contrast with the kind of being that subjectivity has; in themselves objects are not non-being at all, on the contrary they are just the being of the 'something' referred to in the maxim that every consciousness is a consciousness *of* something. 'Consciousness is born *supported by* a being which is not itself. This is what we call the ontological proof' (BN lxi). One might object, of course – and Sartre anticipates this objection – that there need not in fact be anything to satisfy this need of consciousness for a transcendent object; but, he replies, an analysis of intentionality (which Husserl after all misunderstood) shows that the only possible being for consciousness is 'that precise obligation to be a revealing intuition of something' – and, he goes on to say, 'a revealing intuition implies something revealed' (BN lxi-lxii). Subjectivity cannot by itself constitute anything objective, so that if objectivity is revealed to it in this way that must be because it existed independently.

On the basis of all this Sartre is prepared to claim a successful transition from pure appearance to a 'fulness of being'. The argument began from the existence of consciousness, a being whose essence is to be consciousness *of*; this essence calls for another essence, namely that of the object of consciousness, and this in turn implies the existence of that object. Such is the schematic structure of the logical development. But its validity is another question. It is not clear that A's 'calling for' B, B's being 'demanded (*exigé*) by' A, constitute grounds for the inference of B from A. The trouble with all ontological proofs is that what they prove remains relative to the prover; as Marx puts it, in the notes to his doctoral dissertation, all they can assert is that 'what I conceive for myself as actual, is an actual conception for me' (Marx 1967: 65). And similar difficulties attend other efforts to establish being by argument. Sartre wishes to show, for example, that the theological concept of creation cannot apply to being-in-itself: a world created out of the subjectivity of God would, he says, remain intra-subjective, and there could not be, in such a subjectivity, even the representation of objectivity. This conclusion seems quite gratuitous and to beg once more the question of the ontological independence of the in-itself. Such independence is a *nominal* necessity – if properly called the 'in-itself', then the in-itself cannot have been created, cannot even be *causa sui*, must simply be itself. 'Even if it had been created, being-in-itself would be *inexplicable* in terms of creation, for it assumes its being beyond the creation. This is equivalent to saying that being is uncreated' (BN lxiv). But none of this guarantees to us anything properly called 'in-itself'. If there were such a being it would be, as Sartre goes on to say, massive (having no interior, simply presenting itself for what it is) and self-identical (never setting itself forward as *other* than some other being); but these properties have no more ontological force than transcendence or objectivity.

Now all this could be cut through – and in practice this is what usually happens – by the hypothetical assertion of being-in-itself as the substance of a world in reference to which our own being is to be understood: in this way there is no longer any need to strain an epistemological sequence by trying to make it carry ontological weight. Granted that we first become aware of our own awareness in something like the pre-reflective *cogito,* granted that the intended objects of consciousness are posited as other than the intending subjectivity, granted that the appearance of these objects suggests (although it cannot be said to *require*) a domain of being to which they give access but which they cannot exhaust, then it makes very good sense to conclude that this domain has ontological priority, that it outreaches and will outlast us, that we come upon it as contingent spectators of its necessities. There is every reason to think that as an agent (to use a distinction of Hume's) Sartre too regards the world in this way, although as a philosopher he cannot indulge such naturalistic tendencies. The in-itself, therefore, becomes the first object of his philosophical interrogation in *Being and Nothingness.*

The outcome of this interrogation, however, throws more light on the interrogator than on the being he confronts. For it is a *questioning* of being; the answer is not known in advance, and it is the possibility of a negative answer that is of the first importance for Sartre. Out of this situation, in fact, he produces three distinct negations: one belonging to the inquiring philosopher, who does not know the answer to his question, which Sartre calls 'non-being of knowledge in man'; one in the world questioned, since something or other may turn out not to be the case there, which Sartre calls 'possibility of non-being in transcendent being'; and one in the truth that results from the inquiry, which must be expressed in a formula of the type 'it is thus and not otherwise', which Sartre calls 'the non-being of limitation'. As he represents the state of affairs, we have penetrated to the heart of being only to find ourselves surrounded by nothingness. We encounter here that peculiar taste for philosophical melodrama which has so alienated sceptical Anglo-Saxons from their excitable Continental colleagues: Nothingness seems to loom up, or to yawn at our feet, when we supposed that we were just people of average ignorance confronting average uncertainties and drawing from them some approximation of the truth. It is as though Bishop Butler's important truism, 'everything is what it is and not another thing', were seen to contain, in its final phrase, matter for cosmic wonder and alarm. What might this other thing be, that the thing in question is not?

It is therefore tempting to dismiss nothingness as yet another example of the tendency of existential philosophers to attach ontological significance to what we think of as merely linguistic. But this way out is perhaps too easy. Melodrama apart, the relation between language and being in this particular connection is worth looking into. Is nothingness just a by-product of a propositional function, or is this propositional function made possible in the first place by nothingness as a structure of the real? The fact that we can cast propositions in negative form presumably shows something about our conception of reality, and other philosophers have sought the origin of affirmation and negation in something extra-linguistic (cf. for example Cassirer in *Language and Myth*, where he traces these functions back to *mana* and *taboo* (Cassirer 1946: 66)). And Sartre goes on to draw attention to some obvious facts about human involvements in the world, which, if they do not sanction the reification of nothingness after the manner of Hegel or Heidegger, do suggest that there is more to it than a mere linguistic device. He points out that negative judgments (e.g., that something has been destroyed after a storm or an earthquake, or that someone has died) can only be made by people who are in a position to know how things were before the disaster, who knew the person in question when alive. (This puts the point too strongly – the evidence of ruined buildings or dead bodies would presumably be convincing even for somebody who had not known that particular city or that particular person, but that would depend on his having learned the general connection, and the point is that in the absence of such additional knowledge there is nothing in the world at any moment to indicate that it was different at another moment.) Destruction and death have to be 'lived as such' if what died or was destroyed is to be seen now as 'no-more'. But seeing them now in this way means seeing beyond what is positively given, and this involves a transcendence of which only man (i.e., consciousness) is capable.

The classic example of the kind of 'negative fact' or '*négatité*' offered by Sartre in *Being and Nothingness* is Pierre's absence from the café. I have entered it to look for him; it is in its own right a fullness of being, with its customers, furniture, smoky atmosphere, and noise; but Pierre is not there. In his analysis of this case Sartre relies heavily on a distinction between '*forme*' and '*fond*', roughly equivalent to the English expressions 'figure' and 'ground'. The café is the ground against which the figure of Pierre would stand out if he were there. I am not interested in the café as such, only in Pierre, by contrast with whom the café is negated as an object of interest, becomes a nothingness. But as things stand Pierre is negated too, by his absence – he is also nothingness.

> So that what is offered to intuition is a flickering of nothingness, it is the nothingness [*néant*] of the ground, whose nihilation calls for, demands the appearance of the figure and it is the figure-nothingness which glides as a *nothing* [*rien*] over the ground. What serves as the foundation for the judgment: 'Pierre is not here', is therefore the intuitive grasp of a double nihilation. (*EN 45*)

The style is convoluted (and is complicated by an obvious printer's error which has led the English translation (BN 10) into further obscurity) but it says something important: that I have, by my expectation of meeting Pierre, brought something new and quite definite to the café, namely Pierre's absence. But it is my real expectation, and not simply a description, that has contributed this absence, because if I now go on to play with other names – Wellington is not in the café, Paul Valéry is not in it – it is obvious that no real relation of absence comes into being. 'This example is sufficient to show,' says Sartre, 'that non-being does not come to things by a negative judgment; it is the negative judgment, on the contrary, which is conditioned and supported by non-being' (BN 11).

It is to be noticed that Pierre's absence, in this example, is quite different from absence as the mode under which the other (or transcendent) manifestations of something present appear to us, as described earlier in this chapter. For even if Pierre were present he would be so only under one aspect, as seen from the vantage-point of my subjectivity, and all his other aspects – his past, his future, those features of his mind and body actually or metaphorically concealed from me – would be absent in the latter sense; as it is, however, he is wholly absent, and hence has no ontological standing, with respect to the being of the café, except as my expectation confers it upon him. Neither Pierre himself, perhaps, nor the other people in the café have any idea that I am looking for him, and yet my world contains as a salient fact the relation between him and it that I call his absence. The essential point to be grasped here is that the world described positively (the café with its fullness of being) is humanly empty, and the world described formally (Wellington, Valéry, St Paul, Bertrand Russell and the remainder of mankind, all absent from the café, and absent too from all the other places where they are not, in a multiple infinity of negations) is inhumanly full; the balance of being and nothingness is struck only in my interested selection among the facts, positive and negative, that are available to me.

The fundamental philosophical problem that these considerations bring to the surface might be called the problem of the mind-dependence of the relational structure of the world. It is Sartre's merit to have seen that negation does not belong in the objective world at all, although it enters into the determination of that world by the subject. 'Determination' here is to be taken in its strict etymological sense: every boundary includes and excludes (whence the Spinozistic formula *omnis determinatio est negatio*), but boundaries are not natural features of the world except in some conceptually primordial cases (the surfaces of physical objects, of the sea, etc., and the divisions between night and day, life and death, and so on). But if this is true of negation it is true of other relations also, which are to be seen as the super-imposition on the world of other grids, reflecting other interests. If the very existence of the grid as a way of determining the contents of the world were to call into being, as timeless features of the ontological domain, all the possible relations truly determinable by it, we would have metaphysical proliferation beyond necessity or reason; it is much more plausible to suppose that the relations simply do not exist until summoned up by a specific application of the conceptual grid by a particular human subject.

The difficulty with this is that many relations, especially those described by the sciences, have come by their repeated invocation to seem to be objective features of the world, so that there is a great deal of resistance to the view that they are products of our interest. Sartre's analysis makes the case so clear for negation, however, that it lends credibility to the hypothesis of mind-dependence in other domains (geometrical, statistical, etc.). The clearest examples, and the easiest to assimilate, come of course from the social sciences, but the sciences of nature are themselves infected with subjectivity to a surprising degree. Not that there are no true relations in the world – but the task of distinguishing between those we discover and those we invent is harder than has been supposed. (Consider for example the concepts of 'information' or of 'entropy'.)

Needless to say, this line of argument is not one that Sartre follows up; instead he proceeds to a discussion of nothingness as dialectical. In Hegel's view, being and nothingness are two abstractions, one full, one empty, dialectically opposed to each other, and entering jointly into the determination of everything that is the case. But to use them as thesis and antithesis in this way, says Sartre, is to mistake their logical relation to one another. Hegelian being and nothingness are contraries, the extremes of a logical series going all the way from affirmation to denial. Sartrian Being and Nothingness, on the other hand, are according to him contradictories, and 'this implies that logically nothingness is subsequent to being since it is being, first posited, then denied' (BN 14). This rather idiosyncratic use of logical terminology apart – for contradictories, as the name implies, stand in a formal relation to one another, while contraries exclude one another materially, and one might have expected Sartre's ontological interest to find the latter more satisfactory – the insight involved here seems to be sound, namely that it is necessary to avoid at all costs the assumption that nothingness is on a par with being, or might have been prior to it (as for example of creation *ex nihilo* would require). Nothingness is a function of being, not the other way round.

The question that now arises is: what is it about being that might generate nothingness? Through what kind or activity of being does nothingness come into the world? Being-in-itself can hardly be expected to play this role, since it is full and positive; whatever turns out to be responsible will have to show, in some metaphorical sense, suicidal tendencies, since the negation of being must involve to some degree its own annihilation. Can a being or beings be found thus carrying within themselves the seeds of their own annihilation? Sartre's obvious answer is that human beings have just this property. He has already shown how we characteristically relate to the world through *négatités* – absences, lacks, and so on – and while this does not amount to a power of negation over the being that actually confronts us, which is massive and inert, it is a power of changing our relationship to that being: we can refuse things as they are, putting a kind of buffer of nothingness between us and the world. Human being, says Sartre, can 'secrete a nothingness which isolates it'; this isolation is presumably a means of detaching human being from the causal nexus of events, since Sartre identifies this power with what the Stoics, and later Descartes, called *freedom*.

Freedom defined in this way is not so much freedom of action (since for action the isolating buffer would have to be broken through again in order for the agent to have a real effect in the world) as freedom of attitude. As such it is for Sartre not merely a contingently true description of how human beings are, but an essential defining feature of what it means to be human. For the one thing a human being need not do is to accept itself at the hands of other agencies in the world, as causally determined to be what it is. The primary function of freedom is to cut off the past, to negate its determinations, to put it out of play. Now if freedom is the mode of being of human consciousness, the structure of consciousness must be such as to take conscious account of this freedom; there must therefore be a phenomenological content of consciousness that will give an indication of its status as free. Here Sartre, borrowing from Kierkegaard, introduces the concept of *anguish*. Anguish, or dread, describes a spectrum of human feelings, running from mere unease to terror, whose principal ingredients are uncertainty, loneliness, and responsibility: I am in anguish when, left to my own devices and without help from any quarter, I am nevertheless under the necessity of choosing, of deciding, of committing myself (and perhaps others also) to courses of action heavy with consequences. Anguish is not to be confused with fear – I can be afraid of threats from other people, or dangers from things, but anguish arises from confrontation with myself, not from any confrontation with the rest of the world. (Fear may lead to anguish, as in the case of my first being afraid of falling over a precipice, then suddenly realizing the possibility that I might jump.) Both anguish and fear refer to the future; but I am afraid because I know what my values are and anticipate a threat to them, whereas I am in anguish because I do *not* know what they are – my uncertainty about the future attaches not to the being of the world but to my own being. I do not know what I shall be, but I do know that it will not be what I now am, and also that nothing I now am or can know will determine what I shall be. My anguished being, therefore, is the freedom to become what I am not, to be it already under the mode of not being it (BN 32).

The insulation that nothingness provides surrounds me on all sides: it separates me from my past, from my future, and from the present world. I am not what I experience, nor am I obliged to be what I was, nor can

I count on what I will be. Yet in spite of this isolation I shall inevitably become what I am not, and in this becoming I can freely exercise choice, indeed I must do so – and bear the consequent responsibility. Choices as to the future are taken to be guided by values, values being precisely the expression of fundamental preferences, and hence the determining factor in decisions. But if there is determination here, it can only be self-determination, for the world is given without values, it just *is*, and the fact of our freedom simply expresses the world's indifference.

Ordinarily, of course, this fact is concealed from us by our engagement in a social world in which values are prescribed. But when we look more closely we find that *these* values are not in any objective world, they are created and sustained in being by other people whose ontological status is no more fundamental than our own, and they become values to us only by the exercise of our own freedom. This truth does not strike us as we go about our daily business in our own situation, constrained by conventional values 'sown on [our] path as thousands of little real demands, like the signs which order us to keep off the grass' (BN 38); it only appears on reflection: 'anguish then is the reflective apprehension of freedom by itself' (BN 39). The origin of anguish is the sudden realization of freedom on the part of a subjectivity that naïvely supposed everything to be ordered and stable, only to find that this order and stability were its own creation, able to be discarded at will. This realization is vertiginous, and involves a shift of *Gestalt* which may, if it comes at the wrong time, have dangerous consequences, as in the case of a man who suddenly realizes that he is on a tightrope; it may even (as in the anecdote of the rider who crossed the frozen lake of Constance) affect retroactively a life formerly lived in confidence.

The danger and unpleasantness of this situation is fully recognized by subjectivity, which might prefer to be (as many metaphysical theories say it is) merely the spectator of an unfolding determinism. Such a spectator would have no responsibility either for himself or for the course of events, whereas Sartrian subjectivity is constantly obliged to remake itself and to deliberate about what it ought to do. One natural consequence is that it is tempted to use its power of negation to relieve this very discomfort, by denying its own freedom and refusing to be what it existentially is. The chief strategy of this refusal is our tendency to look at ourselves as though we were other people, and to view our freedom as though it were the freedom of another, with respect to which the only problem is to calculate, from the known essential characteristics of the person in question, his likely behaviour if free. It involves, in other words, a recourse to the notion of the Me as an object for the interest of the I. This brings us back to the problem of the identity of the agent: once again, Sartre will be in difficulty if subjectivity is impersonal, because then the Me *would* be other than the I, would require observation, could do surprising things, and might be determined, whereas under the personal interpretation given in the last chapter there is available a locus for anguish and for freedom.

Negation, as an active power of human subjects, makes our human world what it is and also helps in the constitution of those subjects themselves. In *The Words* the young Sartre is intrigued by absence. Monsieur Simonnot, who used to come to lunch on Thursdays, occupied his place in the world firmly enough in his own right, but became transfigured when at some celebration or other he failed to appear. 'There's someone missing here,' said Sartre's grandfather, 'it's Simonnot'; for Sartre suddenly this negative fact overwhelmed all the positive ones that claimed his attention; 'Monsieur Simonnot himself, absent in flesh and blood', appeared like a column in the centre of the room; the other people present merely existed, he was the only one to be *missing*. His actual appearance would have been a disappointment, since he would then have been present on his own account, as it were, whereas, absent, he was sustained by the disappointed expectations of the others, entering their world as a *négatité*, the most meaningful mode of being for a human consciousness. 'Reduced to the purity of a negative essence, he retained the incompressible transparency of a diamond' (WO 91). Later in the book the episode is repeated, this time in connection with an engraving showing a crowd on a quay in New York awaiting the arrival of Charles Dickens: 'There's someone missing here, it's Dickens!' said Sartre to himself, the tears starting to his eyes (WO 168). Such a mode of being as absence was something he himself aspired to, as an antidote to a sense of superfluous presence; in fantasy he stood in the wings of scenes of adventure and danger, waiting for the sign 'there's someone missing here: it's Sartre!' to leap forward in imagination and commit deeds of heroism.

Here we have the converse of Pierre in the café: it is as if Pierre appeared to claim his absence, to stand as figure against the ground of the café, to determine himself in relation to it. The determination of the self is achieved, in Sartre, against some quite specific feature or features of the objective world. These features constantly change, as time passes and the subject moves from situation to situation, but they provide as it were the point of reference in being-in-itself for this subject whose facticity they constitute. 'Facticity' is the aspect of the objective world that, together with the subject, makes up his situation. It is, in consequence, just that aspect of the world he knows himself not to be; in the polar relationship of consciousness to its content, of subject to object, the differentiation between the poles is in the first instance a simple exclusion or negation. Whatever I am, I am over against the particular corner of the world I happen to inhabit. The contents of this corner are, as we have seen, encountered as 'for-me'; I myself, encountered reflexively as apprehending (and hence as being other than) these contents, appear as 'for-myself', a formula which, generalized to the kind of being that I am, may be called 'for-itself'. The in-itself (the objective world) is an essential mediation between the by-itself and the for-itself: only on the basis of the permanence of the in-itself can the former transcend its momentary and isolated character to become an identity and a project. The for-itself is not just given, it is active, undertaking its own realization as a form of being.

The elements of the foregoing account are relatively abstract, with the exception of anguish as the phenomenological correlate of freedom. But being in-itself also has its phenomenological aspect, briefly alluded to in *Being and Nothingness* but developed in a more familiar form elsewhere, especially in *Nausea*. 'Being will be disclosed to us by some kind of immediate access – boredom, nausea, etc.' (BN xlviii). This queasiness or lassitude of the conscious subject confronted with the indifference of being is a dominant theme of Sartre's early fiction; it seems to represent the recognition at once of the alien character of being-in-itself and of the hopelessness of becoming or conquering it. Boredom and nausea are not, of course, the only or even the primary forms of evidence for the existence of the in-itself, indeed it is not clear that they constitute *evidence* at all in any strict sense. The initial realization of the inertia of being-in-itself might, perhaps, have a depressing or even sickening effect on a subjectivity used to thinking of the world as vital or responsive; animism dies hard, and a religious or even a naturalistic upbringing is a poor preparation for Sartrian ontology. But it seems likely that it is the independent realization of the ontological condition, and not the experience of any phenomenological content, that produces this reaction. Tree roots and bits of muddy paper do not, to those who have no other reason for thinking so, provide convincing grounds for the conclusion that things are wholly inert and subjectivity merely fleeting.

VI

Bad Faith and
the Existence of the For-Itself

To summarize the structure of being as it emerges from the foregoing considerations: each of us, exemplifying in his own as yet unreflexive and undifferentiated way the transcendental field of the by-itself, encounters the for-me which, under its aspects of opacity and inertia (productive in us of nausea, boredom and the like) leads to the construction of the transcendent in-itself, and then by inference of the for-itself; the form of this inference (i.e., the logical relation of the for-itself to the in-itself) proves to be negation. Ontological priority belongs to the in-itself, which is what it is, absolutely and timelessly. If the for-itself is a negation of this, then it cannot be what it is, not at any rate where 'is' is construed as meaning participation in the kind of being exemplified by the in-itself.

This way of talking sounds perverse to those for whom the verb 'to be' has a primarily logical force. Not to be what it is can only be the mark of the impossible or the non-existent, since everything possible or existent is what it is. Now with respect to the in-itself, the for-itself might be said to have just those properties of impossibility and non-existence, and the way Sartre chooses to speak of it plays on the double sense of 'to be' as logical and ontological: existence as an essential property of the in-itself is denied to the for-itself, which is not/is (in terms of its own being) what it is/is not (in terms of the being of the in-itself). An element of temporality has to be invoked in order to de-mystify this paradox; this provides a dynamic relation between the present 'is' and the future 'is not (yet)' which when realized will in turn be linked by negation to a still further future.

But in fact hardly any subjectivities consciously represent the state of affairs to themselves in this way. Rather than such a precarious temporality they consider their mode of being to be stable actuality; they are what they are, solid citizens, leaders, professors, philosophers and the like. If their truth is fleeting, if they are freely suspended rather than firmly grounded, these facts seem to be concealed from them. This however need not surprise us: since Freud the notion of a lived deception, resorted to as a protection against a truth glimpsed and quickly repressed, has been a familiar one. The truth, unacceptable because of an ethical shrinking from unnameable desires, an ontological horror of the abyss, is relegated to the domain of the unconscious, and conscious life is dominated by falsehood, in the form of pathological behaviour (which includes a great deal that passes for normal).

According to the Freudian account there is nothing blameworthy in this. There is a state of affairs to be described, and if possible explained; if the products of libido, trauma and the rest are repression or flight, that is how the world contingently and neutrally is in the person of the patient in question. But for Sartre this view is both morally and metaphysically objectionable. (The metaphysical objection would be enough by itself, but Sartre cannot resist giving it a moral overtone as well.) The Freudian account requires a substantial self that exists prior to and independently of its formation by experience, because it can be acted upon by experience (and is therefore also, to some degree at least, passive). But for Sartre there can be nothing of the self that is not for-itself, and nothing of the for-itself that has not been won actively by negation of the in-itself. The for-itself having made itself in this way, it is as it were wholly responsible for itself, and can hide neither behind prior and independent determining forces nor behind a pretended ignorance of the state of affairs. It *knows* itself, and knows all there is to know about itself; and if it fails to acknowledge something about itself, or acts out of character with itself, this can only be because it is knowingly deceiving itself. It is this deception that Sartre names *mauvaise foi*, 'bad faith', 'faith' having here the sense of something one keeps (with another person, or with oneself) as well as something one has.

Although '*mauvaise foi*' involves self-deception, its translation as 'self-deception' is unsatisfactory, because this expression fails to catch just those nuances of meaning that give the concept its specific force. *Mauvaise foi* is a natural condition of the uncritical for-itself, just as *mauvaises herbes* (i.e., weeds) are the natural product of unattended gardens – in both cases the more desirable condition, the 'good' state, is rare, difficult to achieve or maintain. And then also – as Sartre points out later on – 'bad faith' is a form of faith (*foi*), not just a cynical deception practised by the self on itself but a genuine belief that it entertains about itself. And yet in some sense or other it knows this belief to be mistaken, and it knows that it knows this, so that holding the belief does involve the maintenance of the deception. At a sufficiently advanced stage of self-awareness, then, bad faith passes over into downright dishonesty. The condition described in the previous chapter, in which the subject knows but is terrified of its own freedom, which it proceeds to deny, is a familiar case of this.

How can the for-itself, whose very being consists in its self-productive activity against the facticity of the in-itself, undertake an additional project of self-deception? This puzzle can only be resolved if we are clear about the subject-matter of the self-deception of bad faith. For in bad faith we do not necessarily misrepresent to ourselves the objective state of affairs, nor even necessarily our situation – it is our own being that we dissemble, and this in two ways: by denying the fact that it is in question, and by attributing to it fixed properties. Both are comforting strategies, the first avoiding distress and the second providing stability. But for Sartre there is no such thing as a *property* of being-for-itself, unless it is precisely its being in question. 'Our way of being is in question in our being. Nobody is cowardly or brave in the way that a wall is white or a blanket green. To the most cowardly man, cowardice always manifests itself as a *possibility*' (SG 60). So it is not that bad faith gets hold of the wrong attribute, it is that any attribution to me of determinate charactistics is deceptive. Such an attribution, however, is quite compatible with complete lucidity about the truth of the world. Bad faith is not a *lie*, if that means refusing a known truth about the in-itself. If I lie, I lie to others, trying to convince them that I hold beliefs I do not in fact hold, but I cannot do this to myself. I cannot not know what I know, or that I know it. Even the psychoanalytic censor, says Sartre, must know what it is repressing, so if consciousness itself is not in bad faith the censor must be; and since it, as the doorkeeper of the unconscious, cannot itself be unconscious, the translucidity of consciousness and its bad faith cannot be escaped by this route.

There is a sense, Sartre admits, in which bad faith is a kind of lying to oneself – but only on condition that lying does not mean what it ordinarily means; for if I lie to myself I know not only that I am lying but also that I am lied to, and I must therefore be in good faith to the extent that I acknowledge my own bad faith (BN 49). But this opens up the possibility of an infinite regress; and of course it is not inconceivable that I might choose to believe another person whom I knew to be lying. The refusal of truth, or the conscious embracing of falsehood (while at the same time refusing the consciousness of the untruth of what it asserts) may suit my purposes. Sartre's classic example is the woman who knows the intentions of her companion when he takes her hand, but refuses to make the choice (disengaging the hand, or consenting to physical contact) that this knowledge imposes. It is to be noted, however, that her bad faith consists, not in deceiving herself about the companion or their situation as a couple, but in allowing the hand to become an inert thing (like someone else's hand) while she distracts herself with witty conversation.

The two concepts that are played upon in bad faith are *facticity* and *transcendence*, the immediate constraints of the situation and the projection of a self-image independent of these constraints; they might in good faith be brought into coordination, but in bad faith they are exploited alternately as circumstances require. At the same time a second duplicity may come into play, between one's being-for-itself and a being-for-others. Circumstances often require us to behave in ritual ways that other people count on: the waiter must behave like a waiter, the grocer like a grocer. But the waiter, inside himself, cannot *be* a waiter, even though he knows, and performs and expects, the duties and perquisites of being a waiter; or if he *is* one (if he achieves the status of waiter as in-itself, as it is attributed to him by others) he can manage this only in bad faith.

The problem for the for-itself is to think its own existence when the only kind of existence it has at hand as a model is that of the in-itself. Its temptation is to play at being in-itself, and this is the usual mode of bourgeois existence. Lucien, the partly autobiographical hero of 'The Childhood of a Leader', comes to awareness of himself in this mode:

> It was amusing because everybody was playing. Papa and mama were playing papa and mama. . . . And Lucien was playing too, but finally he didn't know at what. Orphan? Or Lucien? He looked at the water bottle . . . Lucien suddenly felt that the water bottle was playing at being a water bottle. (WA 87)

Under this fictional cover Sartre seems, unintentionally perhaps, to admit what was said in the last chapter, namely that we do not really know the in-itself as such, we do not know its transcendence but only its appearance of inertia. We encounter it as Roquentin in *Nausea* encounters the soiled papers or the tree, as indifferent, but this indifference is not an adequate model for existence. Lucien also encounters a tree, and tries with futile anger to get it to respond to him:

> He repeated, louder, 'Nasty old tree, nasty old chestnut tree, you wait, you just wait and see!' and he kicked it. But the tree stayed still – just as though it were made of wood. That evening at dinner Lucien told mama, 'You know, mama, the trees, well . . . they're made out of wood.' . . . Lucien became a little roughneck. He broke his toys to see how they were made . . . each time he was deeply disappointed, things were stupid, nothing really and truly existed. (WA 89)

The *existence* of the for-itself, as opposed to its constitution, is to be looked for elsewhere than in its relation to the in-itself, whose objectivity and inertia prove merely frustrating (even though, as we shall see, they remain a perpetual lure). Other Sartrian formulas therefore appeal to language or to society. In *The Words*, for example, existence derives from being named, and because the for-itself has the power of naming it seems to acquire, in the person of the writer, a position of dominance:

to exist was to have an official title somewhere on the infinite Tables of the Word; to write was to engrave new beings upon them or – and this was my most persistent illusion – to catch living things in the trap of phrases. (WO 182)

The problem is that what is written takes on, after all, the character of the in-itself, in contrast with which the reader (whom every writer becomes) falls back into dependence:

Gliding over that incorruptible substance, the *text*, my gaze was merely a tiny, surface accident; it did not disturb anything, did not wear anything away. I, on the other hand, was a dazzled mosquito, pierced by the rays of a beacon. I would put out the light and leave the study: invisible in the darkness, the book kept sparkling, for itself alone. (WO 183)

As a further example, in the case of Genet, rejection from the social world leads naturally enough to the formulation of existence in *its* terms: 'To Be is to belong to someone' (SG 6). But this dependence on others is double-edged; it allows us to disavow aspects of ourselves that others ignore. 'To the child who steals and the child who masturbates, to exist is *to be seen by adults*, and since these secret activities take place in solitude, they *do not exist*' (SG 16). This truth has been recognized by moralists of all persuasions, whether religious ('Thou God seest me' used to hang as an admonitory text in many evangelical houses) or psychoanalytic (the Superego as the 'generalized Other').

To refuse to recognize one's own actions is bad faith; but so it is to recognize them only in the judgment of others. This however is a very frequent condition. In particular it is characteristic of a special class of persons whose relation to others is one of oppression, whose being is parasitic on that of their victims; Sartre calls them collectively *salauds*. '*Salaud*', which is derived from *sale*, 'dirty', and has the worst connotations of that word (as e.g., in 'dirty trick'), has no obvious polite equivalent in English, but typical candidates for the epithet in Sartre would be policemen, capitalists, anti-semites and so on. The cases vary: an especially striking one is that of the '*chef*', the leader or boss who is recognized by others as occupying a position of power and who comes to see himself as being what his position has made him. Here the playing of a role, which was merely banal in the waiter's case, becomes deadly serious, having consequences not only for the person in question but for the rest of society. 'If you want to command,' says the father in *The Condemned of Altona*, 'think of yourself as someone else' (CA 11). For other people have the objective status denied to the subject, are marked by enviably definite characteristics, have firm convictions and solid reputations. The subject cannot think of itself in this way without bad faith, but it very much wishes to do so and will adopt oppressive views, such as anti-semitism, just for the sake of experiencing its own definiteness in relation to the oppressed. Lucien, in 'The Childhood of a Leader', is again a perfect example: a sense of well-being, of respect for himself, comes over him when he commits himself by a violent action to a pure and pitiless anti-semitism.

> The real Lucien – he knew now – had to be sought in the eyes of others, in the frightened obedience of Pierrette and Guigard, the hopeful waiting of all those beings who grew and ripened for him ... he was and always would be this immense waiting of others. (WA 142-3)

Simonnot, Dickens, Sartre, Lucien – the attempt to occupy a fixed place in the world, through the eyes and at the expense of others, is doomed either to failure or to dishonesty. In the case of the anti-semite, the chosen belief involves manifest irrationality. And 'how can one choose to reason falsely? It is because of a longing for impenetrability' (ASJ 18). Impenetrability is the mode of being of the in-itself, as opposed to the transparency of the for-itself (the mosquito penetrated by the lighthouse beam), the latter's quality of existing as a surface rather than as anything solid ('I have nothing behind me' (PL 92)). The for-itself can maintain itself in existence only dynamically: it is thrown out into the world (*cf.* the essay on intentionality quoted above), and its only hope of authenticity is to enter into this condition of thrownness, to ride as it were its own contingency, to exploit the layer of nothingness that separates it from the determinism of the world and hence from any inevitability in its own future, to be the free project that all this makes possible. (The etymology of 'project' is to be taken seriously.) This directedness, this tension, this controlled mobility, are incompatible with the 'thereness', the inertia, of the in-itself; the for-itself is permeable, and it permeates, it is the presence of the world to consciousness and the intention of consciousness in the world.

The existence of the for-itself is therefore vertiginous; the constant shifting of ground, the repeated encounter with our own otherness, engenders a desire or a nostalgia for the permanence and fixity of the in-itself, and a corresponding fear of the unknown being one discovers oneself to be. So the 'decent' man, i.e., the conforming and substantial citizen, denies his own otherness, which he identifies as Evil: 'it is what he wants but does not want to want', and by its denial he becomes 'the most abstract negation, the negation of negation' (SG 25-6). (Note that Sartre is here employing 'the negation of negation' neither in its analytic sense as the restoration of identity nor in its dialectical sense as the *Aufhebung* of an antithesis, but is playing on the double sense of 'negation' as refusal and as otherness.) This craven refusal of the risk inherent in human existence is quite understandable, indeed a sincere acceptance of that existence is extremely difficult. For sincerity means being what I am and acknowledging it for what it is, but if I am a for-itself then there *is* not anything that I *am* in this changing world, there is only what I am to be (but as yet am not) and what I am not (because I am conscious of it). Hence the necessity and universality of bad faith.

A form of sincerity is nevertheless possible, provided that it rests not on my being what I am but on my not being it and acknowledging *that* – or, better, acknowledging a constant oscillation or 'play of mirrors' between being what I am and not-being it. (But the project of sincerity may itself be undertaken in bad faith. There can, it is true, be an unproblematic *retrospective* sincerity, but that is because my past being, for Sartre, has become being-in-itself, which is what it is.) Bad faith is the inverse of this; it involves a claim to be what I am not – not just not being a coward, for example, but constituting myself as courageous and taking pride in this fact. It is positive beliefs of this sort about oneself that constitute the 'faith' of bad faith. Sartre's attitude is equivocal: on the one hand he regards bad faith as a feature that is 'essential to human reality', on the other he assumes a frankly moralizing tone in condemning its products. The concept thus has something in common with that of 'alienation' in Hegel, which while a necessary step in the dialectical separation of object from subject also becomes, especially in the hands of Marx, a source of human inauthenticity.

The antitheses of bad faith are on the one hand 'good faith' and on the other sincerity. The latter are both ideals realizable only in the in-itself; the for-itself is constantly caught in the play of mirrors: 'To believe is to know that one believes, and to know that one believes is no longer to believe' (BN 69). This seems just a plain mistake. To *know what* one believed – i.e., to know *x*, where *x* is also what is believed – might be 'no longer to believe', since belief would be superfluous in the presence of knowledge, but there seems nothing odd about knowing *that* one believes something, and in this belief's surviving as such. The usefulness and penetration of the concept of bad faith lie, it seems to me, not in the mirror-game, whose elaboration leads Sartre into some rather complex preciosities, but in the realization that I always want to be something in the mode of the in-itself, and that I often take myself to have succeeded in this, even though the strict impossibility of doing so is a condition of my being the kind of being that can even have such a project in the first place. That is why bad faith is an 'immediate, permanent threat to every project of the human being': falling into it destroys the character of the project as such and renders it static. But its possibility is inscribed in the nature of consciousness as the 'instantaneous nucleus of this being' (BN 70).

The central problem in all this is the old one of personal identity, but under a characteristically existential modality – the problem is one not of individuation or of reidentification but of self-identity in the moment, of ontological status. Now, as I have argued, the by-itself is already individuated by the time it emerges in pre-reflective awareness, and this individuation becomes self-conscious along with the realization of the transcendence of the in-itself, a realization which is at once natural and conjectural; if Sartre would allow a similar natural conjecture to establish a transcendental for-itself, then the problem of identity would be less pressing – (my) Self and (my) World would be intentional correlates, and a personal (not an impersonal) consciousness would have something to fall back upon, as it were, as well as something to reach out to. But all this is just what he will not allow. The for-itself can therefore have no being of its own, ontologically it must be a Nothingness in relation to the in-itself. If we accept this it explains neatly how the for-itself can 'secrete' Nothingness, since that is what it is made of, but it does not explain the agency of this 'secretion' or of any other activity.

Sartre's rooted objection to the Freudian unconscious, which provides a solid if sometimes alien grounding for consciousness, no doubt finds an implicit explanation in the fact that Freud is a scientist and hence precisely at home with hypotheses. And this mistrust of the hypothetical is more serious in the case of the for-itself than in that of the in-itself, where as we have seen Sartre practically, if not avowedly, has recourse to it. For the for-itself is by definition consciousness, and consciousness of consciousness; it is therefore bounded by the limits of the immediate, whereas the hypothetical necessarily transcends those limits. At the very end of *Being and Nothingness*, Sartre does, it is true, entertain a hypothesis *about* the for-itself: 'Ontology will ... limit itself to declaring that *everything takes place as if* the in-itself in a project to found itself gave itself the modification of the for-itself. It is up to metaphysics to form the *hypotheses* which will allow us to conceive of this process as the absolute event which comes to crown the individual venture which is the existence of being. It is evident that these hypotheses will remain hypotheses since we cannot expect either further validation or invalidation. What will make their *validity* is only the possibility which they will offer us of unifying the *givens* of ontology' (BN 621). I shall have occasion to return to the 'existence of being,' but note for the moment that, according to this passage, there is no suggestion that there is anything hypothetical about the for-itself that I am, or that I might resort to conjecture about its current status: about its origin in the metaphysical scheme of things, perhaps, but not about my consciousness of it or of its nothingness with respect to the in-itself. It is to be noticed also that in Sartre the for-itself is distinct from, and on the transcendental plane replaces, both the Ego (which for him is transcendent) and subjectivity (which for him is an illusion).

What being can this immediacy of Nothingness possibly possess? Sartre is anxious not to commit the obvious absurdity of attributing Being to

81

Nothingness, but this anxiety produces remarkable conceptual contortions. The for-itself exists, he says, as presence-to-itself, and this is the prime characteristic of consciousness; but this involves a gap between the subject and itself, a gap which however on examination proves to consist of nothing (*rien*): 'this fissure is thus pure negative (*le négatif pur*)' (*EN 120*). From this it is a short step to seeing in it the emergence of nothingness (*le néant*), which is found here in its pure state – 'everywhere else we are obliged, in one way or another, to confer on it being-in-itself as nothingness. But the nothingness that springs up at the heart of consciousness *is not*. It *is been*' (*EN 120*). This conscious violation of grammar turns 'to be' into a reflexive verb, and thus makes vivid the Sartrian conception of the for-itself as a self-sustaining reflection of Being upon itself. (The English translation corrects it by rendering '*est été*' as 'is made-to-be', which misses this nuance; I have therefore not used it for these passages.) So it is not that we come upon Nothingness – it is rather, if I may so put it, self-inferred:

> One does not find, one does not *uncover* Nothingness as one might find or uncover a being. Nothingness is always an *elsewhere*. It is the obligation upon the for-itself never to exist except in the form of an elsewhere with respect to itself, to exist as a being which is perpetually afflicted with an inconsistency of being. This inconsistency moreover does not refer to another being, it is only a perpetual reference of the self to itself, of the reflection to the reflector, of the reflector to the reflection ... thus nothingness is this hole of being, this fall of the in-itself towards itself by which the for-itself is constituted. But this nothingness can only 'be been' if its borrowed existence is correlated to a nihilating act of being. This perpetual act by which the in-itself degenerates into presence-to-itself we shall call an ontological act. Nothingness is the putting into question of being by being, that is to say exactly consciousness or the for-itself. (*EN 121*)

Here, as is so often the case, Sartre's insight seems better than his argument. The latter is extraordinarily vulnerable: Nothingness first emerges 'at the heart of consciousness' but is then equated with consciousness, and there is an explicit appeal to an undefined concept of the 'self' ('the fall of the in-itself towards the self') which if admitted undermines the whole project of subjectivity as Nothingness. And yet, as a strategy for making sense of the anomalous situation of consciousness in the world, its construal on the one hand as a Nothingness with respect to the being of the world, and on the other as a self-generating double (reflector/reflection) has the merit of a kind of desperate plausibility. These two aspects are conceptually distinct; and the latter is independent of the former, although the reverse is not the case – one might have a self-generating double in some other ontological modality than Nothingness, but in that modality some mechanism of pure self-generation is obviously required.

This mechanism is reminiscent of an equally desperate attempt on the part of physics, in recent years, to ground itself materially rather than lose itself in an infinite regression of ever more fundamental particles; known as 'bootstrap theory', the strategy in question makes the particles functions of one another rather than of some more basic stuff. I say 'desperate' in both cases because the alternatives involve an abandonment of a belief cherished by the inventors of the theory, respectively Sartre himself and a certain school of physicists; if one did not happen to share that belief the situation would not, of course, seem particularly problematic, let alone desperate. The alternative in the case of physics is the theory of quarks, which is problematic but not paradoxical. But in Sartre's case the alternatives bring with them an old and stubborn philosophical dilemma: if consciousness is not self-generating, then what does generate it? And if it is not Nothingness, what substance does it have? The weakness of his position is that he has no recourse if somebody chooses to relativize his Nothingness to one form of being (his 'in-itself') and then populate it, as it were, with another, perhaps a spiritual one; this has been done, for example, by the so-called 'Christian existentialists' with their 'vertical dimension' and the like. The trouble with holes, in other words, is that people are tempted to fill them. It is to Sartre's credit that he has resisted this temptation, even if his insistence on their emptiness seems Quixotic. At all events his view explains, as others do not, why at death the world persists, but consciousness vanishes without any other trace than it may have been able to inscribe in that very world.

As we saw in the last chapter, the for-itself defines itself not only against the facticity of its present situation but against its own past and future; these too are actively negated and yet, as negated, indispensable to the ontology of the for-itself: 'I am what I shall be in the mode of not being it' (*EN* 69). And this inevitability of temporal development is another object of avoidance for bad faith – Sartre points out, for example, in the case of the woman whose companion takes her hand, that it is the future implication rather than the present character of her behaviour that she dissembles to herself. But the inevitability of a future is not to be construed as determination, which would obviously be quite incompatible with Sartre's view of time. The specific content of my future exists as 'my possibilities': 'human reality both is and is not its own possibilities' (BN 96).

The concept of 'possibility' at first gives Sartre a certain amount of trouble: 'there is the greatest difficulty in understanding its being, for it is given as prior to the being of which it is the pure possibility; and yet qua possible, at least, it necessarily must have being' (BN 96). But after an elegant short essay on Leibniz and Spinoza (a good example of a typical Sartrian device, turning aside from the arguments to summarize classical positions, not necessarily in order to refute them but as a counterpoise to his own) he sets out clearly the opposition between possibility as a function of subjectivity and ignorance on the one hand, and possibility as an objective feature of the world on the other. It certainly appears to us as the latter: if I say

> it is possible that it may rain, this possibility belongs to the sky as a
> threat; it represents a surpassing on the part of these clouds, which I
> perceive, toward rain. The clouds carry this surpassing within
> themselves, which means not that the surpassing will be realized but
> only that the structure of being of the cloud is a transcendence
> toward rain. (BN 97-8)

The risk here, as Sartre acknowledges, is of introducing an Aristotelian potency of the for-itself, the in-itself being 'in act'; if possibility as subjective is a merely logical concept, possibility as objective may be a merely magical one. Sartre calls these alternatives 'Charybdis and Scylla', but in fact – as we saw in an earlier chapter – the magical was at one time for him an acceptable concept under which to analyze the relation between the subject and its world. It would admittedly be wrong to represent clouds as having magical powers, and yet in the absence of scientific under-standing their production of rain *is* magical (can be prayed for, etc.). Sartre has recourse here, exceptionally, to scientific language, speaking of 'a certain quantity of water vapour, at a given temperature and a given pressure'. But this is only to explain how, in the attempt of the scientists to 'dehumanize the world', real possibilities have been dismissed as subjective. The choice of example is unfortunate, for rain is not one of *my* possibilities, it is not one of the 'options' that Sartre goes on to identify with the self-transcendence of the for-itself. He might have accepted the scientific account and still been able to maintain the view that there is something magical (something, that is, the recognition of which called in primitive times for magical explanation) in the transcendence of the for-itself towards its undetermined but at the same time to some extent chosen future.

It is not yet this future; its future is once more a lack. 'Each *for-itself* is a lack of a certain coincidence with itself' (BN 100). The in-itself is fully presence to itself, or would be if it could (impossibly) confront itself after the manner of the for-itself. *This* presence-to-itself is denied to the for-itself, whose perpetual self-transcendence towards the future means that it is, as it were, never there to be confronted – and yet this very lack is an object of self-confrontation. The for-itself *is* its lack of presence to itself and is present to itself as this lack, the specific content of which consists precisely of its own possibilities. The question remains as to the mode of inscription of these possibilities in the world. 'World' for Sartre necessarily means 'human world' – as is clear from his objection to science as 'dehumanizing' – and a human world requires a human being: can the for-itself adequately play this role? It defines itself against *my* facticity, and as we have seen there is a sense in which human individuality is presupposed in Sartre's argument from the beginning.

The implicit circularity in all this is recognized by Sartre under the description 'circuit of self-identity': 'without the world no self-identity, no person; without self-identity, without the person, no world' (*EN 149*). Here Sartre finally admits explicitly the personal nature of consciousness in its most primitive form, and reduces the possession of an ego to a *sign* of personality:

> far from the ego's being the personalizing pole of the consciousness which, without it, would remain at the impersonal level, it is on the contrary consciousness in its fundamental self-identity that allows the appearance of the ego, under certain conditions, as the transcendent phenomenon of this self-identity. (*EN 147-8*)

What the ego now is, or why it should be necessary, becomes problematic: a 'transcendent phenomenon' seems to be a contradiction in terms, and if consciousness is personal, self-identical, present to itself, and oriented towards transcendence, the invention of an objective pole to lend substance to that transcendence seems superfluous. But Sartre's insistence on the transcendent ego may be the illustration in his own person of what he considers a universal weakness of the for-itself, namely its rooted conviction of its own ontological inadequacy. In another brilliant aside he invokes as evidence for this conviction Descartes's second proof for the existence of God: a being that can form the idea of perfection would, if efficacious, have made itself perfect, and by its failure to do so it stands condemned.

Even when bolstered by the transcendent ego the ontology of the for-itself remains shaky, because it lacks any *necessary* connection to the in-itself; its own facticity, the bit of the world against which it defines itself, seems arbitrarily chosen and could well do without it. The for-itself 'has the sense of its complete gratuitousness, it grasps itself as being where it is pointlessly, as being superfluous' (*EN 126*). It is not an established bit of the world that happens to be conscious, but a consciousness desperately trying to get a foothold in a world its own project has determined it not to be. It is *necessarily* prey to contradictory desires. Not that it wants to *be* its facticity – on the contrary it wants to be itself, and the *totality* of itself, yet in the mode of the in-itself; an 'impossible synthesis', says Sartre, but not an inconceivable one, since if we generalize it to the whole of the world we find a conceptual model to hand, namely God. In our own more modest case the being that the for-itself can never be also has a familiar name: it is *value*.

Value and possibilities: Sartre is undoubtedly right to distinguish the two cases, since not all possibilities are values, and values need not be possible, indeed there is a sense in which, as *unattainable* states of the for-itself, they cannot be. Sartre seems here to subscribe to the view that for a value to be actualized has the effect of destroying it *as a value*, the essence of value being temporal and furthermore future-referential. Still the for-itself belongs in the same dimension, namely in time, and must seek its ontological stability there. And there is in time an entity with which it can be identified, namely the totality of its own past. In *Being and Nothingness* Sartre does not quite reach the concept of 'totalization' that becomes so important in the later works, the moment-by-moment summation of the complex diversity of personal or historical determinations, but he does stabilize the for-itself enough to lay the basis for the moral stance of *Existentialism is a Humanism*: I am the sum of my actions and nothing else; I am responsible for what I have done, and can lay no claim to what I might have done but did not.

How is this to be reconciled with the claim that I am my possibilities? Clearly by an invocation of the formula: I am not what I am and I am what I am not. I *am not* my past (being cut off from it) in the mode of *being* it; I *am* my future (having to be it) in the mode of *not being* it. Grasping the sense of such formulae requires a considerable loosening of normal standards of argumentative rigour, but that may be a criticism as much of those standards as of the formulae; Sartre is struggling with the difficult task of characterizing the ontological status of his (or my, or our) subjective immediacy, which is presupposed as a condition of all argumentation, rigorous or otherwise, and which like all immediacy is transient, so that, as soon as it is fixed for attention, it has become past. The past has the status of the in-itself. The in-itself cannot *have* a past, it can only be what the past has determined it, mechanically, to be; the for-itself has a particular past, and is that past in so far as it can be anything – and yet cannot be it, since the past is precisely what it *was* and is no longer.

Part of the problem here is to distinguish what *is not* from what *no longer is*. Consigning the past to simple non-existence obscures that distinction, whose importance for the for-itself is obviously capital. The contrast between 'not' and 'no longer' superimposes itself on the earlier contrast between negation and nihilation: the status of the for-itself, and its power. Both status and power, as we have seen, pose a problem about the *origin* of the for-itself. If the for-itself *nihilates* some aspect of the in-itself as a means of asserting or producing itself, it must have prior being in order to exercise this power; this prior being is what it no longer is, i.e., what (in that mode) it *negates*. But in order to be negated, this prior being must in turn have asserted itself by a nihilation, and so on.

Sartre's strategy for avoiding this regression seems, again, to involve some sleight of hand. In his discussion of the necessary temporality of the for-itself he makes 'having a past' constitutive of the latter, a past from which it 'stands forth' in the present.

Here Sartre borrows the Heideggerian concept of '*ek-stasis*', exploiting an ambiguity in the Greek prefix which allows 'standing out' in its own right to be read as 'standing forth' from a previous existence. The three ekstases in Heidegger are past, present, and future, each a 'standing out' of *temporality* (*Zeitlichkeit*) (Heidegger 1964: 329). In Sartre they become ekstases of the *for-itself*, which, to the extent that it is temporal (and without temporality, it cannot be) forms as it were an ontological couple with time (BN 136). In Sartre the three 'first ekstases' of the for-itself are (i) not being what it is, i.e., 'having its being behind it' or in the fixed past of facticity, (ii) being what it is not, i.e., being the lack either of a fixed past or of a desired future, and (iii) being dispersed, or 'fleeing itself' in the game of mirrors – fleeing and pursuing at the same time, because it wishes to find and to grasp itself but is perpetually frustrated in this. The for-itself is thus 'Present, Past, Future – all at the same time – dispersing its being in three dimensions' (BN 142). These are 'first' ekstases because later on Sartre finds the concept useful to characterize the development of the for-itself in terms that are no longer exclusively temporal: its three ekstases become, first, the constitutive nihilation, or 'internal negation', of the in-itself; second, the nihilation of this nihilation, i.e., the reflexive establishment of the for-itself; and third the 'external negation' that establishes the being of the Other (BN 298-9). (It is worth drawing attention here to the etymology of '*ekstasis*' and 'existence', both of them deriving — the first in Greek, the second in Latin – from the combination of the prefix 'out' or 'from' with the verb 'to stand'. A conjectural link is provided by the Greek verb *existemi*, whose active meaning is to put out of place, to change, to alter, hence to drive someone out of his senses, to astonish, to bewitch, and whose passive meaning is to stand out of the way, to make way for; also in other forms to retire from, to lose one's senses, to be out of one's wits, to be astonished, to give up one's pursuits, to change one's opinion – a gallery of existential themes from absurdity to the free project.)

This standing forth of the for-itself from its past constitutes the link between past and future that is missing from the Cartesian account of the past as being no longer, and from the Bergsonian or Husserlian account of it as being, but in a different mode from the present. These accounts 'cut the bridges' (BN 110): the past cannot be the past *of this present*, anything might be true of it and the present still be as it is. This last point seems to me correct, but not to have the consequences Sartre fears. It is essential, he believes, that the for-itself should be responsible for itself as the totality of its past, and consequently it must know that that *is* its own past. But it would be quite compatible with his view of the for-itself as project if it were to assume responsibility for the consequences of its presumed past, without insisting on a solution to the very difficult problem of internal temporal relations. Part of my freedom, as we shall see in chapter VIII, must in fact be my future freedom to disavow my present project, and by parity of argument I must surely now be free to disavow my own past – which amounts to the same thing as not caring which past is actually mine, since I have in any case, moment by moment, to choose what I am henceforth to be.

The fundamental problem of temporality – namely why time passes at all – is untouched by all this, although it is surely crucial to our understanding of action and intention and responsibility. Sartre, however, thinks it a pseudo-problem; what he calls the 'dynamic character of temporality' (BN 147) is puzzling only if we attribute it to the in-itself, and what would be puzzling in the case of the for-itself would be rest or permanence rather than motion or change. Since the for-itself never rests and is essentially impermanent (never being what it is, always in flight towards the future) this difficulty cannot arise. Blindness to the problematic of physical time seems to me a chief failing of phenomenological theories, and Sartre's is no exception. (It is worth noting that one of the main historians of phenomenology dismisses Sartre's entire treatment of temporality as resting on a misunderstanding of Husserl and Heidegger (Spiegelberg 1965: 491).) The problematic has two principal aspects, one concerning the passage and the other the continuity of time, neither of which is amenable to phenomenological treatment since both are presupposed in the given structure of the phenomenal world. What is amenable to such treatment is the subjective experience of temporality, the ordinal sequence of past, present, and future. It would be philosophically modest to leave the other problems alone, but Sartre is not content to do this. Not only does he dismiss the dynamic of time as unproblematic, but he also presumes to dissolve the problem of continuity (or Zeno's problem) in both its forms, that of pure temporality or spatiality – the impossibility of traversing any continuous interval – and that of motion in a given place. The former is dismissed *ambulando*: the unity of the act of inscribing the line is taken to be prior to the line's divisibility. (Here Sartre seizes on Poincaré's definition of continuity as an example of one of his fundamental ontological principles: a series a, b, c is continuous, says Poincaré, if $a = b$ and $b = c$ but $a \neq c$:

this definition is excellent, in that it gives us a foreshadowing of a type of being which is what it is not and which is not what it is. By virtue of an axiom, $a = c$; by virtue of continuity itself, $a \neq c$. (BN 134-5)

This discrepancy between the axiom and 'continuity itself' is not further

88

illuminated.) The latter is circumvented more plausibly by insisting that 'to be' does not imply 'to be in a place', since a thing may equally well 'be in motion' (*être-de-passage*). Here again, however, Sartre takes on more than he is equipped to handle, and proposes a theory of motion, in terms of a thing's 'exteriority-to-itself', which mixes phenomenology with physics in a thoroughly muddled way. 'Motion is in no way similar to becoming', as he rightly insists (BN 212) – but the confusion of categories involved in representing motion as a kind of self-transcendence of the moving object is just as erroneous.

If however we restrict attention to the for-itself, and do not try to develop an existentialist physics, this way of putting things is much more helpful. The for-itself is given as spontaneity – which is just the by-itself in its personal mode, i.e., grasped as my project – and as such enters the world with a momentum towards the future. But just as there is a difference between the pre-reflective *cogito* and the reflectively constituted self, so there is a difference between the *original* temporality that we spontaneously are and the *psychic* temporality that we observe ourselves to live out. The latter is derived, the former immediate. The parallel with the case of reflection is not exact, for reflection itself comes in two forms, pure and impure: the former the 'simple presence of the reflective for-itself to the for-itself reflected-on' (BN 155), the latter a form of self-knowledge, rather than of self-awareness. (It could be made more exact by the addition of a form of pre-temporal immediacy.) Self-knowledge occurs when I take myself as an object for myself, and this 'for' is of capital importance for Sartre, representing as it does the defining mark and the perpetual risk of the for-itself.

If I remain on the level of pure reflection I cannot achieve psychic temporality, but if I move to impure reflection this temporality will come to appear as someone else's history, not my own. 'Impure reflection is an abortive effort on the part of the for-itself to be another while *remaining itself*' (BN 161). The narrow line I must walk between mere nothingness on the one hand and bad faith on the other, the necessity at the same time of a temporal play between the reflexive and the reflected if a personal history (as opposed to a disconnected series of fragmentary awarenesses) is to be lived at all – these make vivid the tense yet ephemeral quality of human existence. But walking a narrow line is perhaps the wrong image: my existence is more like that of the subject in Wittgenstein, which 'does not belong to the world: rather, it is a limit of the world' (Wittgenstein 1961: 117). To project myself into the world (rather than, in time, along this limiting boundary) is to objectify myself and fall into bad faith, but to hold back passively so as to be carried by events, rather than appropriating them, is in some sense not to exist at all.

The existence of the for-itself, then, is spontaneous but future-directed, and occupies the tension between reflective and reflected. Yet Sartre ends his chapter on temporality with a new description of the Ego, with its qualities, states, and acts, one class of which (the cognitive acts) gives access to the domain of the 'psychic', with its population of objects such as hatred, exile, systematic doubt, sympathy, and love (BN 163). These objects form an organized totality, the Psyche or 'reflected for-itself' – the Ego, in short, as known to itself. Once again the self is seen to have two contradictory modes of being: it is already constituted and yet must constitute itself in every moment. We have a sense of the ever more elaborate description of something stated more simply much earlier, of a paradox never resolved but repeatedly insisted upon. And yet Sartre does manage a further ontological claim as he concludes this discussion. For my own prior states, populating psychic temporality, 'whose phantom flow does not cease to accompany the ekstatic temporalization of the for-itself insofar as this is apprehended by reflection' (BN 170), constitute a being, albeit a virtual one, which stands *outside* my present being and thus transcends it.

The ontological status of the in-itself remains in question – the interrogation has not yielded an answer – and hence the for-itself, as we saw above, is thrown back upon its own temporality as the dominant mode of its self-construction. And the nature of this past being which the for-itself is and is not is now said to be 'psychic', to consist, that is to say, not of former bodily states but of former mental ones. There is a hint here, whose clarification must wait until the discussion of the free project, that it may be easier to disavow former actions than former states of mind; I am to be sure the sum of my actions, I cannot claim credit for what I might have done but did not do – but at the same time I am nothing, I need not claim credit (although I must accept responsibility) even for what I in fact did, I can start again from scratch. But the 'phantom flow' of my previous psychic states continually accompanies me.

The for-itself having acquired a foothold in its own world, the question of the world of being in itself can now be raised again. Sartre reverts to the phenomenological principle that consciousness is consciousness *of*, this time however in the confidence that consciousness has a being of its own on the basis of which it can reach out to the being of its object. The mode of this reaching out is *knowledge* – intuitive knowledge, for Sartre the only kind of knowledge there is (BN 172), and knowledge of a being no longer posed as negative but as other, as a plenum, as a world. Epistemology is, after all, the road to ontology, and what might be called the epistemological definition of the for-itself finally restates the relation between for-itself and in-itself in such a way as to turn the original negation into an affirmation: 'The for-itself is a being such that in its being, its being is in question insofar as this being is essentially a certain way of *not being* a being which it posits simultaneously as other than itself' (BN 174). 'Knowledge', says Sartre, 'appears then as a mode of being' (ibid.): the being of the for-itself as 'presence-to ... ', but also the presence of being to the for-itself (BN 216).

The affirmative role of negation here seems paradoxical, but is to be understood as a contrast to the earlier preoccupation with absence, lack, and the rest. The *négatités* that mark the human world do not mark the physical world – negation here goes the other way, throwing into relief not the world's failure to meet my expectation but rather my non-being in the presence of its plenitude. Sartre still uses the term 'absence', but now with a positive emphasis: I am 'the absence which determines itself in existence from the standpoint of this fullness' (BN 177). Where knowledge is concerned there is only one ontological component, the *known*; what knowledge does is to locate it with respect to the knower, to render it present, to turn its unqualified being into a 'being-there' (ibid.). The being I thus confront, however, is no longer the 'for-me' of the first encounter with particular things, nor can it be the totality of the in-itself as transcendent, since totality can come into being only through the mediation of the for-itself. Sartre speaks of it simply as the world, which on the one hand makes possible the presence of particular things (of a 'this' and a 'that') but on the other is made possible only by the presence of particular things. The ascent from particular things to being as a totality is the 'totalizing' work of the for-itself, which 'has to be – in the mode of being what it is not and of not being what it is – its own totality as a detotalized totality' (BN 181). What this seems to mean is that the for-itself realizes its own deficiency of being just to the extent that it apprehends the fullness of the world's being; as the 'unachieved totality of negations' (BN 182) it makes itself, to paraphrase only slightly, 'everything that is not the case', and being, the finished totality of affirmations, stands before it as everything that it is not, i.e., as everything that is the case. The point about totalization is that this 'everything' can be thought only from the point of view of a nothingness – not a nothingness out of which human reality springs but a nothingness that constitutes that reality.

If the world is the totality of things, their presence to the for-itself implies also their presence to one another; being, to borrow structuralist terminology, is a synchronic totality. The presence of things to one another is space, which in Sartre as in Leibniz is therefore purely relational. This too is expressed paradoxically: 'Space ... is a moving relation between beings which are unrelated' (BN 184); the elements of the in-itself, in other words, have no internal connections, they are completely independent of one another and enter into a kind of relatedness only through their presence to the for-itself – which is a demonstration of their essential unrelatedness. The mutual exteriority of things in space is repeated in the case of time, a series of 'nows' each populated with independent 'thises'. We cannot speak of *the* future, because 'every future "state" of the world remains foreign to it, in the full reciprocal exteriority of indifference' (*EN*

266); there are thus many futures, all merely possible, and time is the passage from these possibilities to an actuality – again a classical position. What remains wholly unclear is how this universal time 'comes into the world through the for-itself', as Sartre says it does (BN 204); 'universal temporality is *objective*', things carry their temporality with them (in the sense that their permanence argues a future, their presence a past) so that it appears outside us, on the surface of being; true, time would not appear to pass without us, so that it is correct to say that temporality is not at the disposal of the in-itself – and yet once again the status of the for-itself, and the power implicitly attributed to it, seem incommensurate.

The difficulty here is endemic to Sartre's philosophy. It is a question of how seriously we are to take the remark that 'it is through human reality that there is a world' (BN 307). Sartre has a rather loose way of inter-changing terms like 'world' and 'being' (unmodified by a suffix); this means that my world, which I take to be correlative to my consciousness, may be confused with an ontological domain that transcends it, so that the truth that, without me, my world would cease to exist, may translate itself into the falsehood that whatever there is somehow depends for its existence on my awareness of it. It may indeed be – and this is one of the chief conclusions of Kant's work – that I can know nothing about what there is as it would be if nobody had ever come to know it, which is equivalent to saying that whatever I can know must be couched in terms that are intelligible to me. If Sartre's doctrines of space and time are simply echoes of Kant's (in which these categories are forms of the understanding rather than properties of things in themselves) then they pose no difficulty; but he is critical of Kant precisely for presupposing a temporality of the 'I think' as a means of linking essentially independent instants (BN 132-3), and this criticism would lead us to conclude that the for-itself really *produces* time, as if by an act – and similarly for space and all the other features of the world, such as quantities and qualities and potentialities and uses.

The conflation of types of attribute in .this list may give a clue to the problem: while the for-itself, we might argue, genuinely does produce potentialities and uses and perhaps some qualities, it does not produce quantities and the objective relations we come to describe as spatial and temporal. This assertion is, I admit, highly controversial, but its defence would take me too far outside Sartre's philosophy and too deeply into my own; it will be enough, perhaps, to show that in Sartre's own terms either everything is ontologically prior to consciousness and the for-itself nothing but a nothingness that reflects being passively, or everything is on-tologically coeval with consciousness and being is dependent on the active nihilations and negations of the for-itself as it spontaneously produces itself. The former is wholly unacceptable to Sartre, the latter wholly implausible to us, but at the epoch of *Being and Nothingness* this tension is left unresolved. The resolution that would consist of placing consciousness *in* the world as an active and directive participant in complex but natural processes (which would lead to a simple categoreal distinction between episodes that belong to the physical world and are unmediated by consciousness, forming the domain of what are usually called the natural sciences, and episodes in whose determination consciousness plays a part, forming the domain of what have come to be called the human sciences) is not available to Sartre, nor for obvious reasons will he ever entertain it; the burden he places on each individual for-itself to be, as it were, its own demiurge and spontaneously create the universe – to be God, not as the ontologically impossible In-Itself-For-Itself but in the more onerous role of the Ground of Being – is however somewhat lifted in his later work when he forgets the natural world and concentrates on the historical one. For in the historical world the for-itself is not alone, it is accompanied and sustained (as well as threatened) by others like itself. It is to their status in the Sartrian scheme that we must now turn.

VII

The Existence of Others –
Sartre's *Prise de Conscience*

Sartre is not an idealist; the dilemma on which the foregoing account of the for-itself closed cannot be resolved by giving the whole of being the ontological status of consciousness. But the horn of the dilemma which seems to lay upon the individual for-itself the burden of all creation might seem less preposterous if it could be construed as referring to an activity of some For-itself in general, and Sartre does at times seem to mean it in this way; sometimes he capitalizes the term (*Pour-soi*) and sometimes he does not, and the former cases seem to be those on which the ontological weight bears most heavily. What the For-itself might be in general is, however, given the existential and personal mode of its construction, something of a conundrum. It resembles Hegel's Spirit, if this can be understood as knowing the world rather than being it; yet the world *is* not independently of its being known – what *is* is just its being-as-known.

> We shall grant to idealism that the being of the For-itself is
> knowledge of being, but we must add that this knowledge has being.
> ... In a word, by a radical reversal of the idealist position, knowledge
> is reabsorbed in being. It is neither an attribute nor a function nor
> an accident of being; but *there is* only being. From this point of view
> it appears necessary to abandon the idealist position entirely, and in
> particular it becomes possible to hold that the relation of the
> For-Itself to the In-itself is a fundamental ontological relation. At the
> end of this book we shall even be able to consider this articulation of
> the For-itself in relation to the In-itself as the perpetually moving
> outline of a quasi-totality which we can call *Being*. (BN 216)

The emphasis on '*there is*' is instructive; it is the *thereness* of being, not the Being of being, that is conferred on it by the for-itself, or as was seen earlier it is the 'existence of being' which constitutes the 'individual

94

venture' of the for-itself (BN 621). But in that late passage it is the modest lower-case for-itself that is in question, whereas here the For-itself, Sartre goes on to say, is 'the only possible adventure of the In-itself' (BN 216), and this clearly requires greater generative resources than my own small for-itself can muster.

One obvious problem arises in the case of my own body – it would seem odd to say that I have a body because I am conscious of it, even though that is true if the emphasis falls on 'having' as one of the relations the for-itself enters into (so that the elimination of the for-itself would eliminate not the body, but only the 'having' of it). Sartre himself comments (BN 218) on the absence from his treatment of the for-itself of any consideration of the body, but that, he says, is due to the fact that the body is part of the known, not like the for-itself part of what makes knowledge possible. And furthermore my own body has this peculiarity: that it is primarily *known to others*, so that I know it mainly by analogy to my knowledge of their bodies. (This seems to me, as a generalization, quite false, but Sartre's reasons for asserting it are as usual personal; of his own body he says 'we formed an odd pair, it and I', going on to point out that children often take account of their bodies only in sickness or in relation to hunger or other bodily needs, and then citing his own experiences in infancy – the taking of pulse and temperature, the watchful attention adults paid to *his* body (*MO* 77).) The existence of my own body is therefore of a new type, neither in-itself nor for-itself but *for-others*. Before going into the special features of this new variety of existence, however, it must be noted that its introduction is of no help in solving the problem we have been, parenthetically, engaged with: the For-itself that confers the fact of being on the In-Itself cannot be just the sum of a lot of individual for-itselves; the collectivity of human beings can no more sustain the physical world ontologically than a single human being can sustain his own body.

But as remarked in an earlier chapter, in practice Sartre is as sure as the rest of us of the being of the in-itself. The phenomenological clue to that being, to a world which is stubbornly independent of me and against which I define myself, is as we have seen the experience of boredom or nausea. It has sometimes been objected that this is a pessimistic view of man's relation to the inanimate, but there is nothing in Sartre to suggest that no other forms of experience enter into that relation – these particular ones have the force in his scheme of *Grenzsituationen* or limit-situations in Jaspers, except that Sartre's are less cosmic and melodramatic, more apt to be encountered in the everyday. Death and pain are nobler categories, no doubt, than the unyielding there-ness of trees, the viscosity of mud, but it has been part of Sartre's genius to show that the latter can bring us up just as abruptly against the limits of our subjectivity, indeed the very lack of social devices for neutralizing such banal existential encounters intensifies their force. Nausea and boredom are what Sartre calls 'primordial reactions' (*réactions originelles*); they mark the most fundamental relationship of consciousness with being, on what has come to be called the 'visceral' level. While however they remind us forcefully of the existence of Being-in-itself, they tell us nothing whatever about it; they do not have the status of scientific evidence, since they count not as observations of things as they are but as realizations of our own finitude.

In accepting the limitation of Sartre's world to the human, the social, and the historical, and abandoning any hope of finding in his work a philosophical view adequate to physical reality, we must take clear account of the systematic incompleteness that results, especially in view of his occasional appeals to modern science. These are usually eclectic, as in the case cited above where the possibility of rain is objectified in terms of the temperature and pressure of water vapour; another case occurs in the discussion of the facticity of the body, where the 'pure exteriority' of Newtonian science is contrasted unfavourably with the observer-dependent physics of de Broglie and Heysenberg [*sic*] (BN 307). (Sometimes they are just wrong or confused, as when he makes Einstein's theory a reaction to the Michelson–Morley experiment in an attempt to show the historical relativity of knowledge (S VIII: 186), or tries as in the preceding chapter to treat physical motion phenomenologically.) The real issues, in the philosophy of science, stirred up by all these allusions can be of little comfort to Sartre: granted that our formulations of the way the world is cannot be rendered free of the human perspective our interest haplessly intrudes into them, still that does not mean that the way it is depends on that interest. What is thus independent, it may be said, is not *world* as that term is phenomenologically understood. So be it – but then we are back to the covert shift from 'world' to 'being'.

The physical sciences deal, we might say, with being before it has become world. The status of this domain cannot be left aside if our goal is an understanding of the universe as a whole. If, as I believe, individuals and societies are the natural product of material things and their behavioural dispositions, given the prevailing conditions in this corner of the universe, then the truths of the physical sciences (and of the biological and social sciences positivistically construed) may make an essential difference to our grasp of lived social relations. By taking his stand at too high a level of abstraction, and refusing an analytic of material causes and parts, Sartre risks the collapse of his scheme of explanation in the light of a new reading of the genesis or synthesis of the human. He would of course dismiss this criticism as irrelevant, and it certainly need not be fatal: like any other phenomenological enterprise his work may bracket all that, treating analytic complexes as lived simples. It is true that lived simples (such as the experience of perplexity or wonder) normally precede inquiry into the complex foundations of our own physical, biological, or psychological nature, and that Sartre's concern is in any case to free us from determination by that nature. But our freedom might be more complete in the light of a fuller knowledge of its material setting and limitations. Sartre's in-itself (or even In-itself) contributes nothing to this at all, his for-itself (or even For-itself) if possible still less. Beginning with the hypothesis of a material world it is, I think, possible to give a plausible although not conclusive account of subjectivity, but beginning from subjectivity it is not possible to give even a plausible account of the material world – except as a hypothesis.

While we do not create physical objects by our look, however, there is a sense in which we do create one another in this way; while we are not necessarily nauseated by an encounter with the indifference of objects, we are almost certain to be shamed – or at any rate not to remain indifferent – if treated as an object by another subject. The primordial reactions of nausea and boredom are joined, when our attention shifts from the physical to the social world, by another and far more convincing group of such reactions that mark the relationship of consciousness to other consciousnesses, and whose chief members are shame, fear, and pride (BN 291). Just as nausea is a means of self-recognition in contrast to the otherness of the inert, so shame is a means to self-recognition in contrast to the otherness of the Other. The mode of my own being yielded by nausea is the for-itself, the mode yielded by shame is the for-others (*pour autrui*). Note that this is not a mode of the *other's* being, but of my own as seen by the other – or rather as seen by me through the mediation of the other:

> The Other is the indispensable mediator between myself and me. I am ashamed of myself *as I appear* to the Other. By the mere appearance of the Other, I am put in the position of passing judgment on myself as on an object, for it is as an object that I appear to the Other. (BN 222)

It would be hard to overestimate the importance of this juncture in Sartre's development, even though its full implications were not available to him at the time of *Being and Nothingness*. It represents the emergence of the existential subject from its quasi-solipsistic isolation, but at the same time it calls in question the significance and uniqueness of that subject. The trouble with discovering that one is an object for another subject is that one's own subjectivity makes no contribution whatever to the character of that object; as far as the other is concerned, one might be just anybody, even a robot or a mannequin. In fact coming to realize that he was 'just anybody' (*n'importe qui*) was, later on, to be a step of great moment to Sartre, as he testifies in an interview with Simone de Beauvoir (L/S 96). His acceptance of this condition dates, he says, from about the age of 40, that is, roughly from the Second World War, which, as he says elsewhere, divided his life in two: 'It was then ... that I abandoned my prewar individualism and the idea of the pure individual and adopted the social individual and socialism' (L/S 48). Socialism involves, as we shall see, a positive sense in which the individual is 'just anybody', but the emphasis in *Being and Nothingness* is more on the negative sense reflected in the celebrated line in *No Exit*: 'Hell is – other people!' Others force us to react to ourselves with the distaste we would feel for strangers whom we observed performing the vulgar or clumsy acts we ourselves perform; they deprive us not only of our uniqueness but of our protected interiority, into which negation finds its way no longer as an external relation between the subject and the world, but as an 'internal relation' between a subject and another subject.

Sartre is not wholly lucid as to the nature of this 'internal negation', although he compares it to Leibniz's concept of God: a witness is needed to testify to the subjective difference between myself and the Other, which otherwise remains merely a function of our physical distinctness. But if the Other is to play any role at all, it is at least essential that he should *actually exist*, and Sartre's attention is thus directed to solipsism, and the criticism of various standard philosophical arguments against it. Husserl, for example (as we saw above), calls upon other subjects to confer significance on my world, which becomes a world in common; but, says Sartre, the subjectivity of the other remains unreachable as long as my own has the character of the transcendental ego, hardly distinguishable, for him, from the Kantian subject. Such a subject can at best take note of its association with its own body, perceive the similarity of that body to the body of the Other, and then argue by analogy to the subjectivity of the Other. Hegel does anachronistically better, because the relation between Master and Slave is at least one of direct dependence, but the subject in his case is seeking to be established as a *truth* for the other, to be *recognized*, so that the relation remains nevertheless on the epistemological level; the other is a knower, but I still have no access to his being. Heidegger does better still, providing a genuine ontological relation between subject and other in his category of *Mit-sein* or 'being-with'; Sartre illustrates this relation with the image not of a struggle (as in Hegel) but of a team, whose being implies the being both of the subject and of the Other. But even this is un-satisfactory, since the new kind of being, being-with, gives the being of the Other only in a kind of indissoluble coupling, not in its own right.

The problem remains problematic, but Sartre has at least identified some of the solutions that will not work. He does not want a *proof* of the existence of the other, a better *refutation* of solipsism; solipsism is to be rejected not because its absurdity or impossibility can be demonstrated, but because the Other has his own grounding in his own being, an independent *cogito*. It is no use either actually producing the other as object. 'In my own inmost depths I must find not *reasons for believing* that the Other exists but the Other himself as not being me' (BN 251). The For-others is one of the modes in which the For-itself appears; all the Others, for each for-itself, form a totality, but it is what Sartre calls a 'detotalized totality', because there is no independent point of view from which all the subjectivities can be seen as cohering; all of them combine to characterize each in its mode as for-Others, but this totalizing is done afresh from each vantage-point and does not confer any objective totality upon the whole. (The For-itself, itself, has just this kind of detotalized totality, as we saw in the previous chapter.)

The principal form of the subject–other relation is seeing and being seen, and Sartre devotes a long analysis to 'the look' as the phenomenological occasion for my recognition of the other. One of the most interesting results of this inquiry follows from the fact that we may suppose ourselves to be looked at, and have the appropriate reactions of shame, fear and the like, only to discover that we were mistaken – perhaps, says Sartre, what 'I took for eyes were not eyes; perhaps it was only the wind which shook the bush behind me' (BN 276), and yet my conviction of the reality of the Other was just as strong as in the actual presence of another person. 'Therefore, it is impossible to transfer my certainty of the Other-as-subject on to the Other-as-object which was the occasion of that certainty' (ibid.). This however helps to make things clearer: it was not the Other-as-object we were after in the first place, since it remains physical and therefore merely probable; the ontology of the matter attaches precisely to the Other-as-subject and myself-as-object, an *ekstasis* of the for-itself which is possible only by the mediation of the Other. For the latter the actual presence of the Other is not required, as long as my conviction of his presence operates this mediation and yields me to myself as object. In cases other than the primordial reactions already mentioned – for example in the case of friendship or love – the Other-as-object may be absent (as Pierre was absent from the café), and that absence be a mode of presence, in the sense that his absence at a particular time from a particular place changes my relation to that place and makes his absence present there (remember 'There's someone missing here!'). The subjectivity of the Other is in such cases transcendent, in the sense that it does not appear in my world although it may profoundly modify the sense of that world (among other things by putting me into it as an object, as in the familiar desire to be seen, in a new home, a new situation, a new article of clothing, by some person whose regard one values or whose judgment one respects, before being quite able to believe that one belongs in it).

'The Other' is therefore a regulative concept, in Kant's sense, in that it confers intelligibility on the world, or at any rate produces in us a conviction of intelligibility on the ground that the world, however confusing to us, must have been organized by some other subjectivity. The concept is thus a very powerful one: on the one hand it extends to the idea of God, on the other it accounts for alienation. Sartre's relation to God is of central, although largely implicit, importance throughout – not God as the impossible in-itself-for-itself, but God as a historical presence in human culture. Sartre is an atheist, but he is like the atheist described in *The Words*: 'a God-obsessed crank who saw His absence everywhere and who could not open his mouth without uttering His name' (WO 98); somebody, in other words, who, unlike the believer, has religious convictions. The unsupported character of the world in God's absence haunts him; without Him there are no 'values in a heaven of ideas' (E 26). The absence of God (of which Sartre had a kind of revelation – see WO 251) is however that of God the Father, the All-Powerful; for a long time after his disillusionment on this score 'the Other one remained, the Invisible one, the Holy Ghost, the one who guaranteed my mandate and who ran my life with his great anonymous and sacred powers' (WO 251). In *Being and Nothingness* God has become a 'purely formal notion', the 'omnipresent, infinite subject *for whom* I exist' (BN 281). Only in the later period is the sense that meaningfulness must be conferred by this Other finally replaced by the full realization that it is social and must be constructed.

The social construction of the intelligibility of the world brings problems of its own, also adumbrated in *Being and Nothingness*. For if the world is organized by the Other it ceases to be *my* world and becomes *his* world, or *their* world. The 'universal superaddition of sense' of which Husserl speaks may not be such a welcome route of escape from the isolation of the *cogito* if the sense is somebody else's sense. To be sure, it is by this route that I enter into the objective domain of space and time; but in that world what I experience as my possibilities are experienced by the other as mere probabilities (BN 265) – what for me is constitutive of freedom is for him constituted on the basis of empirical evidence. For the Sartre of *The Transcendence of the Ego* this is of course to be expected; for the Sartre of *Being and Nothingness* it is a source of alienation, since my 'being-other' or 'being-outside-myself' which is the object for the Other is 'radically different from my being-for-myself' (BN 273). The inescapable existential unity of the subject is at stake, and its metamorphosis into an object is in the first instance strictly impossible, a dialectical contradiction. This problem leads Sartre into some contradictions of his own; 'in no case can I ever alienate myself from myself', he says (BN 275), but then a few pages later the alienated Me (now capitalized) becomes the object of a kind of social exchange between myself and the other:

> I escape the Other by leaving him with my alienated Me in his
> hands. But as I choose myself as a tearing away from the Other, I
> assume and recognize as mine this alienated Me. ... Thus this Me

which has been alienated and refused is simultaneously my bond with the Other and the symbol of our absolute separation. (BN 285)

The alienation and refusal may be muted in special cases such as those mentioned above; where there exists a direct relationship between my subjectivity and that of the other (e.g., of friendship or love) my objectivized self is acceptable or recognizable, but in the absence of such a relationship, i.e., in the case of an *indifferent* other, the contradiction remains unresolved.

At the same time my discovering myself as an object in a world of objects destroys, says Sartre, the objectivity of that world for me, because it forces upon me the realization that the world is not as I see it, that there is a 'transcendence other than my own', not this time the transcendence of the in-itself but that of another subject. My world contains neither the subjectivity of the other, nor the objectivity of his world. My alienation from that world lies precisely in the fact that I cannot recognize myself in it. I may of course yield to this and allow the self as object, not as in the special cases noted above to coexist with the self as subject, but actually to replace it. This, as we have seen, is the classic route to bad faith; it is inauthentic, and it is an evasion of responsibility. But it is also a continual temptation, as in the case of Lucien in 'The Childhood of a Leader' and the father in *The Condemned of Altona* (see above). The problem is to experience my being-for-others without yielding to inauthenticity in either of these dominant forms, religious or social.

This experience is necessary, not in order for me to be myself, but in order for that self to be human. Being-for-others, Sartre observes, is an ekstasis, but not an ontological structure, of the for-itself; a for-itself could be imagined that had no tincture of the for-others, that had no idea it could exist as an object for another subject – the only thing is that it would not be 'man' (BN 282). Since 'man' is an essentially social concept this is of course hardly surprising. Sartre's main point seems to be that I cannot exist in historical time without the mediation of the other. My emergence into historical time is a definite episode in the 'upsurge of my consciousness into being', which 'historializes' me but is also the condition for any possible history; Sartre therefore dubs it 'antehistorical historialization' (*EN 342*), an expression however for which he seems to find mercifully little use in the sequel. As in the case of the emerging Ego the 'antehistorical' aspect seems inaccessible even to philosophical conjecture, since by the time it is possible to raise even the most naive or halting question about history the 'historialization' or 'humanization' of the subject must be a *fait accompli* of long and irrevocable standing.

That the For-itself should have created the historical world is nevertheless a perfectly reasonable doctrine, especially in contrast to the untenable suggestion that it has created the material world. And Sartre gets around the problem of the incommensurable objectivities of radically separated subjects by introducing the category of 'objectness' (*objectité*). While the 'alienated Me' was objective in relation to the subjectivity of the other, and thus not assimilable (assuming the indifference or hostility of the other) by my own subjectivity, the 'Me-object' is something I can manage to identify myself with in a world where the other is also an object on an equal footing. Not that this is wholly satisfactory either – but it is less personal than the look of a particular other-as-subject who objectifies me in a world that is in no sense mine; my 'objectness' is a function of the 'quasi-totality' of other subjects, who are responsible also for all the other objects that fill the social world (tools, for example). My 'objectness' is balanced, not overwhelmed, by the 'other-as-object'; his subjectivity is thereby neutralized – it becomes a known property, like the inside of a box (BN 289), no longer a threat to my own subjectivity. The social and historical world in which we both exist then offers the possibility of mutual or conflicting enterprises and commitments. If I remember that the other has a subjectivity like my own I can view him as committed (*engagé*) in an active sense, although if I reduce him to the status of an object his commitment is like the merely physical 'engagement' of things with one another (Sartre uses the examples of a knife in a wound or soldiers in a mountain pass, but the point is conveyed just as well by the familiar image of the engaging of gear wheels).

The metaphysical question that underlies all this, says Sartre, is 'Why are there Others?' (BN 297). Clearly they are contingently given, just like the by-itself – but is their contingency irreducible or is it derived from something more fundamental? This leads him into a reconsideration of the ekstases of the for-itself: the first constitutive (not being what it is and being what it is not), the second reflexive (trying to describe itself as being/not being in just that way, which leads to a kind of duality of the reflecting and the reflected) and the third achieving being-for-others. Now it has been sufficiently emphasized that the for-itself establishes itself by negation, but the question is what kind of negation. Leibniz's 'internal negation' comes back into play here, in contrast to what Sartre calls 'the ultimate term of nihilation', the exterior indifference of two spatially separated entities in-themselves. The trouble with *that* kind of negation, says Sartre, is that the for-itself cannot realize, with respect to any being, a negation that is in itself (*en soi*, but this time without the hyphen), without ceasing to be a for-itself. But the constitutive negation of the in-itself by the for-itself cannot be wholly internal either. A term seems to be missing from the argument.

We might represent the state of affairs diagrammatically, as in Figure 1. I_1 and I_2 are two elements of the in-itself, and they are the facticities of two corresponding for-itselves, respectively F_1 and F_2. N_e is the external negation between the elements of the in-itself and N_c is the constitutive

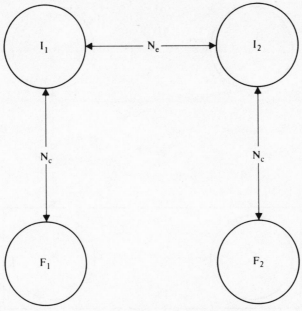

Figure 1

negation by which each for-itself produces itself against its facticity. The question is whether anything in the constitution of the for-others (which is what F_1 and F_2 become in their relation to one another) requires a new kind of negation. For in the first place being-for-others admits me to a spatio-temporal world, the characteristic relations in which are, as we saw earlier, precisely external negations, and in the second place, while the for-itself does not *require* the other for its constitution, the realization that I am not the other plays a constitutive role at any rate where my ekstatic formation is concerned. Sartre even speaks of a 'facticity' of the other and of a nihilation that enters the domain of the for-others (construed now as a plural).

It is in this plurality that the answer to the question of internal negation lies. For what that negation is internal to, says Sartre, is the *totality* of for-itselves which find themselves mutually related as for-others. This totality he is tempted to call 'mind' (BN 301, reading 'mind', wherever it occurs, without the definite article in English), whose function it would be to sustain in being the plurality of for-itselves in their ekstasis as for-others. (Sartre once again uses the locution 'is been' to describe the way in which the for-Others might be constituted by mind, and once again it is translated as 'made-to-be'.) Each for-itself, however, is at the same time paradoxically exterior to all the others as not-being relatively to them, and this exteriority could not have been invented by mind – it is a case of irreducible facticity, all we can say is 'That's how it is'. This situation is

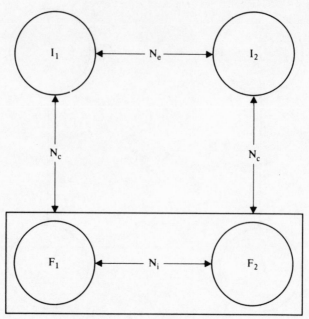

Figure 2

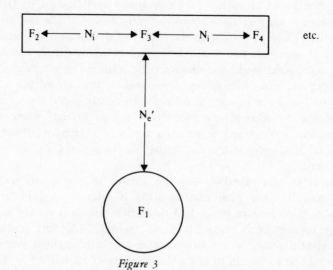

Figure 3

represented in Figures 2 and 3, where N_i is the required internal negation and N_e' the form of external negation that links a given for-itself to the totality of mind, itself excepted. The totality is not the mere sum of these exteriorities – such an aggregation could no more produce mind than mind could produce it. Mind is a synthesis, not a collection. As a totality it is postulated, not conceived, which would be an impossible task for those who, like us, owe their existence to it and depend on it as a condition of their action. Even God could not get outside the totality of mind so as to grasp it as a concept.

We have here for the first time the meeting of two radical contingencies, those of the self and of the (collective) other, the relations between which form one of the principal *motifs* of later Sartrian philosophy. The acknowledgment that 'I exist *as myself* on the foundation of this totality and to the extent that I am engaged in it' (BN 302, emphasis added) is hardly a conclusion argued to through what preceded it, but it throws light on some earlier arguments. It is the force of a transcendental deduction: I need the totality of others in order to be myself, just as I need the facticity of the in-itself in order to be a for-itself. But again the being I might take myself to have been before my encounter with mind, like the pre-personal field of consciousness of *The Transcendence of the Ego*, is existentially inaccessible. The truth of the matter – although Sartre never says this – may well be that the three problematic domains of the Introduction, the subject, the world, and society, come into being *as possibilities for philosophy* simultaneously. Sartre's standpoint in *Being and Nothingness* is that of the subject, which thereby acquires a kind of methodological priority – but now it is seen that the priority cannot be sustained, since the subject becomes what it is through social mediation. The shift into a new philosophical domain is what I have called Sartre's *prise de conscience*. But the further shift to a standpoint from which all three domains could be seen as equipollent is beyond him.

My entry into the social or collective is effected through my body. But – as if to reinforce the point just made – Sartre is at pains to dismiss the scientific approach to the body, in anatomy and physiology, as irrelevant to the subject–other relation, just as he was seen in an earlier chapter to dismiss the scientific treatment of language. Language was said to be dead if not spoken; the body of the other becomes a corpse 'if it ceases to be simultaneously revealed and hidden by the transcendence-transcended' (BN 348). This latter term signifies the symmetrical relation between two for-itselves which are mutually other: I know that the other transcends what I know of him, but at the same time I transcend that knowledge – and I know that he knows this of me, and so on. And this, rather than any bodily contact, is the authentic form of our encounter.

The body locates me in objective space, but at the same time it orients that space with respect to me, and locates other subjects in it at various distances from me. Space is essentially relative – the notion of a Newtonian absolute space was purchased at the expense of expelling human beings from it altogether. But this relation of my body to space and to other bodies is purely contingent, as for that matter is the further fact that *I* happen to inhabit *this* body. 'Being-here' (*être-là*, the equivalent of

Heidegger's *Dasein*; note that the French '*là*' and the German '*da*' can mean 'here' just as well as 'there') experiences its facticity in this double contingence – being *in this body* here rather than in some other, being in this body *here* rather than elsewhere. The orientation of the world with respect to my body imposes an order on things which I can neither escape nor justify, and yet which is in a sense identical with what I am in the world (BN 309). The body, as Plato saw, is the principle of individuation of the soul, but Sartre denies the complementary tenet of Platonic doctrine, the separability of the soul from the body, 'for the soul *is* the body inasmuch as the for-itself *is* its own individualization' (BN 310).

On the physical aspects of the body, therefore, Sartre dwells not at all. Sensation, for example, involves an encounter between a physical body and a physical world; for Sartre it is an absurd notion (*EN* 377), which leads to further absurdities such as interior subjectivity in the psychologists' sense. The presence of the world to the subject is perfectly intelligible to him, but the subject as enclosed, receiving news of an exterior world through the senses, seems a pure invention. In the latter sense the subject is just what cannot get out into the world, while for Sartre we have to be *in* the world to know it:

> it would be impossible for me to realize a world in which I was not and which would be for me a pure object of a surveying contemplation. But on the contrary it is necessary that I lose myself in the world in order for the world to exist and for me to be able to transcend it. (BN 318)

Similarly we act directly in the world, rather than using the body as an intermediary, a tool from which we are in some way distinct – I *am* my hand as I write, I do not observe my actions as I observe those of other people. This is another example of the 'horror of the inner life', and once again it seems to cast the issue too starkly: I do not ordinarily think of my hand as a thing I use, but I can think of it in this way, if for example I perform therapeutic exercises to strengthen it; no part of the physical body is exempt from such provisional detachment, nor could any part of it be the privileged locus of mind, in spite of Locke's fantasy about the little finger (Locke 1894 1:459).

The question of the relation of subjectivity to the body is nevertheless a complex one, and Sartre is undoubtedly right when he insists that for the most part the physical body, like the physical sign (the materiality of words, for example) is '*surpassed toward meaning*' (BN 330). We are not, in other words, aware of our bodies as we go about our daily business in the world, any more than we are aware of language as we use it for ordinary communication; our intentionalities reach through the body or the word to their proper objects. If I become aware, e.g., through eyestrain, of the fact that I am reading 'with my eyes', I am still not aware of them

as physical eyes but only as eyestrain, a contingent feature of the connection of consciousness to the world (BN 333). Such features present
themselves with more' or less insistence; my bodily situation is implicitly
given when it is transcended, but is as a rule forgotten as long as the
intentional activity persists. Even when I stop reading and realize my pain
consciously, however, it is a pain that belongs not to the physical body but
to what Sartre calls the 'psychic body' (BN 337). It is the psychic body
that experiences nausea, for example. Nausea derives in the first instance
from our being reminded that we are also a physical body – it is an
intimate form of the unavoidable confrontation of for-itself and in-itself.
Sartre speaks as if it were a common condition, 'dull and inescapable', and
makes clear that he means by it not a metaphor drawn from physical
nausea but a prior state that underlies physical nausea (and, we might add,
precedes the forms of it he describes elsewhere which bring us up against
an external in-itself) (BN 338). But here again it seems more autobiographical than general, and only Sartre's own nausea can easily explain
his revulsion against all objective discussion of the physical body (except
in the case of sexual relations, with respect to which he goes into some
detail later on). There is, however, a less affective and more serious reason
for rejecting the physical properties of the body as possible clues to
philosophical enlightenment, namely that the existence of the body as a
physical thing poses exactly the same problem as the existence of objects
in the world, other people, and so on, and can therefore contribute
nothing to the clarification of the ontology of the subject.

Other people's bodies are similarly perceived as significant totalities
rather than as physical objects, as a transcendence transcended (BN 348-9).
This leads Sartre into a discussion of 'temperament' and 'character', the
former an attribute of the other's body 'in-itself', as it were, the latter an
attribute of that body in its situation, as freely chosen by the person whose
body it is on the basis of an original facticity. But the symmetry of self and
other means that, as in the case of the look, this notion of the character
of another puts me in a new relation to myself. There are in fact three
'ontological dimensions' of the body, corresponding roughly to the three
ekstases of the for-itself: 'I exist [sic] my body. . . . My body is utilized and
known by the Other. . . . I exist for myself as a body known by the Other'
(BN 351). This development, however, amounts to little more than a
repetition of the earlier one, in corporeal terms rather than in terms of
consciousness, which in view of the transcending of the body towards
signification adds less than the prima-facie contrast of these two categories
might suggest. But this life itself, for Sartre, is a 'set of significations', a
totality of intentional acts, not the history of a body.

If in Sartre, as in Husserl, it is the emergence of significance that marks
the transition to an intersubjective world, it remains true that the world
has to realize itself in concrete cases. When the relation between the

for-itself and the other is no longer an abstractly constitutive one but becomes practical and concrete, an attempted engagement of one subjectivity with another, the mere sense of significance does not suffice and other complications arise. Sartre distinguishes two chief classes of relation that are constitutive of the intersubjective world, two fundamental attitudes of the for-itself to others. Into the first class fall love, language, and masochism, into the second indifference, desire, hatred, and sadism; the first resolves to *capture* the other's freedom, as it were, and turn it towards oneself for the purposes of self-constitution through recognition, the second resolves to *master* the other's freedom, to annul or suppress it and thus constitute the self in defiance of, rather than by means of, the other. Both involve a tension between the self and the other that Sartre describes as conflict.

The intersubjective relation involved in the experience of love has already been discussed in the chapter on language, because Sartre treats it as the basic phenomenon of significance: in the attempt to make my own speech significant I require the presence of an other as interlocutor, but I cannot know whether I have succeeded unless the other responds with a word directed to me. Until that happens language is *holy*, since it indicates the possibility of a silent listener, a transcendence at the point to which it is addressed; when the listener hears it, language is *magic*, because it issues from a signifying object and produces an immediate effect; if the response corresponds to my hopes, language is *love*. But the latter requires a rather complex form of mutuality of intention as between speaker and hearer: the response will be that of a lover (rather than merely of one loved) only if the other undertakes the project of 'being loved' – and yet I do not wish to be loved under this utilitarian modality, I wish to be the object of the love of the other engaged in freely and without expectation of reciprocity. Sartre represents this ideal relation as an impossible game of mirrors, of 'reflection-reflected', and one furthermore that is automatically spoiled if a third person intrudes and objectifies both partners, which accounts for the fact that lovers seek solitude. The inevitable failure of the relationship, due to the fact that the lover is an unsatisfied dupe, perpetually insecure, whose being is hostage not only to the loved one on whom he depends but also to the objectifying regard of the third person, may lead in despair to masochism, the project of losing my subjectivity altogether in that of the other, who is invited to treat me as a *mere* object. But masochism fails too, because in *appealing* to the cruelty of the other it leaves intact the other's recognition of my subjectivity as agent/victim.

Since it is useless to hope to manipulate the freedom of the other, I may be driven to the second strategy, which is instead to defy it. I can try indifference, which Sartre represents as a kind of staring-down: I notice 'the look' and I look at it, in order to 'build my subjectivity upon the collapse of the subjectivity of the Other' (BN 380). I thus practice a *de facto* solipsism, using others if at all as convenient robots with predictable responses. Or I can, through my sexuality – which is for Sartre a fundamental aspect of the human, not dependent on such accidental differences between individuals as the possession of one or another fleshy appendage; in this he consciously disavows the asexuality of Heideggerian *Dasein* – seek to treat the other as mere flesh, incarnate under my caress. Neither of these approaches works, in the end, any better, the first because it just drives me back into my own lonely and insufficient subjectivity, the second because carnal desire, expressing itself in the caress as thought does in language, sets up the old reciprocity of subject-object and object-subject, and even if achieved remains unsatisfied. Not having been entirely sure of what it was that I desired, I may now resolve to force the objectivity of the other through humiliation and cruelty; but the sadistic use of the flesh of another person results either in futility or in the rebirth of desire: 'sadism is the failure of desire and desire is the failure of sadism' (BN 405).

Sartre does not insist that all relations of intersubjectivity are as stark as these – actual patterns of behaviour, because they are conditioned by particular circumstances, may be 'infinitely more delicate to describe' (BN 407), but they all contain a skeleton of sexuality, because that is the fundamental mode of the attempt of the for-itself to realize its being-for-others. The Other is at once elusive and inescapable, setting limits to the possibility of my action, standing as a witness to it in spite of my attempts to remain indifferent, rendering me superfluous in the world, engendering a sense of guilt. It was the presence of the Other that made Adam and Eve realize their nakedness: 'original sin is my upsurge in a world where there are others' (BN 410). The weight of this alien and alienating presence may in the end drive the for-itself, realizing as it does the hopelessness of union, to seek the other's death instead. 'This free determination is called hate' (ibid.). It is not some particular feature of the other that I hate, it is his very existence; it is not even a particular other, it is all others. By now it comes as no surprise that hatred is doomed to failure too – even if I kill the others I am irreversibly contaminated by having once been for-others, and to make it worse I have deprived myself of the opportunity of working, positively or negatively, towards my own constitution through them.

Retreating from the despair of hatred, the for-itself swings back and forth between the two fundamental attitudes: subverting the freedom of the other, or denying it. But is there not an entirely different mode of intersubjectivity, that of the collective, the 'we'? This has been adumbrated in the experience of the lovers surprised by a third person and objectified *together*; the question is whether it constitutes a new ekstasis of the being of the For-itself or is merely an elaboration of the for-others in the individual sense. The point is crucial, since in the former case an opening would be created towards a genuine ontology of the social, in the latter there would be no escape, in the end, from existential isolation. Sartre does not take the question very far in *Being and Nothingness*, but he tends to favour the second alternative – while he admits that the *experience* of the 'we' is authentic, it is just as authentic if only I have it, if it is not shared by the others whom I (mistakenly) take to constitute 'us'. As in the case of the rustling leaves I took for the presence of the other, when I rendered myself an object even though there was no other-subject to objectify me, so now I may constitute myself a member of a collective subject in the presence of other people even if they decline to enter into it as subjects with ·me. But I could not do this unless I had previously experienced myself as for-others; the 'we', whether truly constituted or not, is parasitic on the relation of otherness between its members.

Even if the others participate with me in the subjectivity or objectivity of the 'we' or 'us', each member of the collective will still experience it as an individual. But individual experience is changed by the presence of the Third, and it is on the complexity of this triadic relation that the collective phenomenon is built up. Sartre insists on this complexity in detail – it is one of his virtues to be able to envisage the way in which social relationships are concretely developed, from the look of the Other to that of the Third who sees me with the Other and who may look either at the Other looking or at me looked-at. The Third stands for 'all the others', the background against which my relation to a given other appears, and his look confers an equivalence on me and the other in question; from this point of view I am 'just anybody' (*n'importe qui*), and my relation to the other becomes exterior and impersonal. It is the Third who engenders the phenomenon of *class* (although this engendering is asymmetrical: the oppressor confers class status on the oppressed but not vice versa) and the transcendent Third who goes by the name of God might in this way form the ground of human solidarity in general if only He existed (BN 423). His perpetual absence means that humanism too is doomed to failure.

In the light of the foregoing it is necessary to distinguish between the cases of the 'We-subject' and the 'Us-object'. The latter is a genuine addition to the repertoire of existence, since it is constituted as the for-others was by the regard of an Other (now a Third). The former, however, not only allows for delusion (imagining the others to be participating when in fact they are not), but even in the authentic case when we all participate is nothing but a fortuitous historical conjunction of lived subjectivities. The *Mit-sein* evaporates: 'the essence of relations between consciousnesses ... is conflict' (BN 429). It is true that the collective subject finds an objective expression in the world, through its actions, in the cumulative fruits of human labour – the language, the buildings, the institutions by and in which we all live. (In Sartre's discussion of this topic in *Being and Nothingness* we find an adumbration of the later doctrine of the practico-inert: these things have been created by subjects for the use of other subjects.) But as lived it remains fragmented: 'the experience of the We-subject is a pure psychological, subjective event in a single consciousness. . . . It is a question only of a way of feeling myself in the midst of others' (BN 425).

At this stage, therefore, the *prise de conscience* is not altogether happy. The for-itself has found that there are other for-itselves in the world; its evidence for this is immediate and, in its own terms, incontrovertible. It is linked to them by relations of mutual transcendence, and of equally mutual transcendence-transcended, and so on into the endless game of mirrors. It has acquired a new *ekstasis* and hence a new dimension of self-constitution. On an abstract level this is all very satisfactory: the for-itself finds itself enrolled in the totality of mind, and its body, construed as a 'psychic body', serves to cement these relations in another mode. But in particular cases all turns to ashes: we are left with conflict, with the permanent elusiveness of the other, with the small comfort of objective association under the eye of the Third, accompanied by the realization that this association is illusory on the subjective level, that each of us is living a private life in parallel with the others but without genuine community.

The construction of community requires dialectical resources not yet available at the time of *Being and Nothingness*. And there is a prior problem to be tackled: since the question of concrete relations has been raised, Sartre has to go back to the situation of the for-itself in the physical world. For he realizes that the for-itself is not only the negation of the in-itself but also its determination, to put the matter in Spinozistic terms. Heidegger, says Sartre, fails to take the step from the constitution of an ontology of existents by the for-itself to its equally obvious power of ontic modification, i.e., the fact that people can actually do things that have material consequences. So the discomfort of the failure of social relations is temporarily alleviated by a turning of attention to moral ones, to the question of responsibility for actions – but first to the question of the nature and possibility of action itself.

VIII

Freedom and
Existential Morality

In 1943, when *Being and Nothingness* was published, Sartre considered the philosophy of action to be essentially undeveloped, a view which – given that the major available work in this domain in French was Blondel's *L'Action* of 1893 – seems plausible enough. But such a philosophy was especially needed at that time as a propaedeutic to morality and the philosophy of freedom, because the dominant problems of the moment were problems of the possibility and authenticity of action. (Even though no mention is made in *Being and Nothingness* of occupation or collaboration their presence is often implicit.) Ontology is all very well, but ethics is immediate and pressing when bad faith is rampant and the *salauds* have taken over the world. The individual, Sartre came to see, is the sum of his actions; not the individual as a fleeting for-itself but the individual as a past and therefore frozen element of the in-itself, a personal facticity which is a principal component of the determination of the for-itself and reconciles the apparent inconsistency between its nothingness on the one hand and its effective instrumentality on the other (BN 201). The for-itself can, by the adoption of a new project, start again from scratch, but the constant necessity of choice will soon create a new set of actions – and even the new project cannot so easily get rid of the moral weight of the old actions, though it may be able to shed their ontological weight. (Sartre's evangelism is in this respect the opposite of Bunyan's.)

The essential characteristics of action as Sartre sees them are that it is always intentional and that it always responds to a lack. The latter implies that every action is a venture into non-being. It follows at the same time that no actual state of affairs can determine an action, that as such it cannot even determine that I should see in it the lack that might lead to action. For that matter I cannot even recognize a 'state of affairs' without invoking the power of negation/determination which we have seen to be the defining property of the for-itself and which in the context of action

112

is called its freedom. The latter part of *Being and Nothingness* is devoted to an analysis of 'doing' and 'having' in their relation to 'being', as they depend on and challenge the freedom of the for-itself and constitute its project, i.e., its conscious intentionality towards the future. The book ends with a section entitled 'Moral Perspectives' and the promise of a work consecrated to the problem of morality.

Of this work Sartre wrote, according to his bibliographers, about two thousand manuscript pages (WS 1:228), but only a very few were published (in *Combat*, 16 June 1949, on the problem of blacks and whites in the United States – an indication of the practical and political direction in which Sartre's thought was turning). The dialectical system of morality referred to in chapter I, which needed only to be written up for publication, has fared no better. The absence of any work on ethics as such in the Sartrian corpus reflects one of the basic ambiguities in his philosophy: passionately committed, ready to judge in the most scathing terms bad faith, failures of authenticity, the behaviour of bosses and anti-semites, still Sartre can find no objective ground for these judgments, nor any redeeming explanation for the behaviour. The denial of moral absolutes is not new, but it has often been accompanied by a comforting belief in determinism: men are not evil,· circumstances make them what they are. On the other hand the belief in moral standards is habitually accompanied by a belief in some validating structure, whether involving Reason or God. These strategies are not available to Sartre.

It is nevertheless quite compatible with the absence of strict determination and of transcendent value that men should be held responsible for the consequences of their actions – that is to say, nothing prevents other men from taking this attitude towards the agent. And the agent, if not in bad faith, will hold himself responsible, since his actions make him what he is and authenticity consists precisely in appropriating without subterfuge what one is, to the extent that one can *be* anything, i.e., in the mode of the for-itself. Just what will follow from this responsibility is not obvious, however – there is so far nothing to prevent the response from being smug self-congratulation even with respect to acts judged hideous by ordinary standards. But this would clearly not be acceptable to Sartre, 'the stringency of [whose] moral standards' so struck Simone de Beauvoir after his return from prison camp in 1941 (POL 381). Sartre himself, of course, is by his own account free to be rigidly moralistic if he likes, but no generally applicable ethical consequences would seem to follow from that. The resolution of this difficulty in any philosophically plausible manner cannot be achieved within the framework of Sartre's own views until much later. But he does not hesitate to offer a resolution in the context of existentialism; it is just that its grounds and consequences are not fully worked out and in the event could not be, since the position proves on examination to be philosophically implausible.

Sartre's ethical view, in his existentialist period, rests on his concept of freedom. The fact of the freedom of the for-itself, he says in a famous passage, has serious consequences for human destiny:

> man being condemned to be free carries the weight of the whole
> world on his shoulders; he is responsible for the world and for
> himself as a way of being. We are taking the word 'responsibility' in
> its ordinary sense as 'consciousness [of] being the incontestable
> author of an event or of an object.' In this sense the responsibility of
> the for-itself is overwhelming since he is the one by whom it
> happens that *there is* a world; since he is also the one who makes
> himself be, then whatever may be the situation in which he finds
> himself, the for-itself must wholly assume this situation with its
> peculiar coefficient of adversity, even though it be insupportable. He
> must assume the situation with the proud consciousness of being the
> author of it, for the very worst disadvantages or the worst threats
> which can endanger my person have meaning only in and through
> my project; and it is on the ground of the engagement which I am
> that they appear. (BN 553-4)

This is stirring language even if, under the interpretation of chapter V, the state of affairs is not as drastic as it seems: the for-itself is as it were the occasion of the appearance of the world, not its generator or demiurge; 'situation' consists of 'for-itself plus world' and presupposes 'project', and it is this complex for which freedom is responsible, a complex which, however (as Sartre himself points out), has no meaning unless I decide that it shall do so.

Freedom, as we have seen, is not a *capacity* of the for-itself, but rather a *state*; it arises out of the negation which at once joins and separates the for-itself to and from the in-itself that surrounds it. Freedom is the condition of being undetermined and undeterminable. The breach of determination which the ontological status of the for-itself ensures protects me not only from my present situation but also from my own past. This past, however, includes my motives for action, and this makes action itself a perpetually hazardous, but a perpetually exciting, affair. Not that an action may not proceed conformably with my motives – but it cannot be bound by them. Freedom from this particular form of determination is not a right on the exercise of which I can congratulate myself – to assume this would be to get the whole thing backwards: 'it is not *because* I am free that my act is not subject to the determination of motives; on the contrary, the structure of motives as ineffective is the condition of my freedom' (BN 34). In fact this state of affairs is very unsettling, because it prevents me from being sure as to my own future intentions. If I form a project, I cannot necessarily count on myself to carry it through, and this uncertainty is a source of anguish. It is, says Sartre, as if 'I make an appointment with myself. ... Anguish is the fear of not finding myself at that appointment, of no longer even wishing to bring myself there' (BN 36). Here we see, once again, the emergence of bad faith – but the bad faith does not lie in not keeping the appointment with oneself, it lies (or would lie) in the denial of the possibility that one might not keep it. For I must allow my future self the freedom to be something other than what my present self projects for it. This necessity follows from the simple fact that I am a for-itself and not an in-itself.

What Sartre calls 'original freedom' is, therefore, nothing other than the presuppositionless and undetermined upsurge of the for-itself in every moment of my life. Hence it cannot be represented as a prelude to action, in the sense of something going temporally before – rather it constitutes the foundation for action, whether voluntary or passionate. Sartre differs from many moral philosophers in refusing to oppose will and passion to one another; they differ in manner, to be sure, but may serve the same ends, which neither creates. One man flies in panic for his life, another reasons that it would be better to hold firm, but the fact that the former is governed by his passion and the latter by his will does not mean that one subscribes more fully than the other to the value of life as something to be preserved. It is almost as if will could be regarded as passion exercised calmly, passion as will out of control.

Neither will nor passion, in other words, accounts for the original drive towards projected ends; they are merely its modalities. Nor, however, does freedom as such account for it. Freedom and spontaneity are not identical; this is one of the points on which Sartre proves too subtle for Simone de Beauvoir, who simplifies things in her *Ethics of Ambiguity* to the point of making this identification:

> Every man is originally free in the sense that he spontaneously casts
> himself into the world. But if we consider this spontaneity in its
> facticity, it appears to us only as a pure contingency, an upsurging as
> stupid as the *clinamen* of the Epicurean atom which turned up at any
> moment whatsoever from any direction whatsoever. (EAM 25)

The last part of this is quite correct – the human situation, unmodified by a human project, is absurd or devoid of sense, although this seems obvious if not tautological. But the first part of it suggests that freedom is to be defined in terms of spontaneity, whereas for Sartre the two concepts are equally primordial. Freedom is a state, spontaneity is a drive or a process.

In the analysis of the latter Sartre takes pains to distinguish the two determinants of action known in French as *motif* and *mobile*, roughly equivalent respectively to 'motive' and 'motivation' (or 'drive'), although no simple translation is adequate. In ordinary French usage '*mobile*' occurs roughly where 'motive' would occur in ordinary English usage. This is the equivalence adopted in the English translation of *Being and Nothingness*. Unfortunately it leads the translator to render '*motif*' as 'cause', and although the reader is warned in a footnote (BN 435) the sense is hopelessly thrown off. The *motif* is, to be sure, an objective state of affairs, but it cannot by itself be the cause of an action, since the agent's project is necessary in order for it to be recognized as a *motif* in the first place, and even when so recognized it cannot lead to action without the requisite *mobile*. The *mobile*, it is true, may be just the recognition of a *motif* as such; speaking of the conversion of Clovis to Christianity, the predisposing condition (or, in my reading, the motive) of which was the political and religious state of Gaul (BN 448) which made it advantageous, Sartre says 'we shall say that this first project of his possibilities in the light of which Clovis discovers a cause [read 'motive'] for being converted is precisely the *motive* [read 'motivation']' (BN 449).

Motives imply a project, although even a formed project, as we have seen, cannot compel a *future* action, no matter how imminent that future may be. (There is an echo here of the scholastic debate between Aquinas and Ockham: the former thought God bound by the Aristotelian system, the latter thought such a conclusion blasphemous and argued that God could change his own laws if he wished. The absolute character of God's freedom in Ockham is like the absolute character of man's freedom in Sartre.) 'The internal structure of the for-itself by which it effects in the world the upsurge of causes [motives] for acting is an "irrational" fact in the historical sense of the term' (BN 448), and as such offers no way out of the absurdity. But freedom is among other things freedom to assume the contingency in which I find myself, to adopt (or conversely to reject) the spontaneity I discover in myself. Without the spontaneity there would be no movement at all, without the freedom this movement would be merely random. Both components are needed to make choice possible, and on the possibility of choice depends the possibility of morality.

The *exercise* of choice by the for-itself is however difficult to account for. It cannot arise from deliberation, since the decision to deliberate or not itself results from a prior choice (BN 451). In fact Sartre traces the intentional grounds of choice back to

> the original relation which the for-itself chooses with its facticity and with the world. But this original relation is nothing other than the for-itself's being-in-the-world inasmuch as this being-in-the-world is a choice – that is, we have reached the original type of nihilation by which the for-itself has to be its own nothingness. No interpretation of this can be attempted.... (BN 457)

What can be attempted is a psychoanalytic *discovery* of the 'fundamental act of freedom', although this discovery will not show us a hidden causal mechanism after the manner of Freud, but rather a transparent intentionality – it will offer not an excuse but a self-revelation.

Can the revealed self then be said to be free? Sartre reverts to Leibniz's problem about Adam: could Adam have refused to eat the apple? Yes, but so much would have had to be different that he would have been another Adam, the world another world. Hence the ability to refuse the apple, according to Leibniz, was not Adam's ability, but God's: another world was possible, but once in this world Adam could not choose to be in that one; the essence of Adam in this world involved his eating the apple, he was in fact not free to do otherwise. The difference between Sartre and Leibniz is that for the former there are no human essences that follow from the nature of the world – 'for human reality essence comes after existence' (BN 468) – and no *necessary* implication from one contingent proposition to another; whatever differences there may be in the world in which Adam refuses the apple are future with respect to the moment of Adam's choice, at which no constraint operates apart from Adam's project. It is only theoretically, says Sartre, and in Leibnizian terms, that a different choice would imply another Adam and another world. In the English version of *Being and Nothingness* there is an unfortunate mistranslation here: Sartre says '*En théorie* seulement un autre geste d'Adam n'est possible que dans les limites d'un bouleversement total des fins par quoi Adam se choisit comme Adam' (*EN* 548), but this is rendered '*In theory only*, another gesture of Adam is possible and only within the limits ...' (BN 469); the interpolated 'and' suggests that, practically, another gesture is not possible, whereas for Sartre it is precisely the practical alternative that *is* possible. Sartre's Adam is really free in the only world there is.

The truth of human freedom, we might say, is to turn spontaneity into project, to accept contingency and to ride it, as it were, rather as one might ride a wave. It is in effect to choose the contingency one is with its various possibilities, primary and secondary (those which define the project on the one hand, those among which choice is possible without changing the project on the other). Freedom itself antedates this truth – it is not that we are human and choose and are therefore free, but that we are free and therefore human and must choose. To be free does not mean, Sartre insists, to get what one wanted but to determine one's own desires, even if they remain unfulfilled (BN 483); it does not mean that one chooses the world but that one chooses oneself in the world (BN 521). The resulting doctrine has a familiar ambiguity: on the one hand I am projected into the world, on the other I make my own project in it; on the one hand I am freedom as a negation of determination (i.e., as disconnected from the world), on the other I must be freedom as a determination of negation (i.e., as affirming myself against it). What are we to make of this inspired but incoherent view? It is, it seems to me, a remarkable attempt to give concreteness to what otherwise remains paradoxical, namely the situation of perceived moral responsibility in an apparently determined world, on the part of agents who discover themselves phenomenologically rather than historically.

The question of self-discovery is important. Along with the three metaphysical attitudes distinguished in the Introduction (called there the objective, the subjective, and the collective) are usually to be found characteristic moral attitudes, which might be called respectively conservative, existential, and radical. While this is hardly the place at which to develop these parallels fully, some hint as to what is involved may be helpful. People who find the existence of an objective world both obvious and fascinating are often quite uncritical of the social arrangements in that world and quite willing to accept their 'station and its duties', to use a well-known formula, as given in much the same way as physical phenomena and their native language. In this setting the question of the self hardly arises, and preoccupation with it may be regarded as a form of indulgence; moral responsibility is accepted as a matter of practice, even though the determination it would be natural to extrapolate from the progressive completion of a scientific account of the physical world would make such responsibility empty. Those, however, for whom the objective world is of interest only as it relates to a primary preoccupation with their own state as feeling and knowing subjects may be equally uncritical of social arrangements but are likely to be anguished by the question of moral responsibility as it relates to them personally. Traditional morality is suspect not because of its possibly undesirable social consequences but because of its threat to individual authenticity and freedom; if it is accepted this is likely to be in sacramental form, so that the faith or the commitment of the subject is at least as important as the moral content of what is believed or upheld. From the outside such persons may seem amoral or hyper-moral or perhaps both, adhering passionately as they well may to rigorous but idiosyncratic codes of behaviour designed to satisfy their own moral (or aesthetic or religious) sense. Here the question of the self is paramount, and indifference to it in favour of an objective order will probably be regarded as a form of philistinism. As in the metaphysical case, however, the abstract weakness of these positions is not satisfactory from the perspective of a third possible view which realizes how each of them is dependent on institutions, sensibilities, and forms of expression not of the agent's invention or discovery, themselves proper objects of philosophical criticism. I call the resulting moral stance radical because whatever form it may take it will at all events involve a challenge to the foundations of morality in the other two senses. The difficulty with it is that it has no foundations of its own to propose and threatens to dissolve into mere relativism.

In morality as in ontology Sartre moves between the second and third positions stated here. His later works make a serious effort to reach a dialectical *Aufhebung* of the two in the form of a reconciliation between existentialism and Marxism, the determination of the individual by himself on the one hand, by history and the collectivity on the other. But the theory of *Being and Nothingness* does not provide for the force of the environment; having just emerged from a time of war in which the isolation of individuals, in terror and mistrust, had been one of the dominant facts of existence, Sartre can be pardoned for laying some emphasis, however romantic, on heroic self-determination. The unexpected thing about the moral doctrine of this period, however, is his insistence that the individual in determining his own morality at the same time determines everyone else's as well. In *Existentialism*, for example, he says:

> When we say that man chooses his own self, we mean that every one of us does likewise; but we also mean by that that in making this choice he also chooses all men. In fact, in creating the man that we want to be, there is not a single one of our acts which does not at the same time create an image of man as we think he ought to be. To choose to be this or that is to affirm at the same time the value of what we choose, because we can never choose evil. We always choose the good, and nothing can be good for us without being good for all. (E 20)

This is clearly a form of what is known in ethical theory as the 'generalization argument', the classical statement of which is found in Kant. The most familiar formulation is the categorical imperative: 'Act according to that maxim by which you can at the same time will that it should become a universal law.' Kant's imperative occurs in several versions of varying degrees of abstraction, but it rests on a conception of the agent as a 'universally legislative member of a merely potential realm of ends' whose maxims must harmonize not only with the whole realm of possible ends but also with the realm of nature.

Now in Kant, while the agent is autonomous and responsible, there is always his rationality to fall back on – it is because he, like all other men, is a pure rational will that the concept of universal legislation is possible, that a harmonious realm of ends is conceivable; the universal legislator is not subject to caprice, but on the contrary knows how to judge, of his own legislation, whether it meets the criteria of reason. For Sartre in his existentialist period there is no defining characteristic of the human, not even rationality, apart from existence itself before all possible characterization, i.e., apart from the ability to apprehend oneself as free from all such *a priori* characterizations, to negate all forms of determination. A radical relativism might therefore be thought inevitable. But that is not how it turns out, Sartre suggests; there are certain judgments of value that we simply do not accept as mere private preferences, that we interpret at the same time as adverse judgments of those who disagree with us. The examples he cites, however, are unconvincing. A representative case is found in his UNESCO lecture on the responsibility of the writer. When discussing the merits of books in polite company it is not considered good form to be dogmatic; one does not say of a book that it is good or bad, but that one likes or does not like it, and this is so because the more assertive form would be taken to mean ' "I hold people guilty who do not think that it is good", or if you prefer: "I insist that everybody in the community to which I belong shall recognize this book as good" ' (RW 62), which would be too insistent for politeness. This looks like an appeal to common usage, but that was clearly not tenable from Sartre's point of view of the time. It is no doubt true that an insistence on agreement presupposes the freedom of the other to agree, but the transition from this observation to an anguished responsibility for the whole world is problematic.

What is lacking in Sartre's use of the generalization argument is a class over which the generalization can operate. Short of a Kantian conviction as to the rational status of all men there might still be a form of the argument applicable in more limited communities. Sidgwick, for example, argues that if I judge an act to be right for me I implicitly judge it to be right for someone whose nature and circumstances do not differ from my own in certain important respects. We have seen that there can be no similarity of nature, this concept being for Sartre an empty one; what about similarity of circumstances? We might be tempted to equate Sidgwick's circumstances with Sartre's 'situation' – but to recognize a situation in Sartre's sense we must already have engaged ourselves towards the pursuit of a projected end (since the same objective state of affairs may correspond to very different situations in the light of different projects), and this is something that nobody in like circumstances is obliged to do. To put the matter in another way, Sartre seems inconsistent in his desire to bring action under a *generalizable* description when it is always engaged in under particular contingencies, inaccessible, because of the radical freedom of the agent, to any covering law. Making a law even for myself involves bad faith, since I must be free to break it tomorrow, so it is hard to see why I would want to make one for others. It is to be noted that the enterprise of autonomous action, on Sartre's account, provides plenty of anguish: the man condemned to freedom bears his own weight on his shoulders, and that is surely enough.

It seems reasonable to conclude that Sartre's use of moral generalization is a matter more of evangelistic rhetoric than of philosophical reasoning: he would wish individuals to assume responsibility for themselves in authenticity and good faith, and indeed such an assumption of autonomy is the only hope for morality in a pluralistic world; this would involve the rejection of any imposed system of morals, for even if we have recourse to a system this can only be because we have chosen to do so. 'If you seek advice from a priest, for example, you have chosen this priest; you already knew, more or less, just about what advice he was going to give you. In other words, choosing your advisor is involving yourself' (E 27). Consequently if we wish to preserve the belief that we are operating under a universal law, it can only be one we have ourselves laid down as universal. Why should we, however, wish to preserve this belief? Traditionally, it is true, moral rules have been regarded as given in the form of universal law, or at all events it has been socially and politically desirable, from the point of view of those interested in social stability and political order, for them to be so regarded. But while existential authenticity would presumably require some consistency of rules (in order for a coherent project to be possible) it does not in fact require those rules to carry any universal warrant, even a self-generated one.

One reason for the maintenance of the fiction of universality might be a fear of merely capricious relativism. Another, however, might be a conflation, not to say a confusion, of principles and consequences. One of the cases Sartre envisages in *Existentialism* is that of the worker who chooses to join a Christian union rather than a communist one. 'If by being a member I want to show that the best thing for man is resignation, that the kingdom of man is not of this world, I am not only involving my own case – I want to be resigned for everyone. As a result, my action has involved all humanity' (E 17). It is true that there cannot as a matter of fact be two different and opposing political solutions to the same problem in the same community. It is also true that there cannot be two true but incompatible global religions, and that, if I choose a religious belief that is avowedly prescriptive in morals, then I do subscribe to a form of legislation for all men. But the act by which I seek to further a particular political outcome *need* not be inspired by a universally legislative impulse, even though it *may* be so inspired; I may just want that outcome.

Merely capricious relativism might have been avoided just as well by resorting to a non-fictional universality of human freedom as an essential property of persons, necessarily embodying their highest possible collective value, but as is by now clear this is impossible for Sartre, since his ontology requires freedom to precede the emergence of the human: for him at this epoch freedom is a fact, not a value. Only with the social *prise de conscience* discussed in its ontological aspects in the last chapter does the concrete historical sense of freedom in which it can serve as a value emerge. This is coincident with Sartre's discovery of a new form of universality, which one might characterize as distributive rather than comprehensive, in the doctrine of 'just anyone' ('*n'importe qui*'), where the stress comes to lie not on what everybody should do, but on what anybody might do. And this brings philosophy a step back towards literature again, since the characteristic form of presentation of this kind of universality is paradigmatic rather than schematic, in cases rather than in maxims. There is a genre, whose principal practitioner in Sartre's literary universe was

Flaubert, devoted to what might not unreasonably be called the moral development of characters who stand in just such a paradigmatic relationship to the rest of the species, exhibiting possibilities latent in any individual and hence instructive for each.

Sartre's transition from the legislating individual to the historical individual is effected through the 'case studies' that constitute such an important and significant part of the corpus of his writings – Baudelaire, Genet, Flaubert. Before the first of these, however, comes the highly significant *Anti-Semite and Jew* (1946), in which a case intermediate between the whole human race on the one hand, and a particular individual on the other, is confronted with rare candour. Here again historical circumstances provide the stimulus: the world had just witnessed an insane and tragic and outrageous epic of anti-semitism, and Sartre seems to have had in mind the foundation of a 'militant league' against its recrudescence. His analysis leads him to conclude that it is not up to the Jews to found such a league – the Jews *as a problem* are a creation of the anti-semites, not the other way round. Anti-semitism is an old theme for Sartre – it is by becoming an anti-semite that Lucien, in 'The Childhood of a Leader' (which, it must be recalled, dates from before the war) finds a means of self-identification, in bad faith to be sure but nevertheless effectively – and it is from Simone de Beauvoir that we learn what their joint attitude had been.

> One day she [Olga] asked what it really meant to be a Jew. With
> absolute certainty I replied: 'Nothing at all. There are no such things
> as "Jews"; only human beings.' Long afterwards she told me what an
> impression she had created by marching into the violinist's room and
> announcing: 'My friends, none of you exist! My philosophy teacher
> has told me so!' On a great many subjects I – and Sartre to a lesser
> degree – was deplorably prone to abstraction. (POL 135)

In *Anti-Semite and Jew* Sartre makes important progress towards overcoming that abstractness, taking account of the fact that men must be free to be Jews if that enters into their choice of themselves in the world, precisely without choosing at the same time that all men should be Jews, as would be required by his form of the generalization argument.

The book is, however, less about the anti-semite than about a view of the world that produces at once anti-semitism and other (familiar) forms of life, for example democratic man himself. The anti-semite has, it is true, a pathology all his own, whose structure is recognizable from *Being and Nothingness*: his original choice is to be a Manichaean, to constitute himself as good against an evil he must then identify and embody in an object of hatred. But the attribution of objective characters to others – with its consequent slighting of their freedom – may arise from higher motives, even from humanism itself and its political counterpart, democracy.

122

Humanism is an eighteenth-century abstraction which 'recognizes neither Jew, nor Arab, nor Negro, nor bourgeois, nor worker, but only man – man always the same in all times and in all places' (ASJ 55). While therefore the anti-semite focuses on the Jewish side of the Jew and attaches his hatred to it, the democrat focuses on the human side and attaches his approbation to it. But this strategy is thwarted by the Jew who stubbornly refuses to think of himself as merely human and continues to insist on his Jewishness. 'The anti-semite reproaches the Jew for *being* a Jew; the democrat would willingly reproach him for *considering* himself a Jew' (RQJ 69). Sartre therefore takes a significant step beyond Marx, who in his essay 'On the Jewish Question' took the view that the emancipation of the Jew, like the emancipation of everyone else, would be achieved only when it ceased to matter whether he was Jewish or not, or, to put it more strongly, when it ceased to be possible for him to be Jewish in any important sense; Sartre sees that no theory that prescribes what is to matter to any individual- in a situation is compatible with the radical freedom which is the ontological foundation of the human.

'For us, man is defined first of all as a being "in a situation." That means that he forms a synthetic whole with his situation – biological, economic, political, cultural, etc.' (ASJ 59-60). It does not follow, however, that an individual can be reduced to these terms; Sartre reproaches the democrat (and the scientist) with overlooking the *singular* – 'to them the individual is only an ensemble of universal traits' (ASJ 56). The freedom of the (singular) individual in his (chosen) situation is the most general theme of Sartre's writing, whether that freedom is realized in authentic action or denied in bad faith. I shall not deal here in any detail with the characters of his fiction and theatre, who have been analyzed exhaustively by others – Roquentin's realization of his own contingency, Goetz's ambiguous relation to good and evil, and so on. But the historical individuals whom he chooses as paradigm cases deserve attention in a work on his philosophy because they constitute as it were experimental trials rather than imaginative illustrations – even though some critics have felt that Sartre imagined the Baudelaire, the Genet and the Flaubert about whom he wrote.

It was in his treatment of Baudelaire and Genet that the scandalous side of Sartre exhibited itself, in the opinion not only of a public for whom his (largely fictional) life in the Latin Quarter had already become notorious but also of a considerable body of critically informed persons. For in his studies of these two writers, each scandalous in his own right, Sartre seemed to attack directly French poetry in the former case and French morality in the latter. In fact his interest in both cases was in the 'existential psychoanalysis' of the singular individual, but in the case of Baudelaire the status of his subject as a national literary monument was bound to lead to trouble. The study has a curious obtuseness in its insistence on Baudelaire's failure to choose himself differently when the choice he in fact made resulted in such extraordinary poetry. There is here an old and deep problem for aesthetics and the theory of literature. Baudelaire himself was acutely conscious of the disparity between the condition of his own life – with its disgust, its lassitude, its continual nostalgia for an impossible novelty, and what in Sartre's terms might properly be called its 'nausea' – and his calling as a poet who from these very materials produced miracles of art, and this contrast is a frequent theme of his poetry (*cf.* e.g., '*Bénédiction*', '*L'Albatros*'). That art may often in fact be a product of individual bondage rather than individual freedom is an awkward fact for a liberated history of Western culture – consider for example the immeasurable contributions of Christianity to music and painting. It might of course be argued, and has been (by Hegel among others) that bondage can be perfect freedom, freedom the voluntary acceptance of necessity, and this looks at first something like Sartre's position: the original choice of oneself in one's own facticity, and so on. But for Sartre freedom must be more radical than that, as we have seen, and the Hegelian argument falls into bad faith. I cannot freely choose bondage if I see it as such, necessity once chosen can no longer be represented as having been necessary. There is another tradition that represents art as a mode of liberation from bondage, and Sartre seems to adopt this view, in the person of Roquentin, at the end of *Nausea*: having reduced himself to degree zero, as it were – 'I am free: there is absolutely no more reason for living' (N 209) – he wonders whether an otherwise gratuitous existence might not be justified, like that of the Jew who wrote the song which provides his final epiphany or that of the Negress who sang it, by the production of something that would have *being* beyond *existence*.

> A book. Naturally, at first it would only be a troublesome, tiring work, it wouldn't stop me from existing or feeling that I exist. But a time would come when the book would be written, when it would be behind me, and I think that a little of its clarity might fall over my past. ... And I might succeed – in the past, nothing but the past – in accepting myself. (N 238)

But it is the project of writing that counts here, not the quality of what is written, which does not enter the account except indirectly in the assumption that other people will read it.

Sartre's preoccupation elsewhere with the writer's responsibility has to do, as we saw in chapter II, with the consequences, not the character, of what he writes – the text is an instrument, not an end in itself, the question of the text, in short, is for him a moral and not an aesthetic question. But a writer who writes, without liberating himself, a text to be judged by aesthetic criteria, cannot in terms of his own project be criticized for not being a writer who writes, in order to liberate himself, a text to be judged by moral criteria. Sartre agrees: 'We cannot reproach a poet with denying, in his capacity as a poet, his responsibility as a man. We may reproach him with being nothing but a poet' (RW 166). But on what grounds? Sartre's project as a writer involves the assumption of his responsibilities as a man, Baudelaire's, let us suppose, does not, but what follows from that? Sartre seems to be aware that he will be thought to have missed the point about Baudelaire:

> The reader will have looked in vain for some explanation of the very particular form of Beauty which the poet chose and the mysterious charm which makes his poems inimitable. For many people, indeed, Baudelaire is, rightly, purely and simply the author of the *Fleurs du mal*. (B 100)

And in citing, without commenting upon, Baudelaire's remarkable characterization of the 'poetic faculty' as 'the clarity of one's ideas and the power of hope' which are in danger of disintegration 'in this horrible existence' (B 166-7) Sartre misses an opportunity to acknowledge that the poetic project can after all be charged with the highest human value.

Baudelaire's project apart from his poetry – if it makes any sense to speak in this way, since it seems natural to assume that poetry *was* his project – does offer, it is true, an exemplary case study in bad faith as Sartre has defined it: he tries to excuse his own failings by recourse to 'the hypothesis of the intervention of an evil force which is external to him' (cited B 160), he chooses 'to *exist* for himself as he *was* for others' (B 191), he 'was the man who chose to look upon himself as though he were another person; his life is simply the story of the failure of this attempt' (B 27-8). It appears to be a life of discouragement, of complaint, of evil consciously embraced for the sake of art, a life evoking pity or even sympathy: ' "He didn't have the life he deserved" ' (B 15). But actually, says Sartre, it is all a project of survival, carefully planned (B 191), so that such feelings are quite out of place. 'Supposing after all that he did deserve the sort of life he had? Supposing that contrary to the accepted view, men always have the sort of lives they deserve?' (B 16).

This however is still a very early Sartre; the *Baudelaire* dates from roughly the same time as *Existentialism*. The generalization principle becomes rapidly less important after this period, and the remarks cited above, while still moralistic in tone, suggest that Sartre's intentions are descriptive rather than prescriptive. By the time of *Saint Genet* there is no longer any question of judgment or of deserts – all that remains is the enterprise of understanding. The absence of the *Morale* can now be interpreted as the absence of any legislative desire on Sartre's part: to discuss morality is to presuppose the freedom of the agent to change his conduct, and whereas in 1946 Sartre still believed in radical freedom, in

1952 the point was not quite so obvious. Situations might be more complex, and more confining, than had been allowed for by the heroic version of existentialism. Simone de Beauvoir had already argued, in 1940, that it would not always be equally easy to transcend one's circumstances – how, for example, would it be managed by a woman trapped in a harem? Even that situation, Sartre had said, could be lived in different ways. Simone de Beauvoir, twenty years later, remembered that she had been unconvinced, but had lacked counter-arguments because of the assumption of an 'individual, and therefore idealistic, morality' (POL 346); Sartre himself, later still, was astonished that he could really have believed in freedom of choice under all circumstances. We shall return to this point below.

In *Saint Genet*, while it is not yet a question of the collective – the focus is entirely on Genet himself, whose subjectivity is reconstructed from childhood to fame – the awareness of complexity that will appear so strikingly in the *Critique of Dialectical Reason* is already evident. Not only has Sartre come to see more clearly the determining and confining effect of social origins and situations on the otherwise free subject, but he reaffirms the ambiguity of moral judgments of good and evil and of conventional standards of value. These judgments and standards are in any case imposed from without:

> It is *the others* who prefer a dissatisfied Socrates to a contented pig.
> For if Socrates is dissatisfied with himself and with mankind, that
> means he is not so sure, in view of human folly and wickedness, that
> man is superior to the pig. (SG 190-1)

Better, perhaps, to be an authentic pig than a man in bad faith; the deliberate choice of outright evil rather than qualified good is a recurrent theme in Sartre (as is the pig: in the book on Flaubert it reappears with much the same message:

> For Socrates does not know that he is Socrates – and the others, who
> surround him and condemn him to death, do not know it either.
> Whereas the pig, at ease in its sty, among its fellows, rejoices in
> being a pig. (*IF 631*))

It occurs again, for example, in *The Condemned of Altona*, where Franz remarks that when other roads are closed there always remains that of the worst (CA 130, although the English translation is poor). Good and evil in their pure form seem to meet, criminal and saint to form an 'eternal couple' (SG 73 ff.); like Baudelaire, Genet embraces evil with such genius that it becomes 'akin ... to a work of art. Better still, to poetry' (SG 28). Evil, indeed, strikes like genius and is uncompromising; Sartre repeats the story that Genet

refused to make the acquaintance of Gide, because, he said, 'his immorality is suspect'. I would go further and would say that *all* systematic immorality is suspect and covers up a last recourse to Good. For Evil cannot be system: either it is an explosion or it is nothing at all. (SG 244)

This last remark is an allusion to Breton, of whom Sartre has just been speaking, and to the surrealist insistence on intensity and spontaneity: 'Beauty will either be convulsive, or it will be nothing at all.' So these remarks about Evil are obviously not to be taken as reflecting a decision on Sartre's part that it is equal or preferable to Good; he wishes to raise doubts about the conventional categories, but he himself has no doubt that, for example, authenticity is better than bad faith, and has indeed exhibited in his own life virtues of equanimity, kindness, fidelity and the like which he would not willingly have abandoned for their opposites. His interest in Genet, however, is in the latter's embodiment of free existential choice in spite of his conditioning. Sartre is no longer inclined to make Genet carry the moral burden for all men; it is enough for him to manage the affairs of one man, namely himself. Genet recounts a conversation in prison in which he poses to another inmate the moral problem of whether he, Genet, should steal or not; his interlocutor is puzzled: 'Why you more than anyone else?' he asks, and Sartre says that we recognize the question:

It is the question that Abraham asks himself. When Genet says: 'The question is, for me, whether *I* should steal', and the burglar replies: 'Why *you?*' they are not speaking of the same Self. The burglar has been caught in the toils of the universal. The *self* of which he speaks is the universalizable particular, the one which shares with all others this state of being *self* and other than the others. It is the Hegelian particular, established, supported, transcended and absorbed by the universal. That of Genet is the individual I which has no common measure with the universal and the particular, which cannot be fixed in concepts but can only take risks and live its life. Genet does not resolve the contradiction; he lives it. If it transcended itself within him towards any synthesis, *Jean Genet* would disappear. The terms must be kept together *by means of speed*. If he stops, he is lost. In short, he *exists*. (SG 185)

This text brings into sharp focus an implicit contradiction in the idea of an 'existentialist morality': to be moral means to live according to some code, that is, to have determined in advance one's choice of behaviour under circumstances governed by moral rules. It is to give oneself the appointment in the future already mentioned in connection with anguish – but, as we saw there, it is also to close off the possibility which is the essential mark of freedom. Sartre's ethics, then, is concerned not with morality at all but with praxis:

In an ethic of praxis, the Ego is not distinguishable from its possibilities and projects. It is therefore defined by the complex body of its decisions, which are supported by an original choice, and is revealed only in and by acts. It can be the subject of investigation and evaluation only afterward. As soon as I wonder, *before* the theft, whether *I* should steal, I detach myself from my undertaking, I am no longer at one with it; I separate the maxim of my act from my intuition of myself as if they were two separate realities, and I decide as to their suitability or unsuitability as if they were a matter of a necktie and a shirt. This abstract attitude is called *nobility*; it is ruinous for both the act and the man. (SG 187)

From the point of view of moral philosophy this analysis is less than satisfactory; it appears to require an impossible combination of deontological and consequentialist principles – deontological in that the authenticity of action is all-important, consequentialist in that it must still be possible to denounce an action after the fact no matter how authentic the agent's project. Nobody can say what project a person *ought to undertake freely* – the very formulation is a contradiction in terms. But we must nevertheless be able to say, of a particular project, that it *ought not to have been undertaken*. Perhaps, however, this is an inescapable dilemma of human action, and perhaps the best we can do in particular situations is to live them as they come, matching action to conditions literally moment by moment (so that at any given moment it may be a toss-up whether we opt for good or for evil) and being prepared to answer for the consequences. This is not, to be sure, a description of any recognizable species of *moral* action, but since for Sartre this is an incoherent notion that need not occasion surprise. But it may reflect the manner in which we actually lead our lives more accurately than more conventional moral theories.

From this period in Sartre's thought we have another version of the same subject in the play *The Devil and the Good Lord*, which was inspired by a story of Cervantes in which a pure-hearted but brutal ruffian stakes his future ethic on the outcome of a game of cards: if he wins he will become a monk, if he loses, a highwayman. The 'couple of the criminal and the saint' is like heads or tails – they are practical alternatives, not moral opposites. But Sartre, true to his principles, does not allow the antecedent wager to be wholly determining: in the play the hero, Goetz, chooses the good at the crucial moment by cheating in order to lose. In this play, says Simone de Beauvoir, 'Sartre was once more confronting the vanity of morality with the efficacy of praxis' (FC 242). Praxis is efficacious in the sense that at the moment of choice we do in fact see, immediately, what it is we wish and mean to do, and that that is the only moment at which it is possible for us to see it; we must be plunged into the situation, which must be totalized up to the very moment of choice. But what is there to guide our choice in the moment? The answer is to be expected: nothing but what we have made of ourselves up to that moment. The necessity of choice is a source of anguish. The theme is familiar.

Can moral rules then play no part at all in the determination of action? In his early days Sartre would have been prepared to say of most of them that they merely ministered to bad faith, enabling people to escape as it were by rote the existential burden of free choice. Later, however, he comes to see that the rules themselves - which have, after all, a certain social reality - may authentically be incorporated into a project. In a paper entitled 'Determinism and Freedom' presented at the Gramsci Institute in Rome in 1964 he comments on a poll at a girls' school, in which 95 per cent of the respondents said that lying should be condemned, but 70 per cent admitted to lying 'often' or 'very often'. Clearly this represents a perfectly conscious discrepancy between principle and action; how is it to be interpreted? Sartre decides that freedom means, among other things, freedom to project the good, even if we are habitually evil.

> This is the way the normative actually appears to us: its
> unconditional possibility is imposed upon me as being *my possible
> future regardless of my past*. The fact that the accidents of birth and
> childhood have made me cunning, or that lying has become a habit
> for me, or that antecedent circumstances render such lying useful
> makes little difference: these facts do not touch the possible subject
> of the normative act in his possibility. Thus he constitutes himself as
> a future independently of any past whatsoever. (WS 2:245)

The situation has been inverted: Goetz chooses the good in the moment of totalized praxis even though it does not form part of his project, the girls go on lying even though truth-telling seems to be part of theirs. But both outcomes are surely in keeping with the necessarily undetermined character of human action in the moment of its performance (for if it were determined - or determinable, according to the laws of social science, for example - it would not be action). 'The imperative's *pure future* is *neither knowable nor predictable*. Its character as pure future - that is, as future which nothing has laid the groundwork for and nothing helps to bring about - makes it *a future to be created*' (ibid.). And just as in the days of pure and heroic existentialism, the creation of this future is the work of human freedom - it is only that its power is somewhat reduced.

Ethics, in the later Sartre, yields priority to politics, to which I shall shortly turn. But to the extent that individual behaviour retains its interest - and it does until the end - it is no longer to be construed as the product of a solitary and anguished subject, insulated by its secretion of Nothingness from the facticity of the external world, but as the re-exteriorization of social relations (family relations, relations of production, historical and institutional relations) which have been interiorized by the individual in upbringing, education, and social and political experience. The 'subject' is not central but marginal, 'the small margin in an operation whereby an interiorization re-exteriorizes itself in an act'; it is still free, but freedom is correspondingly redefined – it has become nothing more than 'the small movement which makes a totally conditioned social being someone who does not render back completely what his conditioning has given him' (BEM 35). But this small movement, this small margin, are nevertheless crucial, and they still separate Sartre's view radically from any theory of wholly exterior conditioning, such as he takes those of Freud and Marx to be. The difference between these two, for him, is that Marx at least was right about the form that exterior conditioning takes, to the extent – less than wholly determining – that it really does operate in our lives.

> When I discovered the class struggle, this was a *true* discovery, in
> which I now believe totally, in the very form of the descriptions
> which Marx gave of it. Only the epoch has changed: otherwise it is
> the same struggle with the same classes and the same road to victory.
> Whereas I do not believe in the unconscious in the form in which
> psychoanalysis presents it to us. (BEM 39)

The subject, while marginal, still lives its life consciously, although Sartre's emphasis has shifted from the *conscious* to the *lived* (*vécu*) and with this from the moral to the practical.

IX

Politics and Dialectics

Saint Genet is unique among Sartre's major works in that it deals with a living subject with whom he was intimately acquainted. His esteem for Genet seems to have rested on the latter's living out of the principles of existentialist freedom; but whether because of the paradoxical situation of a man whose project touches the limits of that freedom, or because of the immediacy of the person, there is something unsatisfying about much of the work - the description is rich, the asides brilliant, and yet it is as if Sartre's professed ambivalence about conventional good and evil resulted in a lack of depth, a kind of skating over the surface, a reprise of the 'game of mirrors' in *Being and Nothingness* on a more personal and therefore more disturbing level. The taste for paradox can be indulged without risk in a literary context, and the conclusion of *The Devil and the Good Lord* exploits it admirably. Goetz speaks:

> I shall make them hate me, because I know no other way of loving
> them. I shall give orders, since I have no other way of obeying. I
> shall remain alone with this empty sky over my head, since I have no
> other way of being among men. (DGL 149)

But in a critical work with philosophical pretensions the danger of the paradoxical is that it may seem merely inconclusive. Sartre calls 'whirligigs' (in French *'tourniquets'*) the arguments of Genet that grow out of the paradox of the liar (and which have been developed with some degree of preciosity by R. D. Laing under the name of 'knots'), summarizing them under the 'General Principle': *'If you affirm being, you find yourself in the process of affirming nothingness, but in this movement of affirmation you transcend nothingness and find yourself in the process of affirming being, etc.'* (SG 334). He concludes a sketch of these accelerating and unstable efforts to grasp the real with a masterly comparison of Genet and Nietzsche, but it leads to no positive conclusion.

In fact, of course, as suggested above, Sartre is not in the least ambivalent about good and evil; he himself has none of Nietzsche's moral vertigo, and apart from a mild degree of unconventionality in his personal attitudes none of the social defiance of Genet. These *ad hominem* remarks are relevant to the transition from ethics to politics; to find another philosopher whose personal situation is similar one has to look not to Nietzsche but to Marx. Marx's ethics too, one might say, remained unwritten – and yet there can be no doubt whatever, from reading *Capital* alone, not to mention the earlier 'humanist' works, as to where his moral convictions lie; they are repeatedly proclaimed in the indignation he brings to bear on capitalism as it expresses itself in the exploitation of the proletariat. No ethical theory is required to assure him that the death 'from simple overwork' of the milliner Mary Anne Walkley, who ordinarily toiled for an average of sixteen hours a day during the London season, but was taken ill after more than twenty-six hours of continuous work on dresses for the ball for the Princess of Wales in June 1863 (Marx 1930: 257), was a moral outrage. Nor does Sartre require a theory in order to condemn the arrest of the editor Henri Alleg, who was tortured while in solitary confinement at El-Biar in June 1957 (*S V:72* ff., WS 1:345). The cases could be multiplied indefinitely for both writers – the historical circumstances vary, from the industrial revolution to imperialist oppression, from Paris in 1848 to Paris in 1943, from the Commune to the Algerian or Vietnamese wars – but they have in common the assumption that it is enough to set forth the offence in its inescapable horror, as a manifestly unacceptable *fact*, for the sensitive conscience to rise up in revolt against it. The moral theory here is less Kantian than Socratic: it is impossible to know the better and approve of the worse.

Socrates would have said it was impossible to know the better and *do* the worse. Unfortunately indignation by itself is not efficacious – and both Marx and Sartre were, of course, perfectly aware of this. Plenty of consciences are insensitive, or desensitized. Indeed neither Marx nor Sartre would approve of the term 'conscience' here, since it has been pre-empted by pious rhetoric and has the effect of emphasizing just the wrong things – private virtue, for example, rather than public justice. The remedy, for both writers, lies not in ethical analysis but in political action. 'I think, along with many others,' says Sartre,

> that it is necessary to shorten the convulsions of a dying world, to help in the birth of a producing community and to try to draw up, with the workers and militants, the table of new values. That is why Saintliness, with it sophisms, rhetoric, and morose delectation repels me. It has only one use at the present time: to enable dishonest men to reason unsoundly. (SG 202-3)

At the time of *Saint Genet*, while Sartre had practically abandoned ethics, he had not yet found a definitive position in politics; it was immediately after this that there occurred what his biographers call 'an important turning point in Sartre's political thinking', which resulted in *The Communists and Peace*.

It is not my purpose here to trace in detail the history of Sartre's relations with the Communist Party; what is of philosophical interest is his relation to Marxism. But it is impossible to separate these questions entirely, particularly in view of the fact that one of Sartre's preoccupations during this period was the relation of the Communist Party to Marxism, and that one of the recurrent problems of Marxism has been the relation between philosophical theory and political praxis. Sartre had decided in 1940, after his return from a German prison camp, not to remain aloof from politics after the war was over (POL 342). Politics immediately after the war was dominated by the triangle of fascism, communism, and capitalism: the former crushed, although its legacy among French intellectuals was still bitter; the latter two, after their alliance against a common enemy, taking up once again their traditional antagonism. As we saw in chapter I, Sartre was happy neither with Stalinism nor with free enterprise; but he naturally turned in the direction of socialism rather than capitalism, if for no other reason than that socialism had been the counterpoise to fascism since the Spanish civil war – the capitalist system having opposed fascism only when circumstances forced its hand – and the chief claimants to the banner of socialism were the communists.

The first of the three major texts in political analysis (before *Search for a Method* and the *Critique of Dialectical Reason*) is 'Materialism and Revolution', which expresses Sartre's reservations about dialectical materialism as a philosophical basis for the move towards socialism. As the title of the essay suggests, it is the materialism and not the dialectics that he calls in question; revolution is certainly necessary, but materialism is in danger of 'stifl[ing] the revolutionary design to death' (LPE 256). The philosophical difficulty that Sartre has with dialectical materialism is its claim to scientific status, and the chief culprit is not Marx but Engels. Science can deal with external and abstract relations but not with concrete and historical ones; matter as such has no history and can have no dialectical development. Dialectics, in Hegelian terms, is essentially the working out of *notions*, rather than of *concepts*, which are the stock in trade of science: 'for Hegel the notion organizes and fuses concepts together in the organic and living unity of concrete reality. The Earth, the Renaissance, Colonization in the eighteenth century, Nazism, are objects of *notions*; being, light and energy are abstract concepts' (LPE 209). For those who have read Hegel in English some care is needed here, since in many translations the word '*Begriff*', the equivalent of 'concept' as Sartre uses it, is translated 'notion'. The equivalent in Hegel of Sartre's 'notion' is '*Vorstellung*', whose sense is at once more concrete and less rigorous than that of 'Begriff'. The odd thing about Sartre's account is that in Hegel 'Vorstellung' and 'Begriff' stand for stages in the dialectical ascent towards the Idea, so that it makes little sense to say that the dialectic involves one rather than the other. But 'Begriff' in Hegel does not mean, perhaps, quite what Sartre means by 'abstract concepts' in the natural sciences; he seems tempted to identify them with the objects of which they are the concepts, and objects do not enter into the dialectic. The idea of a dialectics of nature, so dear to Engels, seems absurd to Sartre. In the *Critique of Dialectical Reason*, speaking of the attempt to reduce history to economics and hence to 'the action of a single set of external forces on various objects' he speaks witheringly of Engels as the dialectician who

> crowns his success with the splendid result that he kills the dialectic twice over to make sure it is dead – the first time by claiming to have discovered it in Nature, and the second time by suppressing it within society. (CDR 712)

Ten years later, describing his basic project as the attempt 'to provide a philosophical foundation for realism', 'to give man both his autonomy and his reality among real objects, avoiding idealism without lapsing into a mechanistic materialism', he says that he has come to assign certain limits to dialectical materialism, 'to validate the historical dialectic while rejecting a dialectic of nature, in the sense of a natural process which produces and resolves man into an ensemble of physical laws' (BEM 36-7).

By 'materialism' Sartre seems to understand a kind of positivism; he condemns it to impotence as an explanatory force where human action is concerned.

> [The] possibility of *rising above* a situation in order to get a perspective on it (a perspective which is not pure knowledge, but an indissoluble linking of understanding and action) is precisely that which we call freedom. No materialism of any kind can ever explain it. A series of causes and effects may very well impel me to a gesture or to behaviour which itself will be an effect and which will modify the state of the world; it cannot make me look back at my situation in order to grasp it in its totality. (LPE 235-6)

The problem with this stance is that it calls for an alternative explanation, and, as Kant saw, if materialism cannot account for subjectivity, nor can 'spiritualism' (Kant 1933: 376). The point is important for the later controversy over analytical and dialectical reason: the materialist might wish to say that it is the complexity of the material determinations that makes the concrete historical event inaccessible to explanation in his terms, that no new metaphysical principles need be invoked to explain subjectivity, intentionality, significance and the rest, that the invocation of such principles could in any case throw no light on the question, that the mistake is to try to *explain* such things in the first place, since all of them are prerequisite to the very activity of explanation.

But Sartre simply dismisses materialism:

> In short, it cannot account for revolutionary class consciousness. Dialectical materialism undoubtedly exists in order to explain and justify this transcendence toward the future. But it endeavours to ascribe freedom to things, not to man – which is absurd. A state of the world will never be able to produce class consciousness. (LPE 236)

Sartre's account of this follows, without mentioning, Hegel's dialectic of Master and Slave (especially the aspects of it stressed by Kojève) and issues in the slave's discovery of freedom in his domination of things through work. 'But precisely because he does learn of it through things, he is anything but a thing' (LPE 243), whereas a materialist account of history is bound to regard him as exactly that – otherwise its predictions cannot be relied upon. Sartre wishes to insist again on the intrinsic freedom of man;

> but, say the Marxists, if you teach man that he *is* free, you betray him; for he no longer needs to *become* free; can you conceive of a man free from birth who demands to be liberated? To this I reply that if man is not originally free, but determined once and for all, we cannot even conceive what his liberation might be. (LPE 244)

We have already seen the direction that Sartre's resolution of this opposition subsequently took towards an increased awareness of oppressive determination on the one hand, an attenuated concept of freedom on the other. The oppression as such is already evident enough:

> If a slave's freedom is manifest in his work it is nonetheless true that this work is imposed, nullifying and destructive, that he is cheated of its products, that he is isolated by it, excluded from a society which exploits him and in which he does not share. . . . It is precisely in becoming revolutionaries, that is, in organizing with other members of their class to reject the tyranny of their masters, that slaves best manifest their freedom. (LPE 245)

But the freedom is still of the full existential variety. A revolutionary philosophy, for Sartre, would be one in which the plurality of such freedoms could be reconciled in the construction of a new society; it would transcend both bourgeois idealism and the myth of materialism, and, asserted at first by genuine revolutionaries, i.e., 'men in the *situation of oppressed persons*' (LPE 254), would prove to address itself to the bourgeois also 'as a man among men' (LPE 255). It would in other words be 'the philosophy of *man* in a general sense' (LPE 253).

What the content of this revolutionary philosophy might be Sartre does not explicitly say. But he leaves the way open towards Marxism by insisting that the object of his criticism is not Marxism as such but the communists' version of it: 'the frequenting of communists has taught me that nothing is more variable, abstract and subjective than what is called their Marxism' (LPE 255). The trouble with communism is that it has, out of fear, set itself against the freedom of thought. Sartre's intolerance of this situation comes out starkly in his brief polemic with Lukács in 1949. In response to the latter's criticism that he had changed his mind between a Heideggerian stance in *Being and Nothingness* and a Kantian one in *Existentialism is a Humanism* Sartre alludes to Lukács's own professed renunciation of his early works:

> Lukács condemns me for having changed, but I haven't changed at all. Yet I claim the right to do so if the development of my thinking requires it. Each philosopher has developed during his career, without, however, making the hairpin turns characteristic of thinking subject to a predetermined line. A real philosopher feels no need whatsoever to renounce his earlier works as his thinking develops; Marx changed his doctrine too, but without pronouncing this *mea culpa* which Lukács claims is a proof of his sincerity. Furthermore, the term 'renounce' alone suffices to show that we are in the midst of a way of thinking which is not free; it comes from a medieval and religious attitude and is conceivable only in a scholastic philosophy. (WS 1:221)

Later he implicitly compares the official control of thought in Hungary to the Inquisition, and Lukács to a Galileo who might have insisted on his convictions under his breath, as Galileo did, but for the fact that he had really given them up: 'the earth does not turn for Lukács' (WS 1:222).

The Communist Party, then, is an organ of intellectual oppression; at the same time it is the only source of proletarian hope. This is the dilemma with which Sartre lived in the post-war period. In 1952, however, he became incensed by the smugness and vindictiveness of anti-communism; the event that triggered what he himself calls a 'conversion' (SIT 287) was the arrest of the communist leader Duclos. The details of the episode are not important – Sartre refers to them as only the last straw, the breaking-point in a cumulative process – but its effect was irreversible:

> In the name of those principles which it had inculcated into me, in the name of its humanism and of its 'humanities', in the name of liberty, equality, fraternity, I swore to the bourgeoisie a hatred which would only die with me. (ibid.)

It was this that provoked the second of the major texts mentioned above, *The Communists and Peace*, which represents Sartre's closest approach to the

Party and is in fact an impassioned defence of its title to represent the working class.

In 1952 the Korean War dragged on and the Cold War was in full swing, so that peace was a topical subject; the Communist Party was in principle pacifist, and correctly interpreted, said Sartre, the 'deep-seated pacifism of the masses' (CP 24). But it worked under considerable handicaps: an unfair system of parliamentary representation, an unfriendly press (it was *Le Figaro*'s report of a disturbance in the Renault factory as a 'workers' victory' over the Party that set Sartre off in *The Communists and Peace*), even the hostility of a large proportion of the Left. The chief question for Sartre was that of the identity, interests and attitudes of the working class, and its relation to the Party. A great many people, starting with the editor of *Le Figaro*, seemed ready to speak for the proletariat, but what was it, really? What is the ontological status of a class? It is this problem that constitutes the chief philosophical interest of *The Communists and Peace*, although it is dealt with disconnectedly in the course of a long and more local polemic.

Sartre returns to the question of class in this standard sense at the end of the *Critique of Dialectical Reason*, in the light of the theory of social groups developed there. But the analysis in *The Communists and Peace* has a freshness that makes it especially trenchant. The question has been posed as to the proper and permissible object of strikes: should they be limited to defending the workers' interests or can they serve larger political ends? The bourgeois naturally takes the former position. But what, asks Sartre, are the workers' interests exactly? In the first instance, 'the interest of the worker is to be no longer a worker' (CP 31); but this will be regarded as frivolous – what are his interests *as a worker*? Well, says Sartre, even if we accept (as he does not) the bourgeois relegation of the worker to his ontological status as such, that is still a puzzling question.

> A factory makes a sink available to its personnel: the *interest* of the personnel is that the drain pipe doesn't get stopped up. The country of these workers is swept along towards war by political stupidity: their *interest* is that the war does not take place. Between the first example and the second, there is room for the whole of social life. (CP 33)

The reality of social life is a totality of interests, and it is not so easy to restrict these to following, mechanically, some imagined class line.

'Class' is a sociological concept, but the sociologists who study the working class do so statistically, considering it 'from the outside with a total scientific objectivity and like an inert object' (CP 90), transforming it into 'a zoological species'. 'We thought we were dealing with sociologists; our mistake: they were entomologists' (CP 91). The effect of this treatment is to deny the reality of the worker's *praxis*, to turn human facts into merely physical ones. Unfortunately Marxist theoreticians make exactly the same mistake. Sartre quotes (from Goldmann) Bukharin's definition: 'A social class is a collectivity of persons who play the same role in production and who sustain the same relations of production with other persons participating in the process of production' (CP 93); but a collectivity of persons having functional or social similarities is not necessarily a class; if such a collectivity is just a sum of individuals it is a species again, if on the other hand it is a genuine *totality* (the emphasis on the term is Sartre's) then we have to determine how this totality is generated.

> All these scholars promised to show us the unity of a class, and they showed us the identity of the items in a collection. Now, unity and identity are contrary principles: the first establishes concrete ties among persons, and the second, abstract ties among cases. Thus, in claiming to reconstruct the proletariat, their method destroyed all possibility of any real liaison among its various members. (CP 93-4)

In fact the members of a class become members by meeting one another, recognizing their common interests, taking action in common. They have no class nature before this encounter and this activity. 'Classes don't just happen to exist, they are made' (CP 96). In this Sartre's view is closer to Marx's own than to that of the Marxists, since Marx speaks of the '*formation* of a class with radical chains' (Marx 1967: 262, emphasis added) and does not assume that its chains have already formed it. That is why the apathy of some workers towards a particular strike, for example, cannot be interpreted as an expression of the will or the attitude of the proletariat. To the extent that the workers do form a class, says Sartre, that class supports and is represented by the Communist Party; it is absurd to say that the Party could survive as a major force in France without that support, and it is just as absurd to say that it and the workers are all manipulated from Moscow. But it would be wrong, I think, to construe Sartre's support of the Party as partisan support. *The Communists and Peace* was not, in my view, primarily an intervention in French party politics; it seems to have sprung from a double motivation, partly moral and partly intellectual. The moral motivation was Sartre's outrage at the bad faith of the politicians and the press in their treatment of the Party, which required his defence not so much because of the justice of its cause as because of the injustice of the attacks upon it. The intellectual motivation was his interest in the question of how a number of free existential subjects can form themselves into a cohesive social force, into a 'collective subject'.

Here, to Sartre's credit, he was able to keep his head. Marxist theoreticians have too often fallen into the trap of 'collective consciousness'; since the orthodox view is that even individual consciousness owes its existence to the collective, it is easy enough (especially under the influence of Hegel) to imagine that in some sense the collective has its own consciousness, hence its own purposes, somehow transcending the consciousness or the purposes of its individual members. The abuses to which this view lends itself do not have to be imagined, since they have been realized. Sartre sketches, at the end of *The Communists and Peace*, the emergence of a collective subject, the pressure it exerts on the members of the group to approve unanimously the projects it undertakes, etc., but he adds a note:

I mean by 'collective subject' the *subject of the praxis* and not some kind of 'collective consciousness'. The subject is the group *brought together* by the situation, *structured* by its very action, *differentiated* by the objective requirements of the *praxis* and by the division of labor, at first random then systematic, which the *praxis* introduces, *organized* by the leaders which it chooses for itself or which it discovers for itself, finding *in their person* its own unity. What has been called 'charismatic power' proves well enough that the concrete unity of the group is *projective*, that is to say that the unity is necessarily exterior to the group. The diffuse sovereignty assembles and is condensed in the person of the leader who subsequently reflects it to each one of the members; and each one, to the very extent that he obeys, finds himself, *vis-à-vis* others and outsiders, the repository of total sovereignty. If there is a leader, each one is leader in the name of the leader. Thus the 'collective consciousness' is necessarily incarnated: it is for each one the collective dimension which he grasps in the individual consciousness of the other. (CP 222-3)

Collectivization is not the simple matter social theorists sometimes seem to think; it involves a multiplicity of reciprocal relations between actual persons, it has to be confirmed and lived by each of them.

Here Sartre anticipates to some extent the dynamics of group formation to be found in the *Critique of Dialectical Reason*. But *The Communists and Peace* ends, like so many of his works, on an inconclusive note. His insistence on the real individual self-determination of the workers, on the authenticity of their support of the Party and of its union, the C.G.T. (*Confédération Générale du Travail*), and on their genuine interest in disarmament, is opposed to what he calls the 'Malthusianism' of management, which allows or encourages war and other social catastrophes as a means not only of bolstering the economy and expanding markets but also of controlling the proletarian population, but the argument is left hanging. The impression that Sartre meant it to be concluded practically by rallying to the communists was widely shared. Merleau-Ponty, in particular, decided that Sartre had become an 'ultra-bolshevist', an advocate of Party control and unthinking submission. In *Adventures of the Dialectic* he reproaches

Sartre with having re-invented communism in a form other than the one it had in fact assumed, and against which he himself had turned:

> Such is the situation of the loner who incorporates communism into his universe and thinks of it with no regard for what it thinks of itself. In reading *The Communists and Peace*, one often wonders – without finding an answer, since the quotations from Marx are so equitably distributed – what distinction Sartre makes between Marx, the ideologies of Soviet communism, and his own thought. As a good philosopher, Sartre packs this whole company into his thought. In it and in it alone – once his negation of history and historical truth and his philosophy of the subject and of the other as intrusion are supposed – Marx, Lenin, Stalin, and Duclos are, in the main, indistinguishable from one another and indistinguishable from Sartre. (Merleau-Ponty 1973: 99)

And he puts his finger on a characteristically Sartrian difficulty: 'Someone may object that it is premature to appraise Sartre's first analyses; we cannot know precisely what implications he himself attributes to them, since they are to be completed later' (Merleau-Ponty 1973: 100). His fear is that such first approximations may be taken as definitive and thus harm the prospects of reconciliation between communism and non-communism.

Perhaps all of Sartre will have to be inscribed under the motto: 'to be continued'. That is not necessarily a weakness – it can just as easily be construed as evidence of philosophical vigour and openness. If the analysis given above is correct then Merleau-Ponty's criticism is beside the point, philosophically if not politically. It is no doubt true that Sartre's defence gave aid and comfort to the Communist Party at a time when it was still dominated by Stalinism, so that, given the tensions of the period, an accusation of political naïvete, if not frivolity, was plausible enough. But for Sartre the issue was not one to be taken lightly – it concerned nothing less than the future of the world and of the individual human beings in it, whose lives were (and still are) at risk because of ideological conflicts sustained by leaders whose mendacity, cynicism, and irresponsibility he found unforgiveable.

It may be remarked that, dialectically speaking, the negation of the negation does not yield the original affirmation but something higher, so that to attack anti-communism is not simply to embrace communism. Sartre's attitude to the Party was one of concern and criticism. He shared some of its professed ends and agreed that these justified certain means, 'adding, however, this indispensable corrective: these means define the end' (SS 87) – that is, the adoption of repressive means (as in the Soviet invasion of Hungary in 1956) betrays a repressive end no matter how piously this may be disavowed. From the time of *The Communists and Peace* Sartre had been content to be known as a fellow-traveller, and he adhered

to this position even after his public break with the Party over the
Hungarian episode, when he published *The Spectre of Stalin.*

> In France there exists a Party which will not escape, any more than
> we shall, from guided missiles, and whose enthusiasm would be
> effaced from the earth along with our protests. It is led by a political
> bureau which congratulated the Soviets on their happy initiative, one
> member of which, recently, declared himself much 'cheered up' by
> these exemplary massacres. The Party is our affair, we are familiar
> with it, we have all, for a shorter or longer time, been its
> fellow-travellers: it is on this Party that we must, that we can act.
> (SS 91-2)

The 'criminal folly' of the Soviet invasion had been 'only an involuntary
jerk of dying Stalinism' (SS 33-4), which still however required to be
eradicated in the French Party because it, like other non-Soviet parties, had
organized itself along Stalinist lines and had been thrown into confusion
by Khrushchev's 'secret speech' at the Twentieth Congress of the Communist Party of the Soviet Union the previous February. Sartre's opinion
of the slavish following of Moscow is clear enough when he says of the
Soviets that 'in making a devil of Stalin, they had replaced white Masses
by black Masses, and had not got away from the cult of personality' (SS
83-4).

The philosophical content of *The Spectre of Stalin* is slight but
significant. The cult of personality, says Sartre, is a product of the rejection
of middle-class individualism:

> Each middle-class person resembles all the others in this: that he
> insists on his own difference and on the value of his own personality;
> these barbarous assertions balance one another; the apparent
> reciprocity of relations universalizes them; the middle-class man
> respects in himself, and claims to respect in others, the absolute
> dignity of the human individual. ... Under cover of this respect,
> realist appreciation of one's self and of others will depend on the
> particular content of this universal form: abilities, actions, character.
> These material elements may form the object of a hierarchy, but not
> of a cult: no one of them is valued *a priori.* This individualism
> excludes all possibilities of idolatry. (SS 57)

In the Soviet Union, on the other hand, 'the cult of personality is above
everything the cult of social unity in one person' (ibid.);

> In subordinating his person to the group, the Soviet man avoids the
> preposterous vices of middle-class personalization. ... His reality,
> always subject to recall, comes to him from his very functions; in his
> relations with his equals, it remains a factor of multiplicity, therefore
> an object of distrust; for his subordinates, on the other hand, it is a

hypostasis of Stalin, therefore a factor of unification and an object of worship. At all levels of the hierarchy, we find the same contradiction. . . . In any event, what lays the foundations of the Soviet person and at the same time destroys him is the impossible unity of the group. (SS 58-9)

Sartre's generalizations here seem as dubious as those he condemned on the part of the sociologists in *The Communists and Peace*, but he is struggling with a genuine problem, namely that of the discrepancy between individual and collective being and behaviour; it is the same problem as before and will remain the chief problem in all his subsequent work. Between the self-deception and self-satisfaction of individuals and the oppressive regimentation of the collective, some mediation must be possible, but it must be practical, really involving the individuals in their collective destiny, and hence it must be political.

> Politics, of whatever sort, is action carried out in common by certain men against other men; based on convergences or divergences of interests, relations of solidarity, like those of struggle and of hostility, define a total attitude of man towards man. (SS 4)

But for Sartre the history of this process is identical with the history of socialism, which in each nation is engaged in 'constructing a world with the means available'; socialism is thus in a unique position, since its aim is not partisan but is nothing less than 'to give justice and freedom to all men', and cannot be viewed 'as a fact without privilege' as Merleau-Ponty had argued (SS 89). Socialism however is not some 'absolute principle floating above the fray, but . . . an historical, concrete, positive, total reality' (SS 90).

Historical, concrete, positive, and total – this is the human reality that Sartre wished to grasp. It is a reality produced by collective activity, and not merely that but by group activity, consciously directed towards common ends. But Sartre's ontological project, inactive since the conclusion of *Being and Nothingness*, had established no level of existence beyond the *ekstasis* of the for-itself represented by its being-for-others, with a tentative excursion (described at the end of chapter VII) in the direction of an elusive 'we-subject' (the 'us-object', objectified by the Third, being a mere exteriority, like a thing). The predecessor who had come the closest to an acceptable account of the social was Marx, and Sartre had become convinced that Marxism was the indispensable and inescapable philosophy of the present epoch, the third 'moment' of the history of modern philosophy (its precursors being the 'moments' of Descartes and Locke, and of Kant and Hegel) (SM 7). The inconclusiveness of the philosophical stance in the post-war political works with which we have been dealing sprang from Sartre's failure to resolve the apparent antinomy between existentialism and Marxism, from his lack of a method in philosophy which would do justice to the radical freedom of the subject insisted on by the first, the historical necessity apparently required by the second. The opportunity to confront this issue reflectively, without obscuring it in the passion of some political moment, came a year after *The Spectre of Stalin* with an invitation from a Polish journal to write an article on 'Existentialism and Marxism'.

This article, under the title 'Questions of Method' (changed to *The Problem of Method* in London, and to *Search for a Method* in New York, on its translation into English) was to form the prelude to the *Critique of Dialectical Reason*. In the preface Sartre wrote for the volume in which the two were published together he specifies the question they pose as a single one: 'Do we have today the means to constitute a structural, historical anthropology?' (SM xxxiv). It should be noted that he does not use the more usual adjective '*structurale*' – as for example in the title of Lévi-Strauss's *Anthropologie structurale* – but rather '*structurelle*'; if we assume that he is borrowing this contrast of suffixes from Heidegger's use of them in '*existenzial*' and '*existenziell*' (*cf. Being and Time*) then his emphasis is on a structuring activity rather than on a structured system. Also by 'anthropology' he obviously does not intend Lévi-Strauss's profession but a philosophical theory of man. The question might therefore be re-phrased: 'do we have the means to constitute a theory of man as he structures himself historically?' And the answer is clearly positive: we have a dialectical method, the details of which are to be specified in the two works that follow.

Existentialism, Sartre now says, is not a philosophy but an ideology. Ideologies are parasitic on philosophies rather in the way in which, to use the language of T. S. Kuhn, puzzles are parasitic on paradigms (*cf.* Kuhn 1970: 35 ff.): they come after the 'great flowering' and busy themselves in re-ordering, applying, cultivating, and taking inventory of philosophical concepts and trying out new methods on old problems (SM 8). The philosophy on which existentialism is parasitic is Marxism. This I think represents far too great a concession to Marxism; it may be that Sartre wished to put existentialism in a subordinate position because of the danger of the cult of personality with respect to himself, and he admits to a dislike of the term 'existentialism', which has become a brand name, as for a kind of soap (SM xxxiii), but in view of the way in which existentialism had come to be understood – namely as a fairly well-marked line of thought from Kierkegaard to Sartre himself – it was anachronistic to subordinate it to Marxism (although Sartre does say that Marxism 'gave it a new birth' (SM xxxiv)). In fact in his essay on Kierkegaard he speaks of the transhistorical status of the subject as 'singular universal' (*S IX:175* ff.), and it seems plausible to think of existentialism and Marxism as complementary, just as the individual and the collective are, rather than assimilating one into the sphere of influence of the other. Kierkegaard was scandalized that Hegel should have tried to give philosophy a beginning, and Sartre is the philosopher who seems to have the most difficulty with endings; even if Marxism is a 'moment' in the history of philosophy there seems no reason for the same to be true of existentialism, which one might expect to recur as a problematic in every epoch.

But Sartre holds to his position. As parasitic on Marxism,

> the ideology of existence inherits two requirements which Marxism itself derives from Hegelianism: if such a thing as a Truth can exist in anthropology, it must be a truth that has *become*, and it must make itself a *totalization*. It goes without saying that this double requirement defines that movement of being and of knowing (or of comprehension) which since Hegel is called 'dialectic'. (SM xxxiv)

The point is crucial: in Hegel the dialectic is on the one hand a principle of logic, on the other a principle of ontology. It operates *both* rationally *and* historically, being itself the form that reason and history have in common; their identification is achieved only under the aspect of the Absolute, from whose point of view the whole historical ascent can be seen as the working-out of the Idea. To the extent that philosophy as the 'thinking study of things' (Hegel 1975: 4) takes particular historical developments as its object it has the task of *thinking* these developments *as* rational. It is in this sense that the famous equation: 'what is rational is actual, what is actual is rational', is to be understood – indeed in the preface to the *Philosophy of Right* where it occurs the aim of that work is said to be 'to apprehend and portray the state as something inherently rational' (Hegel 1952: 11). For Sartre, however, to be dialectical means to *be*, not merely to be *apprehended as*, actual and rational at the same time; lived history makes itself dialectically.

The significance of this slight shift cannot be too strongly stressed. It is relevant to the understanding of the other key term in the text cited above, the term 'totalization'. There is a sense in Hegel in which every moment contains exactly what reason has been able to produce in history, the totality of its achievement up to that point, but philosophy understands this only after the fact; it comes on the scene too late to be of any help, the owl of Minerva spreads its wings only with the falling of the dusk (ibid. 1952: 13). One might say that for Hegel the world is already totalized – the accounts are settled, we have only to cast our eye over the reckoning. Marx, in the familiar eleventh thesis on Feuerbach, calls for change, in contrast to the understanding of the philosophers, and this requires the anticipation of events (coming on the scene in time to be of some help) – for him the reckoning is still to come, the accounts are to be settled through critical–revolutionary practice. Sartre however seems to fall between the two: if for Hegel philosophy looks to the past, and if for

Marx (following Feuerbach in this respect) it or its revolutionary substitute looks to the future, for Sartre philosophy is an affair of the present; he envisages a conscious living of the world in the moment, neither leading the event nor following it. What is the case is the product of complex antecedents, the various effects of which are at every location and at every instant re-computed, as it were, to yield the state of affairs there and then, and, by summing over the whole domain of the human, the state of history. We might call these the 'local' and the 'global' senses of totalization. But totalization is more than an automatic summing-up of the past so far; it is also an activity of reason which, taking into account as it can the diversity of the information available to it, comes to understand the necessity of a given outcome. And this is a dialectical activity, because the rational process will itself be temporal and will need to reckon with the continual interaction between the local and the global through the multiple forms that mediate them.

We have already discussed (in chapter VI), the idea of 'totalization' in *Being and Nothingness*, where however it is a momentary or synchronic activity – being stands over against the for-itself as the *totality* of all that the for-itself is not, because the for-itself posits itself as all that being is not, as the 'detotalization' of this totality (BN 181). In *Search for a Method* and more explicitly in the *Critique of Dialectical Reason* a lived or diachronic component is added and becomes dominant; also, as is to be expected, the totalizing relation is no longer between a simple for-itself and the totality of its immediate world but holds within a social context as the culmination of a historical process. This culmination, it is true, achieves its reality only as lived by individuals – it is not supra-personal, as though History had its own being apart from the individuals who live its moments; on the contrary history is precisely what is lived, moment by moment, by those individuals in their relations to one another. But this means that 'the totalization is never achieved and that the totality exists at best only in the form of a *detotalized totality*' (SM 78); here it is no longer a matter of my realizing that I am not the whole of being, but of my realizing that I am not the whole of any collective of which I form part, that the totality is, as it were, distributed among the elements that are united into it.

Speaking of the time when French philosophy had not yet come to terms with Marxism, when its academic organization had indeed made Marxism inaccessible – and speaking also, indirectly, of his own 'merely existentialist' avatar – Sartre remarks that

> for a long time we confused the *total* and the *individual*. Pluralism,
> which had served us so well against M. Brunschvicg's idealism,
> prevented us from understanding the dialectical totalization. It pleased
> us to decry essences and artificially isolated types rather than to reconstitute the synthetic movement of a truth that had 'become'. (SM 20)

The existential subject was taken to be an independent source of free action, but no account was taken of the fact that this subject is also a social product, the outcome or totalization of a sequence of antecedent determinations. Sartre, as we have seen above, still insists that action is not merely reaction, that the individual is free in that he need not re-exteriorize mechanically what he has interiorized, or 'render back completely what his conditioning has given him' (BEM 35). But in order to 'make something out of what is made of him' (ibid.) he must consciously live the latter making, take account of it, move with it, comprehend it; he must continually totalize (although, to borrow what I think is an appropriate image from accounting, it will always be a 'sub-total', never a final one), so as to be aware of everything that has led up to and now constitutes the moment, and thus to be able to act knowledgeably in it. The totality (of the world, of the collective, of a work of art, of a praxis) exists only 'as the correlative of an act of imagination' (CDR 45), it has the projective status we saw above to belong to the group (*cf.* CP 223); 'totalization has the same status ... but it is a *developing* activity, which cannot cease without the multiplicity reverting to its original status' (CDR 46). (I have taken the liberty here and elsewhere of rendering as 'status' the French '*statut*', which in the English version of the *Critique* is translated throughout as 'statute', a hopelessly inappropriate equivalent in nine out of ten cases of its use in the work.) This activity is practical: it is the grasping of the elements of a lived situation of historical becoming in their mutual relations and in their relations to the projected totality; and it is, obviously, dynamic – the free subject must ride its contingency (to recall an image from the previous chapter), but this is a far more complex matter than it was in *Being and Nothingness*, since it must deal now not only with the upsurge of its own being but with the multiplicity of historical determinations with which it is surrounded and which make simultaneous demands on its comprehension and its action.

It is the complexity of the task on which Sartre insists in opting for dialectical over analytical reason. 'Dialectical Reason ... is the very movement of totalization' (ibid.). The significance of his identification of the dialectic with the double movement of reason and history is now clear; it makes a reflective analysis impossible because totalization and resolution and action take place now, and we have neither leisure for a retrospective Hegelian view nor the opportunity for an anticipatory Marxist one. There is a kind of breathless nobility about this new and more challenging Sartrian project. If it were really to be carried through, infinitely many considerations would have to be instantaneously balanced; as it is, practically speaking, a large number of things have to be taken account of in a great hurry; one can imagine Sartre crunching on his daily bottleful of Corydrane pills (FC 289) so as to keep it all going in his head at once, maintaining a vertiginous speed exceptional even for him. The project of dialectical understanding is at its most Herculean in the case of Flaubert, to which I shall return in the last chapter, but the state of mind it generates is vividly revealed in Sartre's exasperated impatience with Lévi-Strauss.

Lévi-Strauss, in the last chapter of *The Savage Mind*, tackles the question of the relation between dialectical and analytical reason and comes out, by his own account, on the opposite side from Sartre.

> Sartre attributes a reality *sui generis* to dialectical reason. ... It exists independently of analytical reason, as its antagonist or alternatively its complement. Although in both our cases Marx is the point of departure of our thought, it seems to me that the Marxist orientation leads to a different view, namely, that the opposition between the two sorts of reason is relative, not absolute. It corresponds to a tension within human thought which may persist indefinitely *de facto*, but which has no basis *de jure*. In my view dialectical reason is always constitutive: it is the bridge, forever extended and improved, which analytical reason throws out over an abyss; it is unable to see the further shore but it knows that it is there, even should it be constantly receding. The term dialectical reason thus covers the perpetual efforts analytical reason must make to reform itself if it aspires to account for language, society and thought; and the distinction between the two forms of reason in my view rests only on the temporary gap separating analytical reason from the understanding of life. Sartre calls analytical reason reason in repose; I call the same reason dialectical when it is roused to action, tensed by its efforts to transcend itself. (Lévi-Strauss 1966: 246)

I cite this passage at length, and match it with another long passage, from Sartre, because they constitute an exemplary misunderstanding, a discussion of which will be helpful in the sequel:

> Lévi-Strauss does not know what dialectical thought is. Not only that – he is incapable of knowing. ... A dialectical thought is first of all, on one and the same movement, the examination of a reality in so far as it forms part of a whole, in so far as it denies that whole, in so far as that whole comprises it, conditions it, and denies it; in so far, consequently, as it is both positive and negative with regard to the whole, in so far as its movement must be both destructive and conservative with regard to the whole; in so far as it has a relationship to each of the parts of the whole, each of which is both a negation of the whole and includes the whole in itself; in so far as all these parts, or the sum of these parts, at a given moment denies – in so far as each contains the whole – the part we are considering, in so far as this part denies them, in so far as the sum of the parts, in

147

re-becoming collectively, becomes the collectivity of those parts joined together, i.e. the whole less this one, in conflict with this one, and lastly in so far as all of this, considered each time as positive and as negative, gives rise to a movement towards a restructuring of the whole. ... Dialectical thought is quite simply a way of using analytical thought; it is a dialectical use of it. This is what I tried to explain in *A Critique of Dialectical Reason*. Dialectical thought is not opposed to analytical thought. Analytical thought is thought that renders itself inert so as to be competent to deal with the inert, whereas dialectical thought is the synthetic utilization of the collectivity of inert thoughts which themselves become part of a whole which shatter their determination and negation in order to re-belong to the whole, etc. (PL 117-19)

Just as in the complaint about linguistics in chapter II, Sartre here is invoking his Bergsonian mistrust of science. The man of science, says Lévi-Strauss, is bound to place himself outside the situation in order to get at the truth. Sartre remains inside, he takes himself to be experiencing the truth, 'but it does not follow that his meaning, just because it is the richest (and so most suited to inspire practical action), should be the truest' (Lévi-Strauss 1966: 254). For Sartre this criticism is quite beside the point. The '*temporary* gap separating analytical reason from the under-standing of life' is for him an absurdity, for while analytical reason was catching up life would have gone on, more totalizations accumulated, new practical problems presented themselves – and in any case it could not catch up, even with a single totalization; nothing worth saying could be said from the outside, everything would be false.

The dialectical knowing of man, according to Hegel and Marx, demands a new rationality. Because nobody has been willing to establish this rationality within experience, I state as a fact – absolutely no one, either in the East or in the West, writes or speaks a sentence or a word about us and our contemporaries that is not a gross error. (SM 111)

This, says Sartre, is just because contemporary thought is not in move-ment – its ideas are dead.

What does it mean for thought to be in movement? It is clear that for Sartre it means engagement is praxis, as opposed to the contemplative quiescence of theory. American sociology, for example – he mentions Lewin and Kardiner – can be understood historically as the product of 'a country whose History is relatively short' (SM 71) (which, having nothing much to attend to dialectically, can presumably afford to overlook the past), but while it can provide useful empirical findings it simplifies too much to be adequate to the 'real level of life' (SM 75). Psychoanalysis is in a better position, indeed it is needed as a practical mediation in particular cases, but it has no theoretical principles, only a 'completely innocuous mythology' (SM 61). Marxism itself, in the hands of people like Lukács, is 'frozen' (SM 28). It is because 'Marxism stopped', because 'there arose within it a veritable schism which rejected theory on one side and *praxis* on the other' (SM 21-2), that the ideology of existentialism was able to survive. 'A philosophy remains efficacious as long as the *praxis* which has engendered it, which supports it, and which is clarified by it, is still alive' (SM 5-6); the task is to restore Marxist praxis, because Marxism, although moribund, has not been superseded, indeed it cannot be until the problems that gave rise to it are solved or themselves superseded. Existentialism is the route to this restoration, because while 'historical materialism furnish[es] the only valid interpretation of history ... existentialism remain[s] the only concrete approach to reality' (SM 21). Sartre continually emphasizes that existentialism requires to be supplemented by the dialectic in order to grasp this reality, that it attends to 'the specificity of the historical event' and seeks to understand the role of the individual in it not so much because that is its task as because Marxism is in default (SM 124, 128, 133). 'From the day that Marxist thought will have taken on the human dimension (that is, the existential project) as the foundation of anthropological Knowledge, existentialism will no longer have any reason for being' (SM 181).

We may accept all this (or some of it – for a Frenchman of Sartre's orientation to suggest that American history is short is to forget the order of their respective revolutions) and still be unsure of the status and role of Dialectical Reason. Lévi-Strauss in the passage cited above does not seem to find the notion of reason problematic, but is concerned only with its status as analytical or dialectical; he even identifies reason with language: 'a non-reflective totalization, language is a human reason which has its reasons, and which man does not know' (Lévi-Strauss 1966: 334). This allusion to Pascal suggests a view of reason as a faculty, and one we exercise in spite of ourselves – and yet it may mean only that Lévi-Strauss thought it clever to echo Pascal. This sort of literary play is such an incurably rooted habit among the French that one may be forgiven for wondering whether Sartre may not have chosen the title for his *Critique of Dialectical Reason* because he thought it clever to echo Kant. The term 'dialectical reason' does not occur in *Search for a Method*, except as part of the title of the following *Critique*, although we find 'dialectical method', 'dialectical totalization', 'dialectical surpassing'; the closest approach is the passage already quoted about the new rationality that is needed for the dialectical knowing of man. The desideratum becomes a problematic in the joint Preface to the *Method* and the *Critique*, where Sartre virtually identifies Reason with the dialectic in the sense in which it was discussed above:

Not even empiricists have restricted the word 'Reason' to some kind
of order amongst our thoughts. And any 'rationalism' would require
that this 'order' should correspond to, or constitute, the order of
being. From this point of view, if the correspondence [*rapport*]
between the historical totalisation and the totalising Truth is possible,
and if this correspondence is a double movement in both knowledge
and being, we shall be justified in calling this changing relation
Reason. Consequently the aim of my inquiry will be to establish
whether the positivist Reason of the natural Sciences is the same as
the Reason which is to be found in the development of
anthropology, or whether the knowledge and comprehension of man
by man involves not only special methods but also a new form of
Reason, that is, a new relation between thought and its object. In
other words, is there such a thing as dialectical Reason? (CDR 822-3)

Such a dialectical Reason is required, says Sartre, in order 'to study a
person, a human group or a human object in the synthetic reality of their
significations and of their relations to the developing totalisation' (CDR
823); it is essential to prove 'that any isolated knowledge of men or their
products must either transcend itself towards the totality or reduce to an
error of incompleteness' (ibid.). This sounds exactly like Hegel, who does
not seem to have found it necessary to postulate two kinds of reason.

In fact there seems to be no need, apart from a stylistic one, for a
separate category of dialectical Reason. One might characterize different
activities of thought, or different kinds of *reasoning*, without invoking
different kinds of *reason*; thus there can be no doubt that analytic thought,
far from being a universal talent, is a late product of human society, and
that a kind of 'reason in act', relativized to particular circumstances, long
preceded it. 'Reason has always existed', says Marx, 'but not always in
rational form' (Marx 1967:213). Analytic thought comes late because it
requires formulation in language – it depends on the concept of contradiction, not merely that of negation – and because it depends on agreed
standards of precision in the use of language. And thought must have been
dialectical before it became analytic, since standards of precision could not
have been conceived of except in reaction to a conscious sense of deficiency
in that respect, i.e., by a negation of previous linguistic practice. But
thought cannot be analytic without knowing that it is so – in the sense
that notions of affirmation, denial, consequence, and inconsistency are
necessarily part of the conceptual repertoire, as a matter of practical if not
theoretical awareness, of everyone who can be said to reason analytically –
although it might well be dialectical without realizing this. It is natural,
therefore, for those who first think about reason to do so in analytic terms,
and for the concept of dialectic to be a later acquisition. And this seems
to hold true in the history of philosophy; as Sartre says, 'Dialectical

150

thought became conscious of itself, historically, at the beginning of the last century' (CDR 823).

At one point, early in the *Critique of Dialectical Reason*, Sartre discusses the concept of dialectical Reason explicitly in terms of its relation to 'positivist reason', that of Kant in his first *Critique*. Kant's transcendental arguments rest, says Sartre, on a fundamental unintelligibility, the brute fact of the experience whose possibility is to be justified by them. On the other hand the 'fundamental characteristics' of dialectical Reason 'imply that it reveals itself to apodictic experience in its very intelligibility' (*CRD 127*; the English version, at CDR 44, has 'appears as apodictic experience in its very intelligibility', which throws the sense off drastically, since Sartre is speaking of the kind of experience we have *of* dialectical Reason). Now the force of this 'imply' is not clear; this is one of the rare places where Sartre actually uses the language of argument, but the grounds of the assertion are unfortunately not provided. What seems to be involved is the analogue on the collective and historical level of the pre-reflective *cogito*: if reason is operating dialectically, it (or we) must be aware of this, otherwise we would not be operating dialectically. This is a rather tangled question. Sartre insists on the double intelligibility of the principles of the dialectic:

> Firstly, the dialectic as the law of the world and of knowledge must itself be intelligible; so that, unlike positivist Reason, it must include its own intelligibility within itself. Secondly, if some real fact – a historical process, for example – develops dialectically, the law of its appearing and its becoming must be – from the stand-point of knowledge – the pure ground of its intelligibility. (CDR 44)

But it is not clear from this whether the process actually forfeits its dialectical status if somebody fails to grasp that intelligibility (is intelligibility an observable property or a dispositional one?). Also all those 'musts' are gratuitous; it would certainly be very satisfactory if historical processes were transparently intelligible in this way, but nothing requires it to be the case, indeed by Sartre's own account it cannot have been the case until the early nineteenth century (*cf.* the citation from CDR 823 above). Of course 'must' might be interpreted conditionally and legislatively: if there is to be dialectical Reason, it must meet such and such conditions, so that if nothing meets the conditions, there is no dialectical Reason. Sartre does in fact go on to say

> thus the basic intelligibility of dialectical Reason, if it exists, is that of a totalisation. In other words, in terms of our distinction between being and knowledge, a dialectic exists if, in at least one ontological region, a totalisation is in progress which is immediately accessible to a thought which unceasingly totalises itself in its very comprehension

of the totalisation from which it emanates and which makes itself
its object. (ibid.)

Note however that nothing is lost here if we speak simply of 'dialectic' and
not 'dialectical Reason'; note also that a process of inquiry might be more
or less dialectical, although it is hard to think of reason itself as more or
less dialectical if 'dialectical Reason' is a distinct *kind* of reason.

There is yet another definition of 'dialectical Reason' in the *Critique*:

if there is any such thing ... it must be defined as the absolute
intelligibility of the irreducibly new, in so far as it is irreducibly new.
It is the opposite of the positivist analytical enterprise of explaining
new facts by reducing them to old ones. (CDR 58)

But again this can be construed as a contrast between uses or activities
of reason rather than between different kinds: reason as future-referential
(or merely as consciously *present* to itself), reason as retrospective. The
analytic or scientific use of reason is in Sartre's terminology 'universalizing',
while its dialectical use is 'totalizing' (SM 25). Without rehashing Bergson
or the arguments about *Verstehen* in the German social philosophers we
can certainly agree that the external, analytic, universalizing mode of the
employment of reason cannot replace the internal, synthetic, totalizing
mode. But of course everything depends on the kind of knowledge that
is wanted and on the degree of vagueness that can be tolerated in its
formulation. Among the reasons why science has pursued and continues to
pursue the former mode in preference to the latter are that it is testable
and corrigible, that it lends itself to quantification and to the use of formal
languages, that it can tackle one phenomenon at a time and get that right
before going on to the next. It is therefore admirably adapted to the study
of events that repeat themselves exactly whenever and wherever they occur
and that are accessible to generation after generation of researchers, whose
work is cumulative because Nature remains conveniently to hand and has
no objection, if reassurance is needed, to displaying the same effects
patiently time after time.

In 1789 Lavoisier published his *Traité élémentaire de chimie*; the principles
it enunciates, suitably translated (and not only from the French), could be
confirmed or refuted by any undergraduate, to whom air, and heat, and
various materials and receptacles are available just as they were to Lavoisier,
and for whom they would obligingly behave in just the same way, other
things being equal – and the point is that with a little effort they could
be made equal. In 1789 various other events took place; Sartre constantly
alludes to them; they form one of the turning-points of modern European
history. How are we to study and understand them? It seems plausible –
although this is not uncontroversial – that if on some experimental planet
in an experimental solar system just like ours we were to reconstruct
France (and the rest of the world) quark for quark as it was in 1789, so

that people bearing the names of Louis XVI and Necker and Mirabeau, and identical to them down to the warts and short hairs, the detailed contents of the digestive tract and of the brain, remembering the same gratifications and fearing the same ordeals, seeing the same patterns in the same sunsets, hearing the same thunder in the same storms and being rained upon by raindrops identically distributed, moved in an exactly faithful replica of the material and cultural setting in which their namesakes moved, in which second by second a precisely similar sequence of events unfolded in every cubic millimetre of terrestrial space up to the moment chosen for the start of the experiment: if, I repeat, we were able to do all this without getting anything even an angstrom or a nanosecond early or late or out of place, it seems possible, although it is by no means certain, that the French revolution would take place once more. (But the presence of an observer would of course throw everything off.) The point does not require further elaboration. The union of carbon and oxygen in combustion happens in a billion identical events every time I strike a match, but the French revolution happened only once.

One may well wonder how any method, however dialectical, can even begin to bridge the gap represented by that contrast. But it would be a mistake to think of the dialectic as an alternative way of looking at the physical complexity of the world; it is a way of looking at a different world, a world in which events do not just happen, but in which they are lived, planned, hoped for, acted out, the world in other words of human praxis. That is why, as we have seen, Sartre is so scornful of Engels's attempt to found a dialectics of Nature, even though he sometimes claims to be agnostic about it (CDR 32-3). Nature has no history, because it has no project.

> Only the project, as a mediation between two moments of
> objectivity, can account for history; that is, for human *creativity*. It is
> necessary to choose. In effect: either we reduce everything to identity
> (which amounts to substituting a mechanistic materialism for
> dialectical materialism) – or we make of dialectic a celestial law
> which imposes itself on the Universe, a metaphysical force which by
> itself engenders the historical process (and this is to fall back into
> Hegelian idealism) – or we restore to the individual man his power
> to go beyond his situation by means of work and action. This
> solution alone enables us to base the movement of totalization *upon
> the real*. We must look for dialectic in the relation of men with
> nature, with 'the starting conditions', and in the relation of men
> with one another. (SM 99)

It is in this light that the otherwise extraordinary insistence on the total intelligibility and necessity of history at the beginning of the *Critique* proper is to be understood. We *must* be able, Sartre says, to assume that

153

the materialist dialectic is true (CDR 15); knowledge of the kind we are seeking 'would be a mere philosophical dream if it did not have all the marks of apodictic certainty' (CDR 21). But this clearly cannot mean that we must ourselves *in fact* be able to reconstruct in all their historical necessity particular past or even present episodes, with respect to which our information is always bound to be deficient. Sartre certainly knows and appreciates one of the things Engels did manage to get right, namely the idea of history as an unplanned resultant:

> History is made in such a way that the final result always arises from conflicts between many individual wills, of which each again has been made what it is by a host of particular conditions of life. Thus there are innumerable intersecting forces, an infinite series of parallelograms of forces which give rise to one resultant – the historical event. . . . For what each individual wills is obstructed by everyone else, and what emerges is something that no one willed. (Engels 1978: 761)

It means rather that just because history is the resultant of individual wills in relation to one another, affirming, negating, negating their negations, we have at hand in principle everything we need to understand it, because that is the kind of relation we live in our own projects. Sartre would, however, presumably disagree with Engels in the sentence suppressed in the quotation just given: 'This may . . . be viewed as the product of a power which works as a whole, unconsciously and without volition'; a historical unconscious is just as unacceptable to him as a psychoanalytic one.

> It is not the dialectic which forces historical men to live their history in terrible contradictions; it is men, as they are, dominated by scarcity and necessity, and confronting one another in circumstances which History or economics can inventory, but which only dialectical Reason can explain. (CDR 37)

The dialectic is the play of these contradictions. In order to perfect it, it is necessary to work out how men in fact relate to each other in groups and under conditions of scarcity. That is the task of the constructive part of the *Critique*. It represents the resumption of the ontological inquiry Sartre had left in abeyance since *Being and Nothingness*, the raising of the characteristic features of the existential subject – lucidity, negation, project – to a collective level.

X

Series and Groups:
The Dialectical World

> We willingly grant that the *group* never has and never can have the
> type of metaphysical existence which people try to give to it. We
> repeat with Marxism: there are only men and real relations between
> men. From this point of view, the group is in one sense only a
> multiplicity of relations and of relations among those relations.
> (SM 76)

The challenge to a corrected Marxism, then, is to show how the men and
their relations operate dialectically in the making of groups which in their
turn make history, so as to guide praxis in a collective project, the
formation of a new society. Its ontological resources consist of a population of 'for-itselves', loosely associated in a somewhat nebulous totality
which might if it could only be grasped be called 'mind' (BN 301) or
'humanity' (BN 423), but each entering into some specific relations with
other individual for-itselves to which it presents itself as a 'for-Others'.
Some of these relations in turn are mediated and objectified by still other
for-itselves who play the role of Third with respect to the for-itself in
question and its original Other. And some Thirds objectify whole collec-
tions of for-itselves into classes, but they are classes without internal
structure: 'the oppressed class finds its unity in the knowledge which the
oppressing class has of it' (BN 421). This unity however is only the unity
of a crowd which for the Third in question is an object, a material object
even depending on the continued interest of such a Third, without which
it would disintegrate.

The argument of the early chapters of this book, from the 'by-itself',
through the 'for-me' and the 'in-itself', to the 'for-itself' and hence the
'for-Others', was represented as an ontological ascent, and it might seem
that the task is now to take the resources sketched above and move to the
next higher levels, that is to collective being. It should be noted, however,

that the ascent may be merely to new levels of complexity and not necessarily to new levels of being: in one sense it has not risen above the level of the for-itself, the for-others being, as we saw in chapter VII, not a new ontological category but an *ekstasis* or mode of existence of the for-itself. The collective entities we shall now be examining, like the 'group' in the citation that opens this chapter, are not on a higher ontological level either; no new form of Being emerges which is qualitatively different from the forms already encountered. Society and history are relational structures which depend for their existence – which is genuine enough – on their being sustained in the consciousnesses of the individuals who compose them. This was one of the great insights of Marx, who reconstructed the propositions of economics and political science that seemed to deal with objective entities of a higher order – property, money, the State, etc. – as propositions about human relations of production and appropriation, exploitation and alienation, etc., that hold because of men's conceptions of themselves and one another and the world.

It would have been interesting, and in the *Critique of Dialectical Reason* one might have expected, to see these Marxist insights reinterpreted in terms of the for-itself, the in-itself and the rest of the ontological apparatus of the early Sartre. In his shift towards the problems of collective praxis, however, Sartre makes very little use of the categories introduced in *Being and Nothingness*; apart from a footnote, especially for those who have read that book, about the self-discovery of the For-itself as a form of inert materiality in the In-itself (CDR 227-8), there is not a great deal of overlap of terminology between it and the *Critique*. This may be because Sartre's attention in the interim had been occupied with concrete problems of biography and politics, so that the starting-point of the later project was among ontic exemplars rather than ontological abstractions. But if there is not much overlap, there is continuity: the investigation of the *Critique* begins with the Other and the Third. The perspective has shifted, however: at the end of *Being and Nothingness* the role of the Third is mainly as the agent who makes of me a member of a 'we' or an 'us', depending on the degree of activity or passivity involved; at the beginning of the *Critique* it is I as observer who make of the others a reciprocity or seriality – Sartre, that is, puts himself in this external position, and I as reader see the world from his point of view, taking the position of the Third. (In the English translation of the *Critique* 'tiers' is rendered 'third party' throughout, which would be appropriate enough in a work on insurance but suggests an accidental status unsuitable to the crucial constitutive role played by the Third in the formation of the social world, so that I have preferred to carry forward the usage familiar from *Being and Nothingness*.)

This external standpoint makes of the *Critique* something more like a treatise in social science than like an existential quest, at least in its early chapters; when groups come on the scene interiority is restored, but at first, with the discussions of the practico-inert and of seriality, Sartre's account is simply an alternative descriptive scheme for some familiar social phenomena. This is quite in keeping with the method announced in *Search for a Method*, a method borrowed from Henri Lefebvre and christened 'the progressive-regressive method' by Sartre. Lefebvre's specification is given in his own words from an article entitled *'Perspectives de sociologie rurale'* in the *Cahiers de sociologie* for 1953:

(a) *Descriptive.* Observation but with a scrutiny guided by experience and by a general theory. . . .
(b) *Analytico-Regressive.* Analysis of reality. Attempt to *date* it precisely.
(c) *Historical-Genetic.* Attempt to rediscover the present, but elucidated, understood, explained.

And Sartre continues:

We have nothing to add to this passage, so clear and so rich, except that we believe that this method, with its phase of phenomenological description and its double movement of regression followed by progress, is valid – with the modifications which its objects may impose upon it – *in all the domains of anthropology.* (SM 52)

It was noted in chapter III, however, that Sartre himself had already juxtaposed the progressive and regressive methods in 1938 in his essay *The Emotions*, although at that time he did not see how to combine a psychological regression with a phenomenological progression.

Regression is characteristic of external, analytic inquiries which begin with data gathered from objects and work back to causes and explanations; progression is characteristic of internal, synthetic enterprises which begin with intentions held by subjects and work out to actions and significations. The progressive-regressive method (actually the regressive-progressive method, but the other formulation is more euphonious) simply puts these two processes end to end, as it were; at the point of juncture or articulation we find the existential subject. The joint method provides the only adequate means of dealing with history because it makes the explanatory-causal chain (which is not, however, deterministic) pass *through* human agents. 'Men themselves make their history but in a given environment which conditions them,' Sartre quotes Engels as saying (SM 85); he explicates this in the light of the method:

men make their history on the basis of real, prior conditions (among which we would include acquired characteristics, distortions imposed by the mode of work and of life, alienation, etc.), but it is *the men* who make it and not the prior conditions. Otherwise men would be

merely the vehicles of inhuman forces which through them would
govern the social world. (SM 87)

The dialectic is the pattern of the historical development of the human
world towards its future, and it is a dialectic of the subjective and the
objective, playing the 'internalization of the external' against the 'exter-
nalization of the internal'. One might be tempted to say that this is just
another and more complicated way of talking about perception and action,
or even about stimulus and response, but Sartre's avoidance of this
language makes sense in the light of his refusal to reify the for-itself as an
object with fixed capacities or reactions – it is not as if there were
something antecedently and independently there which perceives, acts,
responds and the like. The 'inner life', Sartre's horror of which was alluded
to in chapter IV, was suppressed, it will be remembered, only when 'the
existence of consciousness was made to depend on a perpetual transcending
of itself towards an object' (FA 194); now, in addition to having a future
object, consciousness turns out to be conditioned by past objects, so that
it becomes a double process instead of a single one, taking its place in this
world not merely as an original spontaneity but also as a totalizing praxis.
(I say 'not merely' because an element of spontaneity remains.)

'Praxis, indeed,' says Sartre,

> is a passage from objective to objective through internalization. The
> project, as the subjective surpassing of objectivity toward objectivity,
> and stretched between the objective conditions of the environment
> and the objective structures of the field of possibles, represents *in itself*
> the moving unity of subjectivity and objectivity, those cardinal
> determinants of activity. The subjective appears then as a necessary
> moment in the objective process. (SM 97)

The objective process is to be studied for what it is, but it will be
understood only if the subjective moment is recognized. When the
regressive analysis has done all it can, this moment has to be invoked in
order to get the progressive elucidation started. At that point it will,
naturally enough, prove to be embodied in an individual. This may be
Baudelaire or Flaubert, or Robespierre or Napoleon – or, we might add,
Marx or Sartre – but it may also be an anonymous member of some group
who internalizes jointly with its other members its situation and possibilities and externalizes with them its project in the form of practical
activity. In the *Critique* it is cases of this sort – the 'just anyone' so
important to the later Sartre – that are principally envisaged, rather than
those of particular historical figures. No doubt to understand any case fully
it would have to be worked out in individual detail – indeed an attempt
at this is to follow, in the work on Flaubert – but in order to do this the
principles of collective relations in general must be established. (It will be

recalled that from one point of view the *Critique of Dialectical Reason* was a by-product of the Flaubert project – see chapter I.)

The regressive part of the analysis of these relations involves two methodological categories announced in *Search for a Method* in the chapter entitled 'The Problem of Mediations and Auxiliary Disciplines'. The mediations in question are the structures that intervene between the individual on the one hand and history on the other: the political groups, the systems of belief, the family settings, the industries, the cities and so on. These, says Sartre repeatedly, are realities that have to be acknowledged; we must avoid the Marxist temptation of 'totalizing too quickly', of 'replacing real, perfectly defined groups (*la Gironde*) by insufficiently determined collectivities (the *bourgeoisie* of importers and exporters)' (SM 45). The auxiliary disciplines are those, like psychoanalysis and sociology, which if pursued empirically rather than theoretically can help specify these structures of mediation and thus flesh out the 'abstract skeleton of universality' (SM 83) which passes for totalization among the frozen Marxists. The gap that separates individual praxis from the totality of history must be bridged not by theoretical constructs but by real social formations; the auxiliary disciplines improve, therefore, as they approach more closely to 'hyper-empiricism', that is to the detailed and insistent reporting of 'the resistances, the checks, the ambiguities, the uncertainties' (SM 82) which make social and psychological facts relatively 'irreducible'. People who work in these disciplines, however, think of them as theoretical and not merely descriptive. The dilemma here is classical and has been stated in a different context, by Hempel, as characteristic of all theoretical enterprises: either the theory gives a correct account of the facts, or it does not; if not, it is a worthless theory, but if so it is superfluous, since the facts are accessible directly (Hempel 1965: 186). Sartre wishes to insist on the concreteness and complexity of historical fact, and at the same time to have a theoretical account that will show historical necessity, but he does not trust the theory of the auxiliary disciplines.

His position, as it unfolds in the first part of the *Critique of Dialectical Reason*, might be called, paradoxically but not unjustly, a kind of idealized hyper-empiricism: idealized because it does not deal with actual cases (except occasionally by way of illustration), hyper-empirical because it goes into minute and lengthy and realistic detail about relations between individuals in various situations. The cases it deals with, though they may be suggested by real events that Sartre himself observes, are peopled by characters he imagines, each of whom is 'just anyone', or alternatively a 'concrete universal' (another way of saying the same thing). It seems appropriate but then suspicious that this mode of procedure should be adopted by a writer like Sartre. To take one example: he introduces the detailed discussion of seriality with an illustration that no doubt was easily at hand, a collection of people waiting for a bus outside the church of St

Germain-des-Prés (an echo of the 'sad little group' of people waiting for the last tramway under Roquentin's window in *Nausea* (N 9)). Considering that for years he lived just opposite, Sartre could presumably observe these people simply by lifting his eye from the page. Nothing suggests that he actually went down to talk to them, as a true empiricist would have done, and yet he does not hesitate to describe the state of 'semi-awareness' of the others, on the part of a man who stands with his back to them, in these terms:

> it is morning, he has just got up and left his home; he is still thinking of his children, who are ill, etc.; he is going to his office; he has an oral report to make to his superior; he is worrying about its phrasing, rehearsing it under his breath, etc. (CDR 256-7)

Now there is clearly nothing wrong with this from one point of view; as Dean Inge said of the Socratic myth, 'if not this, then something like it must be true'; and yet it does cast some doubt on Sartre's claim, referred to in chapter II, that he preserved such a sharp separation between literary and philosophical prose. And this reflection is relevant to the style of his philosophical argumentation.

Writers as such do not argue for the propositions they assert, they simply assert them; they do not attempt to convince, but count on a general plausibility – of the world described, or, in the limit, of their own literary enterprise – to carry the reader without protest. It would be ungracious on the reader's part to quibble with an assertion about the writer's world on the grounds that it was not true of the real world, although a critic (i.e., a careful and articulate reader) might complain of the work as a whole that it was too improbable and without other virtues, or that, while within the limits of verisimilitude, it contained internal inconsistencies or infelicities of other kinds. Philosophers come in both varieties – writers and critics – but by and large they are not expected to take creative liberties with the world; also it has come to be expected, at least in English-speaking circles, that the philosophical writer will at the same time be a critic, not putting anything forward in the first capacity that would not survive scrutiny in the second and furthermore being explicit about the critical principles involved. If we accept this distinction between writers and critics as it applies to the domain of philosophy we may say that the majority of contemporary philosophers are critics but not writers, whereas Sartre is one of the few who are writers but not critics. This of course oversimplifies considerably – I speak of the emphasis in his work. And I repeat what was already said in chapter II (where it was a matter of style rather than of content), that this need not detract from his claim to philosophical standing – philosophy has too few writers, and needs the accounts of the world they are able to give, if for no other reason than to keep its critical faculties in trim. It might of course be argued that philosophical critics can find plenty of material to work on elsewhere, but the case of a writer like Sartre, who is manifestly as intelligent and quite possibly as learned as his sharpest critic could be, sets a special challenge.

At all events it may be helpful, in following the argument of the *Critique of Dialectical Reason*, to regard it as an account by an inspired philosophical writer of a world – which might be this one – whose history is dialectical and whose inhabitants enter into various relationships which the writer undertakes to describe. Of all Sartre's works (with the exception of the Flaubert) this attitude best fits the *Critique*, especially in view of its mode of writing as described in the Introduction to this book. A world which might be this one: I take it, in fact, that all philosophical writing implicitly offers itself under such a hypothetical modality, the advantage of which is that the reader can accept and profit from the work in just the respects, and to just the extent, that it appears on reflection to be true of or enlightening about his world. Even if, as in the case of Sartre, the whole is offered with characteristically unshakable conviction, so that he himself might be tempted to take an all-or-nothing attitude about it and consider the possibility of such partial acceptance belittling, the respect due him from other philosophers can be paid in no other way. It was on just this point that Hegel lost Kierkegaard's respect:

> if he [Hegel] had written his whole *Logic* and declared in the Preface that it was only a thought-experiment (in which, however, at many points he had shirked some things), he would have been the greatest thinker that ever lived. Now he is comic. (Kierkegaard 1944: 558)

(Sartre is preserved from this fate by having put the whole of the *Critique* in the form of a question, even though there is little doubt as to his answer to it.)

The construction of the dialectical world begins appropriately enough from the individual with his own praxis and its local totalization, which sums up his state of affairs from moment to moment. Totalization is an essentially temporal matter, and the temporal relation of the individual to the world is one of *need*. Need is in the first instance not a social relation but a natural one, which however has the effect of giving Nature a quasi-human status as a 'passive-totality' from the point of view of 'an organic being seeking its being in it' (CDR 81). This organic being transcends its own materiality by totalizing, but at the same time, seen from the outside, it is wholly natural and obeys the laws of Nature. Sartre asserts without argument that 'in the interiority of nutritive assimilation, molecules are controlled and filtered in close coordination with the permanent totalisation' (ibid.), and this seems as reasonable as most attempts to reconcile the fact that human beings are persons with the fact that they are organisms, although it would be hard to know what counted as evidence for it; for the moment, however, what matters is that they are organisms, and therefore vulnerable to Nature as well as depending on it. 'The material universe may make man's existence impossible' (CDR 83), that is, it may appear to be capable of negating man; the relation of negation does not occur in Nature as such, it enters only through man. This is familiar ground; the relation of negation between man and Nature is the 'constitutive negation' of chapter VII, which while human in its origin is then symmetrical: man is not his facticity, it is other than him. The fact that Nature thus constitutes itself a *danger*, with an attributed power of negation, means that man in order to survive must negate its negation. By this second negation he introduces determinations into the world (according to the Spinozistic formula), and he does this by work against Nature.

The first step of the regressive movement, then, goes from an all-encompassing Nature to a human individual. - but not the individual who will appear at the end of the process and from whom the progressive movement will begin. At this point the individual is merely an organic unity, and a great deal remains to be done before we arrive at the social. First of all, the action of the individual in the natural world, which he has now divided up through his work into different domains of materiality, mediates between those domains; an example (to jump a few stages in the evolutionary ascent) is the domain of things and that of words, which are themselves material but would have no connection with the things if it were not for the mediation of human linguistic activity. Second, the individual mediates between other individuals, also material organisms, with which his world proves to be populated. As we saw in connection with *Being and Nothingess,* binary or reciprocal relations between for-itselves are mediated and reified by the Third, with respect to whom their status is that of for-others. So the elementary structure of the social world is the triad self/Other/Third, described by Sartre as a 'reciprocal ternary relation' (CDR 111).

It was remarked above that the Third in the *Critique* is no longer seen as the Other, but that Sartre puts himself in the position of the Third in order to describe the reciprocal otherness of the couple. His first example is of a couple whose members are unaware of one another's existence: from his window he sees a road-mender on one side of a wall, a gardener on the other; he himself is on holiday. The triad thus constituted is in the first instance accidental, but it is nevertheless real - there all three of them actually are - and as such an object for possible understanding.

> In making myself what I am I discover them as they make themselves.
> . . . I realise myself as a member of a particular society which
> determines everyone's opportunities and aims; and beyond their present
> activity, I rediscover their life itself, the relation between needs and
> wages, and, further still, social divisions and class struggles. (CDR 101)

As Sartre points out, the way in which one experiences such an observation depends on the formation and attitudes of the observer – not all holiday-makers have dialectical understanding as their aim. What he does is to become aware of the workers' mutual ignorance of one another, but it is a mutual ignorance that he brings into being as mediator between them. He might arrange a meeting between them and thus mediate actively, or they might meet independently, forming a closed totality and excluding him. Whatever happens, says Sartre, 'each of the two men, in his ignorance of the other – an ignorance which becomes real through me – will interiorise in his behaviour what was an exteriority of indifference, even if they never meet' (CDR 104). It is hard to see quite what sense to give to this, since interiorization can scarcely be affected by an observation on the part of a Third of whom one is not aware. But there can be no doubt that in the world from Sartre's point of view (and the world is always from somebody's point of view) the attribute of ignorance can be predicated of the interior state of each worker as well as any attribute can ever be predicated of any interior state belonging to another person. The point of the example, though, apart from its introduction of the triad, is to show that 'the organization of the practical field in the world determines a real relation *for everyone*' (ibid., emphasis added), even if that relation is negative or as it were virtual.

The two persons who fall under the observation of the Third have either the reciprocity of indifference or reciprocity under one of two other forms, cooperation and struggle, the positive and negative forms of interaction. We might be tempted to think of oppression as a fourth possibility, but Sartre rules this out on the ground that it is not a human relation at all, the oppressor treating his victim as an animal rather than a person. Struggle arises as a function of need under conditions of scarcity, since when resources are scarce it is not only Nature that threatens but the Other also. One would suppose that the reality of struggle would not in fact depend on its being witnessed by a Third, but Sartre suggests that the participants in the struggle cannot totalize it as such – each can do so only from his own perspective, which results in two totalizations, not one – so that its unity requires the Third. It would follow from this that the class struggle, for example, cannot be perceived integrally by anyone who is participating in it. While this would make an interesting (if suspect) defence of Sartre's disinclination to join the Communist Party, it could hardly be accepted by any revolutionary theorist, entailing as it does the necessary blindness of all revolutionary activity, lending weight indeed to Hegel's insistence that understanding always comes too late. Sartre himself could surely not tolerate this implication.

But if we insist that the couple can be intelligible to its members without the intervention of the Third (even though that intelligibility will necessarily be coloured by interest, this need not entail the falsity of the perceptions of *both* parties), it does not follow that the triadic structure is unnecessary. Struggles do not remain private; when they are collective everybody is not wholly committed on one side or the other; in fact the norm in social life is that every dyad is a component of many triads, while the triad itself may not be fixed as *this* couple plus *that* Third. In a society with many members, says Sartre, the triad may be either commutative or hierarchical – we may take turns at playing Third, as in parlour games, or there may be some contingent asymmetry which designates roles in advance. The triad of Sartre and the gardener and road-mender is clearly hierarchical, in the sense that it would be improbable for the gardener to engage in philosophical reflection about Sartre and the road-mender; the historical contingency that determines this asymmetry is the fact of Sartre's having been born a petty bourgeois, having become a philosopher and radical, etc. History is built of such asymmetries; if everybody on earth were interchangeable with everybody else there would be an end of history. (Something like this is evisaged in the final stage of communism.)

Scarcity is a mark of our collective facticity and determines the struggle that constitutes history. We find here an echo of the categories of *Being and Nothingness*; the analysis of the individual case there finds analogous situations among groups in the *Critique*. There Sartre introduced the case of the subject who becomes an object for an object and hence appears as a for-Others; here he describes how social units (nomads and peasants in China, for example) experience 'the Other as the object for which it is itself the object' (CDR 135) in a field of praxis where need has encountered scarcity and thus generated struggle. There he spoke of facticity of the in-itself as negated by the for-itself in its self-productive project; here he speaks of the 'totalized totality' of the material world, which when totalized is found wanting, as the object of negation in the form of a kind of 'war on scarcity' on the part of groups whose survival depends on their cooperation against nature as well as against one another. In this case, though, the situation is modified by the introduction of tools collectively produced and wielded.

At the end of *Being and Nothingness* Sartre gets as far as the encounter with facticity in doing and having, but it is still a question of following given contours (one of his more striking images is that of the skier who has to come to terms with the slope of the hill, the condition of the snow, and so on (BN 582-5)); he does not envisage the practical modification of the situation by effort. Later on he discusses action, especially political action, and our responsibility for its outcome, but there the consequences are social rather than physical. Now however the collective relation to Nature constituted by human labour, aided by tools, produces what he calls 'worked matter', and with this a new consideration enters which has a determining effect on history. When men work on their material surroundings this work leaves traces: a changed landscape, artifacts, buildings, monuments. These traces become part of the environment of their successors or descendants. They are the product of human praxis but they are encountered as part of the 'totalized totality' of the material world, i.e., as inert; since they are simply given and do not necessarily correspond to the needs or the project of those who encounter them they may be experienced as alien. This 'alienated objectification of individual and collective praxis' (CDR 153) is, in the limit where it is simply encountered after a lapse of time, what Sartre calls the 'practico-inert'. (Even language may be encountered in this way, as in the case of the hero of 'Erostratus' in chapter II – although as that example indirectly shows the practico-inert need not always appear as alien.) But it may be that worked matter becomes alienated in the very process of working it – that chains of consequences are started by collective action which turn on their originators and demand further action which was not part of the original project. When this happens matter seems to take over; later on Sartre will call it 'bewitched' (CDR 219):

> when we learn that gas-lighting, which was a consequence of the use of coal as a source of energy, *enabled* employers to make their workers work fifteen or sixteen hours a day, we do not quite know whether it was the industrial ensemble dominated by coal which, through the medium of the men it produced, required a working day of sixteen hours, or whether it was the industrialist, in the coal-based economy, who used gas-lighting to increase production or, again, whether the two formulations do not refer to two aspects of a single dialectical circularity. (CDR 160)

The dialectical relation between praxis and its material object may become inverted, so that matter determines praxis when the function of praxis is to dominate matter.

This situation is only too familiar to bourgeois property-owners:

> To preserve its reality as a *dwelling* a house must be *inhabited*, that is to say, looked after, heated, swept, repainted, etc.; otherwise it deteriorates. This vampire object constantly absorbs human action, lives on blood taken from man and finally lives in symbiosis with him. (CDR 169)

(This has the ring of truth even if it is the outburst of a man who has lived all his life in hotel rooms, and has had such a horror of being tied down by property that he prefers to be able to carry everything he possesses, even occasionally large sums of money, on his person (L/S 69).) In fact history is full of examples in which human praxis went wrong – this appears to be the rule, rather than the exception. Two cases are to be distinguished if the problem is to be understood, since it is one thing for praxis to go wrong in relation to a consciously entertained project, communal and premeditated, and another thing for it to go wrong when nobody is coordinating it and there is no overall plan. Sartre illustrates both of these in connection with the vicissitudes of Spanish gold in the sixteenth century: on the one hand there was Philip II with his advisers and his monetary policy, on the other there were the merchants with their self-interest. But it is presumably the confluence of these two kinds of praxis that guarantees the 'counter-finality' of the historical process, the end that nobody wanted, to echo the quotation from Engels in the previous chapter. As Sartre puts it, 'the synthetic interiority of the group is penetrated by the reciprocal exteriority of individuals' (CDR 171). (This is fairly typical of the style of the *Critique* and means when interpreted that there comes to be conflict between collective interests and private ones. It is a relatively faithful rendering of the original, but like so many other French writers Sartre really needs not merely to be translated but to be re-written in more straightforward and less pretentious prose.)

Worked matter, says Sartre, is the motive force of history. It is a bearer of human meanings but moves according to laws not devised by humans and not even understood by them until grasped dialectically. This movement produces counter-finalities (*contre-finalités*) or unwanted ends, but it also makes possible *finalités contre,* that is to say the manipulation of these ends against certain classes in a society to the benefit of others (an exploiting class consciously or unconsciously abets worked matter in its production of ends unwanted by an oppressed class, because of some advantage that will accrue to the former). Sartre's examples spring, as one might expect, from the industrial revolution, since the machine is the paradigm case of worked matter which becomes exigent and enslaves those who attend it: 'the over-industrialisation of a country is a counter-finality for the rural classes who become proletarianised to precisely the extent that it is a finality for the richest landowners because it enables them to increase their own productivity' (CDR 193). The advantage, however, is short-lived because still other unwanted ends follow, for example the spread of pollution, the flight from the cities, etc.

This sinister power of worked matter no doubt derives in part from a tendency people have to identify themselves with it in a relation that Sartre calls 'interest'. This term is not to be interpreted in the minimal attitudinal sense it tends to have in Anglo-American moral and social philosophy but in a much stronger sense. 'Interest is being-wholly-outside-oneself-in-a-thing insofar as it conditions praxis as a categorical imperative' (CDR 197). The basis of it is laid in the fact that the organism is dependent on its environment and must identify itself, as a possibility of survival, with definite objective conditions, although at this level 'interest' seems to be just another way of expressing the relation of need from which we began. Interest appears in developed form 'wherever men live in the midst of a material set of tools which impose their techniques on them', but is fully realized only in societies based on property. The clearest case is real bourgeois property, in which we see 'the identification of the being of the owner with the ensemble of his property' (ibid.).

The new category of 'being-outside-oneself' is essential for social description, but it is not a genuine ontological category nor even, I think, an authentic *ekstasis* of the for-itself; it is not a mode or condition of being but the identification of the for-itself with something other than itself. It may play a role in the constitution of the for-Others, in that others may also identify a person with his property; property thus becomes a kind of costume or camouflage, whose effect in the sphere of real human relations can only be an alienating one. Interest as being-outside-oneself comes into play chiefly in the sphere of private property in Marx's sense, and especially property in the means of production, where it is in a given employer's interest to install certain kinds of machinery, for example. This interest is one only to the extent that other employers have similar interests; under scarcity, as might be expected, people tend to identify themselves with the same resources of worked matter, so that what looks like a community of interest conceptually may be a conflict practically, producing a structure of negation within the social order, making it a 'milieu of antagonisms of alterity' (CDR 201). (Here the natural difficulty of Sartre's style is not helped by the translator, who takes a relatively straightforward term – '*altérité*', formed on the Latin root of the common word '*autre*' or 'other', and thus meaning in English simply 'otherness' – and turns it into a spurious technicality.) It is the structure of the social order which is at issue in this part of the *Critique*, and it is hardly surprising to discover that it is a structure of Otherness and negation. But the concept of interest has led to the assumption that everyone pursues his own interest, and that there exist class interests, identical in every member of a group, as though these were prior to the formation of the group as such. We saw in the last chapter the scorn with which Sartre treated the attribution of interests to the proletariat on the part of the employers; in fact the worker is not free to follow his own interests at all but is obliged to serve the interests of the employer because of his enslavement to the machine. Here we find a version of being-outside-oneself which is not identical with interest.

The worker who serves the machine *has his being in it* just as the employer does; and just as the employer reinvests his profits in it, so the worker finds himself objectively forced to devote his wages to the upkeep (at minimum cost) of a servant for the machine who *is none Other than himself*. . . . But we must not be misled by this apparent symmetry: the machine is not, and cannot be, the worker's *interest*. The reason for this is simple: far from the worker objectifying himself in it, the machine objectifies itself in him. (CDR 206)

So the worker becomes part of the practico-inert, and from the point of view of the employer is indistinguishable from the machine, except that the latter is more tractable (does not go on strike or join a union); it therefore becomes the interest of the bourgeoisie, which defines itself 'through a common opposition to the common praxis of the workers' (CDR 213), to eliminate the worker in favour of the machine.

> These formal remarks cannot, of course, claim to add *anything at all* to the certainty of the synthetic reconstruction which Marx carried out in *Capital*; they are not even intended to be marginal comments on it. By its very certainty, the reconstruction in effect defies commentary. (CDR 216)

This sounds like a disappointingly craven repudiation of any intent to tamper with Marx; it comes unexpectedly in the middle of the section on interest and seems unmotivated. Sartre claims merely to be describing a social domain which is logically prior to Marx's historical reconstruction, clarifying 'the basic relations between *praxis* and the material environment' as a 'rational foundation for the certainty of dialectical investigations' (ibid.). A certainty which defies commentary but at the same time needs to be provided with a foundation seems an odd kind of certainty. Perhaps the passage signals, without intending to do so, the place in the argument where Marx, or at any rate Marxism, is in fact the most vulnerable. For Sartre goes on to say

> either 'everyone follows his interest,' which implies that divisions between men are *natural* – or it is divisions between men, resulting from the mode of production, which make interest (particular or general, individual or class) appear as a real moment of the relations between men. (ibid.)

The first alternative represents a kind of Darwinian struggle which would entail that 'human relations are *a priori* antagonistic' (CDR 217) but it rests, according to Sartre, on the 'entirely unintelligible *datum*' of interest as a fact of nature; only history as the history of modes of production (and hence of class struggle) can account for conflicts of interest. It seems that by calling it an 'unintelligible *datum*' Sartre is rejecting interest as a fact of nature, even though he has just said that the 'dialectical possibility of its existence is already given with the biological organism' (CDR 197). He then proceeds to criticize some unnamed Marxist writers for hesitating 'between the law of interest and the Marxist conception of History, that is to say, between a sort of biological materialism and historical materialism' (CDR 217). Their mistake is to start with an opaque and again unintelligible concept of need, which they identify with interest (a plausible enough move in view of the remarks above) but which proves inadequate for the comprehension of human conflict because most such conflicts 'seem to involve "interests" of completely different level, complexity and structure' (ibid.).

Sartre is at least consistent: he refuses, as we have seen on more than one occasion, to put the dialectic into inorganic nature, he insists upon it as soon as human individuals come upon the scene. In his own treatment of need he says that it is 'the first totalizing relation' through which 'everything is to be explained' (CDR 80). But on the one hand it is hard to know what he would do with evolutionary developments prior to man (is the need of the amoeba 'opaque' or does it too totalize?), and on the other it is hard to see, if there is any kind of continuous development from the primordial individual to the complexity of history, where the specifically Marxist component enters, since the dialectic has been there from the beginning. Given Sartre's disjunction (between interests as natural or interests as consequences of modes of production) we might opt for the latter and apply Marx's categories. But Sartre's project, as we just saw, is avowedly to fill in the 'logically prior' domain which lies between the material environment and dialectical certainty, so he surely cannot begin with the modes of production already established. We might, again, choose to start a Marxist inquiry with classes in place after a period of primitive accumulation, but this time Marx himself would object; 'the so-called primitive accumulation,' he says, 'is nothing else than the historical process of divorcing the producer from the means of production' (Marx 1978: 432). The question then is, whose interest was served by this historical divorce? and what status can it have had if interests are a consequence of an already-established division between men resulting from the mode of production? If the process occurred blindly then nobody was totalizing it and it was not truly dialectical; if not then some interests at least must antedate the establishment of modes of production.

Marx, to do him justice, would not have been troubled by any of this and would have been perfectly happy if evolutionary continuity had been established from the amoeba to capitalism (his admiration for Darwin is well known). But then Marx would surely not have said that *Capital* 'defied commentary', even if he had at the same time poured scorn on the commentators. Sartre gets himself into a tight corner because of his repugnance for the opaque, his insistence on the transparent and apodictic character of the dialectic, his refusal of surds in history. I have suggested that this is analogous to his view of the total translucidity of consciousness and his rejection of the murky Freudian depths. But while the latter makes a great deal of sense for a fundamentally moralistic and Protestant mentality like Sartre's, which wishes to be totally authentic and responsible and not to hide behind excuses, it is not easy to import such integrity and awareness into a protracted and collective enterprise involving thousands of years and millions of people. Speaking of the dialectic as a parallel unfolding of being and our knowledge of it, in the introduction to *Search for a Method*, Sartre says 'I have taken it for granted that such a totalizaton is perpetually in process as History and as historical Truth' (SM xxxiv); at the end of the *Critique* he suggests that the real problem of history is that of 'totalisation without a totaliser' (CDR 817). Yet we have also seen that he rejects any conscious collective subjectivity. The conjunction of these positions adds up to a formidable philosophical problem, to which I shall revert at the end of the chapter; for the moment it can only be said that Sartre's deference to Marxism as the intelligibility of History argues a level of confidence in it to which Marx and Engels themselves could never have dreamed of aspiring.

When we return to the domain in which Marxist analysis is at home, among the workers and the means of production, we find the old Sartre of *Being and Nothingness* giving a new interpretation of freedom in a situation in terms of the totalization which every subject performs at every moment of self-awareness. My praxis is free, but it operates in an environment of materiality and of worked matter and of the praxis of Others; furthermore I myself am not an empty spontaneity but a product of contingent forces. How then am I to enter with full understanding into my historical condition? By way of answer Sartre offers a portrait of enlightenment:

> the man who looks at his work, who recognises himself in it completely, and who also also does not recognise himself in it at all; the man who can say both: 'This is not what I wanted' and 'I understand that this is what I have done and that I could not do anything else', and whose free *praxis* refers him to his prefabricated being and who recognises himself equally in both – this man grasps, in an immediate dialectical movement, necessity as the *destiny in exteriority of freedom*. (CDR 226-7)

We come to know ourselves as the totalizing movement we are by observing our interaction with the world and discovering, as it were, the mould in which we are cast, the shape of the In-itself that constitutes the facticity of the For-itself. (This, as remarked earlier, is the one place in the *Critique* where these categories are invoked.)

What the worker, in particular, finds out about his situation as free praxis by this process of examination of the historical conditions of his being – a discovery that may be stimulated only by his being thrown into conflict – is that he belongs to a class that is determined by worked matter (the machine) as having a certain destiny without transcendence towards future possibilities, and as denied the opportunity for becoming aware of these very conditions.

> The discovery of our Being is frightening (since it generally occurs in the midst of failure and conflict) – because it reveals that what one

did not know was something one knew all along, in other words, because it retrospectively constitutes our ignorances of our Being as determined and prefabricated by the Being which we are but of which we were unaware. In this way – and this applies to the group as much as to the individual – inert Being can also be defined in terms of the type of practical choice which prevents one from knowing what one is. (CDR 246-7)

The consequences of this discovery will be revolutionary, but for the moment it is hard to see how the condition is to be overcome.

We have seen *class-being* as the practico-inert status of individual or common *praxis*, as the future sentence, petrified in past being, which this *praxis* itself has to carry out and in which it must finally recognise itself in a new experience of necessity. (CDR 250)

How is this self-recognition to be achieved? For what is lacking so far is any mechanism of class solidarity. I am determined by Others as well as by worked matter, etc., but I am still isolated and have no way of making common cause with them, of organizing for cooperative praxis. It is at this point, therefore, that Sartre turns his attention to what he calls 'collectives'.

In the first place collectives are part of the practico-inert; they are social beings encountered in the world as the contingent outcomes of prior praxis. But among them at least three varieties are to be distinguished: collectives which owe their existence to contingent unifying forces outside them; collectives which constitute genuine *groups*, which have, that is to say, a common praxis which provides an inner unity; and collectives which are the vestiges of groups, whose unity is contingent but as it were genetically so rather than in relation to some present, although exterior, object or force. As an example of the latter Sartre cites the Hungarian Social Democratic Party, which even after most of its members had joined the communists, been arrested, or emigrated, kept its name and emblem and headquarters; an equally good but perhaps more striking example might be the many religions which, having lost contact with the sources of revelation that inspired their original group praxis, keep together by a kind of historical inertia and look about them for new external objects (charity, social work) to justify their continued existence. The first of these varieties Sartre calls the *series*. The paradigm case of a serial relation, as we saw earlier, is that which holds between the members of a collection of people waiting at a bus stop. They are turned not towards one another but towards an exterior object, namely the expected bus; they have no project in common, and yet there is a common element in all their projects, namely taking the bus to some destination. The bus and its trajectory through the streets of Paris and the system of tickets that give priority in boarding and the sign marking the bus stop are all part of the practico-inert, conceived, planned, and put into operation in the praxis of earlier Parisians, now probably dead. So this collective satisfies Sartre's definition of 'serial being' as 'the determination of the bond of alterity [read "otherness"] as a unity of plurality by the exigencies and structures of the common object which in itself defines this plurality as such' (CDR 302); the series relates its members to one another and also to the collective itself, but only by means of a detour through the exterior object.

The series is a convenient starting-point for the study of collectives but has no ontological or genetic priority: 'it is no part of our project to determine whether series precede groups or vice versa, either originally or in a particular moment of History' (CDR 65). But Sartre does say that groups 'can arise only on the foundation of a collective' (CDR 253-4), and it seems unlikely that this could happen in a situation not marked in some way by seriality; since group praxis must involve a project which addresses some condition or other in the material or social world one might suppose that at least some members of the group would have been turned towards that object independently of one another before fusing into a group, and this common turning is just the condition for seriality. The members of a series may not, it is true, be aware of one another's existence; for example, the collective which consists of all people who happen at the same moment to be listening to a given broadcast is a series, since each is attending to a common exteriority; similarly all the purchasers of a given commodity form another series, and so on. The fundamental relation between the members of a series is otherness, but otherness within a collective that has the potentiality of organizing into a group. This otherness sometimes takes the form of mutual impotence, and the last example cited, of the free market, is a good case of this.

It is a feature of the practico-inert that it behaves as it if were natural, in the sense that the laws governing its behaviour are just as objective as the laws of nature; and members of a series whose exterior object it is may contribute to the preservation of a particular element of the practico-inert by doing in their turn what is expected of them. Every time I buy something at its marked price I play the part of a cog in an economic machine; but, further, every time I exercise choice about price in a free market I do the same, because consumers and producers form series whose relationship through the exteriority of commodities determines price as a function of supply and demand. Sartre illustrates this point with a table (CDR 283) that seems to have been taken out of a textbook on economics, since it deals with an unnamed commodity over a price range per unit from 1 to 18 francs and yields when plotted perfectly classical curves. It might surprise the ordinary buyer or seller to learn that

everyone determines both himself and the Other insofar as he is

Other than the Other and Other than himself. And everyone observes his direct action deprived of its real meaning insofar as the Other governs it, and in his turn hastens to influence the Other, over there, without any real relation to his intention. (CDR 285-6)

But then it would presumably surprise him also to learn that his mode of being, quite apart from the market, is not to be what he is and to be what he is not. The question for us is not whether Sartre gives a correct description of the workings of the market – economics is clearly not his strong point – but whether there is anything instructive in the description he does give.

What Sartre describes is the situation of the consumer, who finds the apparatus of the market already in operation and is impotent as an individual to influence it. Behind the market of course is the whole system of capitalist production and appropriation. This system relies on a state of competition and therefore antagonism between individuals, but it also relies on their sameness, at least within limits, as buyers and consumers. Its concern then is to preserve the seriality which ensures both these desiderata – their continued interest in the exterior object, namely the commodity in question, and their continued ignorance of one another, since direct acquaintance might evoke sympathy or provoke solidarity. The realization on the part of the consumers of their condition of mutual Otherness and impotence may lead to the abandonment of seriality for group action; the emergence in recent years of so many environmental and public interest groups, consumer and voter groups, etc., is an illustration if not a confirmation of Sartre's analysis. (I have been avoiding the use of the term 'analysis' because of Sartre's opposition between the analytic and the dialectical, but one should perhaps not accept such prescriptive uses too readily, and what he does certainly counts as analysis in one of the most honourable philosophical senses of the term, namely the restatement of familiar propositions in a different and more enlightening way. That enlightenment has to be won in the teeth of a rebarbative terminology does not mean that it cannot be genuine.)

Another familiar phenomenon whose description in terms of seriality proves instructive is public opinion, Sartre's paradigm case of which is the Great Fear of 1789, in which panic spread through the French provinces about an imaginary threat from brigands in the pay of the aristocracy. It is characteristic of public opinion that it is always someone else's opinion, the opinion of the Other. This is a case of seriality that comes into being not through anyone's praxis but by what Sartre calls, by contrast, simply a process. His definition of 'process' is admittedly not helpful at first glance – he says it is 'a development which, though orientated, is caused by a force of exteriority which has the result of actualising the series as a temporalisation of a multiplicity in the fleeting unity of a violence of impotence' (CDR 304) – but one can see at any rate the difference between a seriality that arises from prior praxis (the people at the bus stop) and one that arises from natural causes (people seeking shelter from the rain under a tree, for example). In a long footnote Sartre gives a brilliant account of racism as an example of a kind of seriality of opinion that is not a genuine system of thought seriously upheld by anyone, but which depends for its perpetuation on being repeated and acquiesced in from member to member of the series, each of whom thinks their common interest requires discrimination and repression but no one of whom would accept the authorship of the policy.

> The strength of *this* particular colonialist lies in the fact that the Idea (as a common bond) comes to him as the thought of the Other. . . .
> He affirms himself as the Other who *really thinks it elsewhere* by making himself *the Other who repeats it here without thinking*.
> (CDR 302)

Sartre insists, nevertheless, on the reality of the practico-inert field and of the other determinants of seriality which make of us 'their thing' (CDR 323) and condition our freedom. The familiar theme of the transcendent Ego and the outwardness of the inner life recurs here. When a

> free individual praxis . . . develops as an undertaking which temporises itself in the course of a life, motivations are never 'psychical' or 'subjective': they are things and real structures in so far as these are revealed by the project through its concrete ends and on the basis of them. Thus there is normally no *act of consciousness*: the situation is known through the act which it motivates and which already negates it. (CDR 327)

This seems to fit in well with the views of philosophers of action who deny that there is some separate inner movement of resolve or decision before the act itself, on the assumption that by 'act of consciousness' Sartre means such a distinct episode, but it is a curious position for a philosopher who has always insisted on the translucidity of choice and the respon-sibility of the agent. The context here needs to be noted, however; Sartre is discussing the situation of workers caught by the constraints of the practico-inert, for whom 'freedom . . . does not mean the possibility of choice, but the necessity of living these constraints in the form of exigencies which must be fulfilled by a *praxis*' (CDR 326). And finally the heroic doctrine of *Being and Nothingness* is stood completely on its head – for it is not only the worker who lives under these constraints:

> It would be quite wrong to interpret me as saying that man is free in all situations, as the Stoics claimed. I mean the exact opposite: all men are slaves in so far as their life unfolds in the practico-inert

field and in so far as this field is always conditioned by scarcity.
(CDR 331)

This cannot of course be the end of the matter; freedom can still be achieved by the re-humanization of the practico-inert and the conquest of scarcity. But these things will not happen of their own accord. The trajectory of the *Critique* so far has brought us from individual praxis and totalization with its local dialectic, via worked matter, the practico-inert, and being-outside-oneself, to collective structures and seriality. All this makes up what Sartre calls the 'constituent dialectic', where 'constituent' has the sense of 'constituting' rather than 'being a constituent of'; once again we need expect the emergence of no new elements in the situation – whatever is to come will be put together from the elements already marshalled. Attention now shifts to the 'constituted dialectic', which stands between individuals and series on the one hand and History on the other. Series cannot form intelligible unities for the purposes of historical action, since they exist only thanks to some exterior focus of attention and have no internal structure except that of Otherness; such unity of project is possible only with the emergence of the group. It is through the group that the condition of impotence and slavery imposed by the practico-inert and its attendant seriality can be overcome. The rhetoric is in danger of carrying us away: it should be said, by way of correction, that the practico-inert is not always so sinister; the slavery that consists of having to wait for the bus outside the church of St Germain-des-Prés, rather than being able to flag it down a hundred yards nearer the Seine, is one we may welcome as a condition of having a bus service at all. A good proportion of the practico-inert, in other words, is convenient rather than oppressive. But of course it may become oppressive, especially at certain revolutionary junctures in history. One of these was the French revolution itself, from which Sartre's examples of group formation are largely drawn.

The first kind of group to emerge is what Sartre calls the 'group in fusion', an expression which for some reason the English translator of the *Critique* has rendered as 'fused group', thus suggesting that the process of fusion is complete. The group in fusion is a collective which recognizes not only its common interest in some exterior object but also the potentiality of a common praxis with respect to it. The Bastille is a common symbol of oppression, and the Parisians who look upon it as such are initially in a state of serial impotence. But then – by a complicated sequence of events that Sartre deals with in detail but which are unimportant here – some of them take it into their heads to storm it. No *one* of them does so *by himself*, but each does it by himself along with the others. The group in fusion, as its name suggests, is one that forms more or less spontaneously as a function of the perception by each of its members, at about the same time, of the possibilities of cooperative action.

It has no hierarchical structure and – as we have seen more than once – no collective consciousness; it is a number of people, each a for-itself, each responsible, each caught in the toils of the practico-inert. Each member of the group in fusion, furthermore, is 'sovereign', says Sartre, each is 'the organizer of common *praxis*' (CDR 370). And each is a Third for all the others – or for that matter perhaps a hundredth: if 100 people form a group in fusion they are not ordinally ranked. If there is a gathering of 98 people and two of us join to bring it up to 100, 'each of us is the 100th of the Other' (CDR 375), but the fact that we are latecomers may be accidental, and Sartre might well have generalized this symmetry to the whole group. Such symmetry and equipollence among its members are the chief characteristics of the group in fusion; all are free, all are pursuing the same end, each internalizes the common project; the result is that the one who is the 100th for each of the Others is not the 100th for himself but a single one in the form of a group. 'He joins in the attack neither as *isolated* nor as a *hundredth*, but as the free utilisation of the power he gets from *being*, here and everywhere, *the material strength* of the number one hundred' (CDR 393).

This is heady stuff. But fusion, as physicists know, is a process difficult to contain and to sustain, and the group in fusion is unstable over the long run. There is nothing like it for storming a Bastille, but it will not last out a revolution. Each member is a legislator and a Third to all the others, but each continually risks that status. Sartre imagines himself listening to another member of the group as he harangues the crowd, and feeling at the same time the reassuring interiority of his own situation; but

> if I in turn climb on to the podium which he chose, I am, again,
> inside but my interiority is stretched to the limit, and the slightest
> jolt could turn it into an exteriority (for example, if I make a
> mistake about the common action, if I propose to the group an
> object different from its own). (CDR 408)

The group in fusion is like the series in this respect, that it hangs together by virtue of something outside itself – a common danger, a common enemy, a common objective. But the danger may pass, the enemy be vanquished or flee, the objective be gained. If the group is to achieve stability it must find an inner principle of cohesion. Sartre therefore introduces the second type of group, which is produced by the swearing of an oath by each of its members and is called the 'sworn group'. Here again the translation leaves something to be desired – it renders '*serment*' as 'pledge' rather than as 'oath', which makes everything sound more like the Temperance Movement than the revolution (not that 'pledge' has no nobler connotations, but it lacks the gravity and the implicit violence of 'oath'). Sartre takes the oath, and its consequences, with deadly seriousness, for it is through the oath that Terror enters the picture. The group in fusion arose out of fear (or at any rate for the present purpose it is convenient to assume that it did so), but the fear was of something external – the members of the group feared *it*, not one another. The oath introduces a new fear, namely the fear of the group itself, in the persons of its other members, on the part of every sworn member. By swearing allegiance to the group, I invite it to kill me if I ever fail in this allegiance. This admittedly sounds rather melodramatic, and we might personally be more comfortable in a group united by a simple pledge, in which a fall from grace would bring down upon us nothing more threatening than the sorrowful glances of our fellows. But the bloodthirsty language is Sartre's own. 'The fundamental statute of the sworn group is Terror' (CDR 433, amended); because the members of the group are 'brothers' Sartre some-times refers to this simultaneous condition of solidarity and fear as 'fraternity-terror'. In the context of the French revolution the terms are understandable, although they perhaps render the analysis of this particular stage of group formation less useful than it might have been in its application to other cases. (In fact Sartre does envisage the formation of groups in which Terror would seem, to say the least, an extravagant designation of the principle of unity – for example 'an association for buying and selling property on the moon' (CDR 447).)

The sworn group 'is initially no more than the impossibility for everyone of abandoning the common *praxis*' (CDR 434), but as its project becomes more complex and its membership more numerous its structure begins to evolve; *statutes* are laid down and it becomes a 'statutory group', no longer just a group but an Organization, with leaders, officers, divisions, and other hierarchical apparatus. Sartre is full of detailed examples, but I pass over this rather dense development, which contains little of central importance to the argument, except to alight (perhaps unfairly) at a point where he is discussing

> small, highly disciplined groups, like sports teams, in which every
> movement of a fellow member, seen *in its functional differentiation*, is
> decoded in the very movement which it occasions in another fellow
> member, as a differentiated function, through the practical field
> defined by the action of the group and as a function of all the other
> movements. (CDR 473)

Here the reader is referred to a footnote in which Sartre drily observes, 'In fact, in a football match, everything is complicated by the presence of the opposite team.' The point is for future reference; Sartre claims that 'this complication does not alter our problem in any way', and to the extent that the problem in the quoted passage is one of the dispensability or indispensability of members of the group he is right, but the example is revealing and, I shall claim, symptomatic.

It is characteristic of an organization, with its implicit or explicit

177

statutes, that its existence transcends that of its members; one person may replace another in a particular function and the organization continue as before, until in the limit all the members have been replaced. In this it resembles society itself, in which structural relations persist from generation to generation. One of the few people to whose work Sartre makes specific positive reference is Lévi-Strauss, whose *Elementary Structures of Kinship* describes, in Sartre's words,

> those strange internal realities which are both organised and
> organising, both synthetic products of a practical totalisation and
> objects always susceptible of rigorous analytical study, both the lines
> of force of a *praxis* for every common individual and the fixed links
> between this individual and the group, through perpetual changes of
> both of them, both inorganic ossature and everyone's definite powers
> over everyone else, in short, both fact and right, mechanical elements
> and, at the same time, expressions of a living integration into a
> unitary *praxis* of those contradictory tensions of freedom and inertia
> which are known as *structures*. (CDR 480)

It may be worth recalling that in the interview cited earlier, where Sartre so mercilessly abused Lévi-Strauss for his ignorance of dialectic, he also defended himself against the charge of writing long sentences, on the grounds that the complexity of dialectical Reason required them (PL 118). Part of his disillusionment with Lévi-Strauss no doubt arose from the fact that the latter was not particularly pleased to have his fundamental analyses assimilated to 'strikes, boxing matches, football matches, bus-stop queues ... all secondary incidentals of life in society [which] cannot therefore serve to disclose its foundations' (Lévi-Strauss 1966: 250).

This reaction on Lévi-Strauss's part is certainly understandable, but what must be said on the other side is that all is grist that comes to Sartre's mill; he is not trying to invade the territory of the professional sociologist or anthropologist, but he chooses examples from these domains when they serve his purpose. A culture within which a given set of kinship relations holds *is* a group in his sense; even if there never was a primordial oath not to depart from it, there is an implicit commitment to maintain the collective norm (and it is striking how tempting philosophers have found it over the centuries to explain social solidarity in contractual terms). This implicit commitment is sometimes made the explicit subject of a ritual on behalf of new members of the group not yet in a position to acquiesce in its conventions – baptism is such a ritual, and in another of his luminous footnotes Sartre observes that everyone who grows up in any society finds himself so committed from birth:

> a child must submit either to the baptism of atheism or to that of
> Christianity. The truth, which is very hard for liberals – but then any

truth is hard for tender liberal souls – is that it is necessary to decide the meaning of faith (that is to say, of the history of the world, of mankind) on behalf of the child, and without being able to consult him, and that whatever one does, and whatever precautions one takes, he will bear the weight of this decision throughout his life. But it is also true that it can mark him only to the extent that he has freely interiorised it and that it becomes the free self-limitation of his freedom rather than an inert limit assigned to him by his father. (CDR 486)

This last remark is of great importance; it reminds us that the individual is still there in the group, carrying his private as well as his collective burden, and that (in the face of Terror if need be) his membership in it is always subject to reconsideration. The genuineness of such membership is to be found in common praxis, not merely in the 'agreement of minds', which Sartre regards as an idealist trap. His criticism of a possible conceptual basis for group solidarity is however not entirely fair; 'after all', he says, 'the artillery of two enemy armies will be in complete agreement about ballistics' (CDR 532), but this invites two responses: first that the agreement sought is presumably not only on the universal principles of physics, second that, even so, an agreement of that sort would not be insignificant – such universal principles, analytic and non-dialectical as they may be, have been the basis in recent years for a great deal of *rapprochement* across otherwise intransigent political boundaries, and the artillery on both sides might find more profit in a theoretical discussion of ballistics than in a practical exchange of missiles. At all events, there the existential subject still irreducibly is, and it turns out that after all

the dialectical rationality of common *praxis* does not transcend the rationality of individual *praxis*. On the contrary, individual *praxis* goes beyond it. And its special complexities, its rational knots, and the formal concatenation of its structures derive precisely from the fact that the second rationality is *constituted*, that is to say, from the fact that the group is a product. (CDR 538)

But if constituted on the basis of individual praxis, individual praxis may betray it; so the organization or statutory group is vulnerable too, just as the group in fusion was.

In fact 'organic, practical individuality' forms what Sartre calls the 'untranscendable limit of the constituted dialectic' and he speaks of 'the strange circular conflict, where all synthesis is impossible, which is the untranscendable contradiction of History: the opposition and identity of the individual and the common' (CDR 559). This begins to be really puzzling. We are nearing the end of a book which is a propaedeutic to

History as apodictically certain, and we learn that History contains an untranscendable contradiction which makes all synthesis impossible; if this is the case, how can the dialectic hope to make it intelligible? Contradictions are, it is true, the stuff of dialectic, but its task is precisely to transcend them. It is to Sartre's credit, perhaps, that he allows this admission to stand, or to slip out, but one cannot avoid the impression that somehow the foundations of dialectical reason are crumbling. The foundations of the group, in Sartre's analysis, are crumbling too. Once institutionalized (with conditions of membership, etc.) it has, it is true, strength in reserve by virtue of the fact that it is sustained in being not only by those it includes but also by those it excludes – its unity or being-one' comes to it, says Sartre, from the outside, through Others (CDR 564). If it has no autonomous ontological status it does exist for Others, and hence for itself as meeting their expectations (it invents for itself out of its own ignorance, says Sartre, the meaning and destiny Others in their ignorance imagine it to have (CDR 582-3)); the members may come to feel a loyalty to the group as it presents itself to Others, they may feel themselves constrained to be, at all events in dealings with outsiders, what the Others expect them to be. Inside, however, while 'the movement of mediated reciprocity constitutes the unity of the practical community as a perpetual detotalisation engendered by the totalising movement' (CDR 576), the fatal conflict of individual and collective goes on, and from potential exclusion or elimination as embodied in Terror we move to actual exclusion or elimination as embodied in the Purge. When this stage is reached seriality re-enters the group, for now each member relates to it as an exterior object of fear – each is a potential traitor, each a potential object of the next purge.

At this point the group is likely to feel the need to establish an institutional structure of coercion, some means of exercising authoritarian sovereignty. It cannot appeal to an objective sovereign, whether God or its own totalized-totality, since these do not exist; instead it invents a sovereign, in strikingly Hobbesian manner, as an organ of integration in a group which is in danger of losing its group character (CDR 622). (It may well be that societies in which contract theories flourish are all, as England was at the time of Hobbes or France at the time of Rousseau, societies in which some old-established and formerly powerful order is in decay.) The State itself is a sovereign, but it is also a sworn group (its members swear loyalty to the Crown, or to uphold the Constitution, etc.); the greater part of the population, however, has a serial relation to it, as an external, and feared, force. Sartre refuses both the Hegelian theory of the State as the concrete reality of society and the Marxist theory of it as something that could conceivably wither away – for him it is equivalent to the dominant class, grouped, organized, and institutionalized.

Society, then, is a ramified network of interrelated groups and series –

the series with different unifying objects, the groups at different stages of formation. As usual Sartre's insistence on the real complexity of things is impressive, although the example he chooses for extended treatment is once again a 'secondary incidental'. The complex structure of an advanced technological society such as that of the United States is sustained in being, he supposes, by propaganda and slogans generated by groups whose objective is to maintain various forms of seriality. Since the principle of unification of the series is an Other-directed Otherness, people who care about public opinion and wish to be as much like Others as possible make predictable members of series, to the satisfaction of the manipulating group which wishes to profit from the combined size and impotence of the series, say by persuading it to buy things and thus part with its money. The example Sartre works with is the Top Ten record programme, which he heard on American radio in 1946: each Saturday the ten best-selling records from the previous week are announced, and this means that they sell even better the following week; the listener knows, therefore, that the record in question has already been the choice of a lot of Others, and makes himself like them by going out and buying it in his turn.

> If he listens to the radio every Saturday and if he can afford to buy
> every week's No. 1 record, he will end up with the record collection
> of the Other, that is to say, the collection of no one. . . .
> Ultimately, the record collection which is no one's becomes
> indistinguishable from everyone's collection – though without
> ceasing to be no one's. (CDR 650-1)

Sartre refers also to newspaper competitions in which the object is to predict the order of popularity of some set of objects (buildings, artists, cars) – the competitor whose list is closest to the results of the poll wins 'because he has been more perfectly Other than all the Others' (CDR 651).

There can be no doubt that this is an illuminating way of looking at some marginal manifestations of popular culture, but quite apart from the questions whether these particular mechanisms are determining features of American or any other society, or whether there is a conscious intention on the part of the sovereign group to use them as devices for 'increas[ing] the inertia of collectives and govern[ing] by means of it' (CDR 655), it may be asked whether any culture whatever, in a population large enough to sustain long-range seriality (and such a population is presumably prerequisite for culture) can avoid some such development. The reason, for example, that Gallimard was able to print so many copies of the *Critique of Dialectical Reason* was that a lot of Others had bought Sartre's earlier works; by buying and studying it I have become like them; what are the books in my library, Plato, Aristotle, Kant, Marx, Sartre, but everyone's collection of works of philosophy that is at the same time no one's collection? Some writers, notably Foucault, have recently been drawing

181

attention to the ways in which the institutions of high culture – publishing houses, universities, scholarly journals – exert in their way a control over the Word every bit as sinister as the control exerted by the disc jockeys over popular taste in music (see for example Foucault's inaugural lecture at the Collège de France (Foucault 1972: 215 ff.)). But perhaps this is not intrinsically sinister – it may be an inevitable feature of the practico-inert, like the coercive structure of language itself, which can be sinister or not according to the manner of its use and which, like baptism, need not be oppressive – or at any rate not covertly so – to the subject who has become aware of his situation. At all events it is not clear that liberal or radical dismay at the sheep-like seriality of popular music-lovers is well founded, even if the analysis of the phenomenon is persuasive as an exercise in social philosophy.

There are more serious cases of manipulation on the part of the sovereign group, which has at its disposal a large number of agents distributed through the population – the police, for instance – whose function is, among other things, to prevent the transformation of series into groups that might oppose the sovereign. But these agents have their own forms of seriality, which must in its turn be controlled and directed; they may also form groups which develop their own form of terror, and become organized and institutionalized – in the service of the sovereign to be sure, but the sovereign needs to assert its power from time to time by ordering their disssolution. The resulting complex structure for the exercise of sovereignty in society is *bureaucracy*, which Sartre calls a 'triple relation – other-direction of the inferior multiplicity; mistrust and serial-ising (and serialised) terror at the level of the peers; and the annihil-ation of organisms in obedience to superior organism' (CDR 658). Bureau-cracy represents the last metamorphosis of the group, after which it is ready to fall back into seriality again. But it is not the same seriality, and the process will be repeated. The original project of the group, however, whatever it may subsequently have become, was a noble one, namely 'taking the inhuman power of mediation between men away from worked matter and giving it, in the community, to each and to all' (CDR 672); and history will consist of a kind of circular repetition of this endeavour. The material environment will sometimes have the status of the practico-inert, but sometimes it will be a field of common praxis. The dialectic, however, which is to make these changes intelligible (which by now, says Sartre, has done this (CDR 678)) does not give priority to one state over the other.

The whole gamut of group possibilities is outlined again as applied to the case of the working class – a series *vis-à-vis* the means of production, a group in fusion and then a sworn group when it finds the courage to strike for higher wages or better conditions, an organization and institu-tion when trade unions are formed, a sovereign group and eventually a bureaucracy when the unions produce their own elite with respect to which the rank and file sink into seriality again. The working-class movement is then perhaps on the verge of a new dialectical round – but Sartre declines to prophesy:

> the working class can be said to be a developing totalisation *everywhere*. At the present level of our investigation, this does not mean either that it must or that it can attain a higher degree of integration or militancy; but it does not mean the opposite either. (CDR 706)

As yet we lack 'the perspectives of History'. Now the history of all hitherto existing society, as we know, is the history of class struggles; the difficulty with this formulation, however, is the interpretation which Marx and Engels, but especially Engels, gave it – if reduced to economics it becomes merely mechanical and therefore non-dialectical, no matter how hard a misguided Dialectics of Nature may try to show that mechanics is dialectical too. (Sartre's opinion of Engels on this point was quoted in the previous chapter.) The foundation of the class struggle must lie, on the contrary, in a conflict of interests which arises between two serialities in their exterior relation to the practico-inert; it is a 'reciprocity of antagonisms' (CDR 713) and cannot be dealt with by writing separate histories of capitalism on the one hand and the working-class movement on the other, as some Marxist theorists do (CDR 743).

History as class struggle, in fact, is the history of the real and conscious relations between an exploiting series/group and an oppressed series/group. 'Conscious relations' in the sense that, to revert to existentialist language, not to be conscious of them constitutes bad faith; part of the work of the radical writer is precisely, as Sartre has always insisted, to make the oppressing class aware of what it is really doing, and indeed this is just what he was trying to do at the time of writing the *Critique* with respect to French oppression in Algeria. 'Substituting History for economic and sociological interpretations', which he recommends for understanding the Algerian situation (CDR 733), means for him precisely coming to awareness of one's real relations with the worker or the colonized native, refusing to hide behind public opinion or to accept the status of an Other. But just as in the case of racism, which we discussed above, class relations between the bourgeoisie and the proletariat are marked by attitudes that have the structure of public opinion – workers are lazy, capitalists are rapacious, etc. In particular the Malthusian tactics of the bourgeoisie, to which Sartre returns at length – especially its tolerance of working-class mortality – are regarded as an unfortunate process rather than as a repressive praxis and would be disavowed by anyone who was accused of contriving them; they are always for the benefit of the Others. The bourgeois, for that matter, is perfectly ready to repress himself for the sake of the good opinion of the Others – hence the cult of respectability. To be bourgeois – and Sartre has never, since 'The Angel of Morbidity', wavered on the point – is *automatically* to be in bad faith.

> If we reduce the number of classes to two in order to simplify the scheme, we might say that each class finds its unity in the Other, in a double form and in perpetual disequilibrium – both as a unifying threat of extermination, and as a totalisation which is sovereignly totalised by the action-process whose objective unity lies in the totalised object. (CDR 792)

(Marx and Engels, of course, thought at the time of the *Communist Manifesto* that history had already performed this simplification.) But this mutual dependence of opposed classes is not just a dialectical device, it rests on a 'real project of violence' (CDR 794). The two classes confront each other in their parallel developments, with their sovereign institutions, their pressure-groups, their forms of seriality; each constitutes a part of the practico-inert for the other; each has its tactics, acknowledged and unacknowledged.

> One of the objectives of the employers' *praxis* (and certainly not the least important) ... becomes the introduction of splits and insecurities into the ranks of the workers by infecting the proletariat with a being-outside-itself in bourgeois class-consciousness taken as the absolute standard of what is human and what is not. (CDR 800)

The workers on the other hand seek to maintain their solidarity even at the expense of what the bourgeois would no doubt regard as their own *amour propre*, and Sartre approves:

> If a worker says, 'I shall avoid doing more than the Others, in order not to require the Others to do more than they can, and in order that I shall not be required to do more than I can by an Other', he is already a master of dialectical humanism, not as theory but as practice. (CDR 803)

By the end of the *Critique*, then, Sartre has managed to set the stage for history, if indeed it is the history of class struggle; the antagonists, like two chess players, interpret their own possible moves in terms of the significance the other will attach to them, and vice versa, realizing that each move will rearrange the whole game. The one thing that cannot happen in history is what regularly happens in chess, namely that the players move into an end-game where the remaining moves are all predictable, in which the vanquished adversary has been reduced to the status of inert material obeying objective laws. In History the freedom of the Other is always to be reckoned with, and the only way to deal with it is to deepen one's comprehension of the Other, to grasp his praxis 'as a simple, objective, transcendent temporalization' (CDR 816).

Seven hundred pages earlier Sartre identified a contradiction in the form of binary relation that constitutes struggle: 'it is a totalisation which has to be totalised by what it totalises. It presupposes the complete equivalence of two systems of reference and of two actions; in short, it does not posit its own unity' (CDR 113-14). It was remarked then that the indispensability of a Third for the comprehension of the class struggle would surely be unacceptable to theorists of the revolution. Now he seems to agree: 'for each of the adversaries, this struggle is intelligible; or rather, at this level, it is intelligibility itself. Otherwise, reciprocal *praxis* would in itself have no meaning or goal' (CDR 816). The problem now is whether the Third can actually manage the required totalization after all. Sartre resumes the imperative and hence uncertain tone he adopted in the Introduction to *Search for a Method* and the *Critique*:

> complex events produced by the practices of reciprocal antagonism
> between two individuals or multiplicities must *in principle* be
> comprehensible to the third parties who depend on them without
> participating, or to observers who see them from outside without
> being in any way involved. From this point of view, nothing is fixed
> *a priori*: the investigation has to be continued. (ibid.)

But the end of the book is only two pages away.

That the *Critique of Dialectical Reason* should be unfinished is of course no surprise, and would not be even if it had not been called 'Volume I'. The explanation Sartre offers (in an interview with Jeanson) is a modest and straightforward one: 'in the second part it would be a question, to put it briefly, of explaining what history is: and I consider that I do not know enough history to undertake that' (*Jeanson 1974: 298*). But the *manner* of its being unfinished – its theoretical inconclusiveness and its systematic incompleteness – is troubling for Sartre's philosophical project. He can hardly, one feels, have been quite as much at sea as he appears to be at the point where the argument is cut off. One of the ambiguities that is left hanging is the one just alluded to – whether historical totalization is to be carried out by the participants in the dialectical development or by some Third. A second, and related, ambiguity is whether the totalization is to be achieved on the side of knowledge at the moment when it comes about on the side of being, or whether it can be a matter of rational reflection after the fact, can as it were be recollected in tranquillity. It is one thing to reconstruct Flaubert with a century's hindsight, another to understand the Algerian war while it is in full swing. We know, of course, that the historical totality can never be *finally* totalized, a 'totalized totality' corresponding rather to the old 'in-itself' and hence being incapable of further dialectical development, which in the case of History can never be ruled out. But if we are to take seriously the notion of the dialectic, with which the *Critique* and *Search for a Method* began, then the dialectical intelligibility of History must surely mean, if it means anything, the possibility, not just once but always, not after the fact but in its presence, of grasping the complicated strands of the dialectic and holding on to them long enough to totalize provisionally at least, to see the situation of the moment as the rational outcome of the moments that led up to it, and as rationally related to the whole of which it is a part. This is admittedly a gigantic task, which would by Sartre's own account require a specification of the material environment as the starting-point of the dialectical relation of need, a clear perception of the practico-inert because of its determination of seriality, full knowledge of the projects and intentions of all the relevant Others, whether in series or in groups, and deep comprehension of the class strategies of participants in the struggle which can alone claim to constitute History. A gigantic task, but one that must be possible if the avowed purpose of the *Critique of Dialectical Reason* is not to be decisively vitiated; one also that, according to the original notion of totalization, can only be carried out by an existential subject, and an individual one at that, the concept of a collective subject (except as a subject of praxis) having been declared empty.

For History as a whole (as distinct from some particular episode of it) there might be two kinds of candidate for the position of such a totalizer: he might be a super-historian, of the sort that Hegel felt himself to be in that moment of realization as Napoleon rode through Jena, or he might be a cosmic Subject of History, God himself, perhaps, or the Hegelian Absolute. None of these possibilities is acceptable to Sartre, who is more modest than Hegel and an atheist to boot, so that when he comes, in the very last paragraph of the *Critique*, to talk about History as such he suggests in passing that it is to be thought of as 'totalisation without a totaliser' (CDR 817). Either this means a resolution of the ambiguities stated above in favour of a Third who totalizes after the fact (construing 'totalisation without a totaliser' to mean without one *at the time*, although later on someone capable of the task might come along), or it means abandoning the subjective side of the dialectic altogether, in which case the objective side would inevitably reduce to a play of mechanical determinations, suitable for treatment by positivistic science. The latter Sartre must again find unacceptable, but the former, while consistent with the use he practically makes of dialectical reasoning (to throw light on Flaubert, or the French revolution), concedes to Hegel the chief point of argument from the beginning: philosophy does, after all, come on the scene too late to be of any help.

I leave this problem in suspense, as Sartre does. If we turn now to what the *Critique* offers in the way of a world, following the strategy suggested earlier in the chapter of regarding it as hypothetical, two things are strikingly evident: on the one hand how much it gets in, and on the other how much it leaves out. The regressive movement is complete; it has demonstrated, says Sartre, 'the intelligibility of practical structures and the dialectical relation which interconnects the various forms of active multiplicities' (CDR 817). Within the limits of the work this seems right: it does provide a way of thinking intelligibly and freshly a whole range of social and political phenomena, and the sketch I have given in this chapter has not begun to do justice to the rich and detailed way in which Sartre builds up the social structures of his dialectical field. But if we ask whether this field corresponds at all closely to the world as it is, Sartre's comment about the football match comes to mind: in the real world 'everything is complicated by the presence of the opposite team'. There are other agents in the field of praxis (terrorists, negotiators, environmentalists, madmen, philanthropists) whose simplest moves may muddy the historical waters beyond hope of intelligibility: there are historians themselves, whose investigations and interpretations make an essential difference to subsequent perceptions of events; there are other philosophers (utilitarians, structuralists, critical theorists, not to mention analytic philosophers – and still less *nouveaux philosophes*, who to do Sartre justice were still in their cradles when the *Critique* was written) who will give sharply differing accounts of the principles at work and of the language required to deal with them and of the standards of inference and argument that are required if pronouncements on matters of public importance are to be responsibly made. Sartre has proceeded, since his earliest successes, in relative indifference to the political and philosophical world outside the circle of his chosen concerns, and for those whose formation and preoccupations have been elsewhere this results in a curious sense of unreality when his system is confronted in its entirety.

Nevertheless the system repays study, even when its claims seem excessive and even when it seems to fail totally in its announced intentions. That human beings do not always achieve what they set out to achieve cannot alarm Sartre, for whom the principle of 'loser wins' has always made sense if the stakes are high enough and the game played with sufficient intensity. Sartre's world may not be ours in all its details or even in its outlines, but enough of it is an exact likeness to produce a frequent sense of recognition, which when it occurs is always enlightening. As he himself says of Genet, he 'holds the mirror up to us: we must look at it and see ourselves' (SG 599); the image would be banal if it were not for the fact that what Sartre shows us is often what it might never have occurred to us to look for, and that having seen it nothing can be quite the same again – we have a new sense of freedom, or of responsibility, or of shame at our own bad faith, or of the complexity of private or political life. Sartre is, of course, as is the case with most writers, also holding the mirror up to himself; his last and longest work, to which I turn in conclusion, is a study of a writer who has come to be almost his *alter ego*, Gustave Flaubert.

XI

History and the Universal Singular: Sartre and Flaubert

This final chapter will be brief, in contrast to Sartre's last major work with which it deals. But the philosophical content of *L'Idiot de la famille* ('The Family Idiot'), while far from insignificant, is not in proportion to its bulk. The book does not, like the *Critique of Dialectical Reason*, offer a hypothetical world, which might be this one – it offers, in this world, a hypothetical person, who may be Flaubert. Sartre of course believes that it is Flaubert, although he does not insist as he did in the *Critique* on apodictic certainty; on the one hand he would like the *Idiot* 'to be read as a novel', on the other he 'would like it to be read with the idea in mind that it is true, that it is a *true* novel' (L/S 112). The book announces itself as the sequel to *Search for a Method*; the question with which it opens – 'What can we know of a man, today?' – echoes Sartre's remark in that work about the common aim of Marxism and existentialism, namely a knowledge of man:

> but Marxism has reabsorbed man into the idea, and existentialism
> seeks him everywhere *where he is*, at his work, in his house, in the
> street. We certainly do not claim – as Kierkegaard did – that this real
> man is unknowable. We say only that he is not known. (SM 28)

The project of knowing such a man 'comes down to *totalizing* the information we have about him' (*IF* 7); nothing proves that this is possible – perhaps personality is irreducibly multiple; certainly the available information is heterogeneous and it may add up to no single result. Sartre however is confident; what he wanted to show, he said at the time of the publication of the book, was 'that fundamentally everything can be communicated, that without being God, but simply as a man like any other, one can manage to understand another man perfectly, if one has access to all the necessary elements' (L/S 123). But the man in question must be dead, which answers one of the questions left hanging at the end of the last chapter, at least as far as individual totalizations are concerned: 'it is impossible to totalize a living man' (L/S 122).

The information, in the case of Flaubert, consists largely, of course, of what he wrote. But Sartre does not treat Flaubert's writings as *texts* in the new-critical sense; he 'is completely opposed to the idea of the text' (L/S 123) and draws on the juvenilia and correspondence in search of 'the equivalent of a "psychoanalytic discourse" ' (ibid.). Everything about Flaubert is available for exploration; one goes in and looks around, in a finished life as in an old mill (*'on entre dans un mort comme dans un moulin'* (IF 8)). The method to be applied to the study is of course the progressive-regressive method. It will yield Flaubert, but not, says Sartre, as an individual;

> for a man is never an individual; it would be better to call him a
> *universal singular*: totalized and, in virtue of that, universalized by his
> epoch, he retotalizes it by reproducing himself in it as a singularity.
> Universal by the singular universality of human history, singular by
> the universalizing singularity of his projects, he demands to be
> studied simultaneously from both sides. (*IF 7-8*)

Flaubert, says Sartre, because there has from very early on been a personal score to settle with him, because he is accessible in his writings above all as the author of *Madame Bovary* but also through the juvenilia and correspondence already referred to, because as the originator of the modern novel he is a pivotal figure in contemporary discussions of literature.

Sartre has attached immense importance to the work on Flaubert, which he envisaged as early as *Being and Nothingness*. At the time he conceived of it as case study in existential psychoanalysis,

> a method destined to bring to light, in a strictly objective form, the
> subjective choice by which each living person makes himself a person;
> that is, makes known to himself what he is. ... This psychoanalysis
> has not yet found its Freud. At most we can find the foreshadowing
> of it in certain particularly successful biographies. We hope to be able
> to attempt elsewhere two examples in relation to Flaubert and
> Dostoevsky. (BN 574-5)

(As far as I have been able to discover nothing came of the second project.) By the time of *Saint Genet* a Marxist component had been added to the method, although Sartre was perhaps less confident of its adequacy. At the end of that book he says: 'I have tried to do the following: to indicate the limit of psychoanalytic interpretation and Marxist explanation and to demonstrate that freedom can account for a person in his totality' (SG 584). *Search for a Method* brought the existentialist and Marxist interests into balance and relegated psychoanalysis to the status of an 'auxiliary discipline' in the process of totalization. The *Critique*, as we saw earlier, was a way of working out the philosophical problems unearthed by digging into the social origins and historical setting of Flaubert, who appears in it as 'a small landowner outside Rouen' (CDR 754). After the *Critique* Sartre worked almost exclusively on Flaubert, and the project became for him the one he hoped to see through to the end: 'I told myself that I couldn't go on abandoning my projects in the middle. . . . I decided that for once in my life I would have to finish something' (L/S 110). The question to which finishing the book was to provide an answer was precisely the question of the relation of a writer to the particular works he produces: why *Madame Bovary* and not some other novel, given that Flaubert in his own eyes at least was not writing on his own account but *as a writer*, that is to say a practitioner of a pure Art? 'That is what we shall try to decide in re-reading Madame Bovary', says Sartre (*IF* 3:665). The *explication de texte* of the novel projected as the fourth volume of *L'Idiot de la famille* was in fact to be the fruition, at last, of the progressive part of the method; having in the first three volumes situated Flaubert exhaustively with respect to his family, his epoch, his education and his acquaintances, and shown the manner of his neurotic life and how this established itself, Sartre took himself to be in a position to replay, as it were, the sequences of determinations that led to the project of *Madame Bovary* and to its realization.

In its audacity this enterprise has something in common with the fantasy in chapter IX about the experimental recreation of the French revolution: Sartre is resolved to make this the totalization *par excellence*. What is its value for a study of his philosophy? He himself takes it to be a philosophical rather than a scientific work.

> 'Scientific' would imply rigorous *concepts*, As a philosopher I try to be rigorous with *notions*. The way I differentiate between concepts and notions is this: A concept is a way of defining things from the outside, and it is atemporal. A notion, as I see it, is a way of defining things from the inside, and it includes not only the time of the object about which we have a notion, but also its own time of knowledge. In other words, it is a thought that carries time within itself. (L/S 113)

And this time is double: it is the time of the production of a certain character – say passivity, for Sartre the great key to Flaubert – and it is the time of living it. But even Hegel, for whom as we saw earlier *Vorstellung* is less abstract and more informal than *Begriff*, would not have considered that *Vorstellung* required the kind of mimetic representation of the temporality of its object that Sartre seems to engage in in the *Idiot*: for the reader who undertakes the somewhat daunting task of working through its

2,800 pages the book sometimes feels as if it is quite as long as the life with which it deals.

And the book is a life, a biography, not a work of philosophy. (It might be looked upon as a philosophical exercise – the working out in practice of something Sartre claims to be philosophically feasible, namely the total characterization of a life with respect both to what produced it and to what it produced, its historical determination and its existential project.) But it should not be ignored by students of Sartre's philosophy, because while it contains no systematic development of anything new it incorporates a number of philosophical essays which, if excerpted and bound, would make a good-sized book in philosophy in their own right. These constitute, as it were, peaks in an extended landscape; there is a second level of philosophical interest, in the application to Flaubert's case of Sartre's theoretical categories – imagination and the *analogon*, negation, seriality, totalization, etc. – but this in turn is embedded in a mass of anecdotal detail about Flaubert and his minor works that will have little or no interest for philosophers as such: the fact that he masturbated, that he looked at himself in mirrors, that his father cried or did not cry (Sartre has conflicting opinions in different parts of the book), along with questions about the exact nature of his malady, whether the crisis of Pont-l'Évêque was between 20 and 25 January 1844 or before 15 January, and so on. Sartre's almost obsessive interest in Flaubert sprang apparently less from intuitive sympathy (indeed he claims to have been quite unsympathetic at first and to have arrived eventually at empathy rather than sympathy) than from some objective contrasts – Flaubert's mother was not loving, Sartre's mother was; Flaubert had a dominant father, Sartre had no father, and so on – together with an affinity arising from the fact that Sartre had been brought up to belong in Flaubert's time rather than his own: he describes his grandfather's influence on him as that of

> a man of the nineteenth century . . . foisting upon his grandson
> ideas that had been current under Louis Philippe. . . . I started off
> with a handicap of eighty years. Ought I to complain? I don't know:
> in our bustling societies, delays sometimes give a head start.
> (WO 40)

There is an echo here of the theme 'loser wins' that has surfaced several times and will again be significant for Flaubert, whose decision to be a writer in a bourgeois family was at once defeat and victory. It is of course Flaubert's status as a writer, and a writer whose writing constituted his private solution to the problem of personal being, that brings him closest to Sartre. For all these reasons one can understand if not welcome the fact that the vehicle for Sartre's last extended philosophical writing should be an even more extended psychological, sociological, and literary study. I shall not attempt to indentify and discuss all the pockets of philosophy it contains, even though many of them show the philosopher as writer at the top of his form, but some representative passages in each of the categories described above – the illustration and sometimes the modification of familiar Sartrian positions in terms of Flaubert's life and character, and the digressions on more narrowly philosophical topics stimulated by various turns in the biographical development – deserve attention even in a cursory reading. Flaubert's life is segmented by Sartre into 'constitution', 'personalization', 'fall' or 'crisis', and 'neurosis'. Sartre's concern is to show not only how the circumstances of Flaubert's life *determined* what his personality would become, but also how, at the same time, he *chose* that personality. The powerful father, a doctor caught up in the mechanistic ideology of the positive sciences (to the supplanting of which by the dialectic, as Sartre sees it, he devotes one of his philosophical vignettes, *IF* 73-7); the conventionally religious and conventionally submissive mother, more like an elder sister to her children than like a parent, loving them in her husband 'as Christians love one another in God' (*IF* 95) but not with maternal warmth; the conventionally successful elder brother, who had already won all the prizes at school by the time Gustave arrived – all this produced in Flaubert his passivity, his femininity, his hebetude, his '*bêtise*'. The conflict of the two ideologies, that of the father and that of the mother, put him in a classical situation of internal discomfort; convinced by the one and attracted by the other, he played the role of the passionately theological atheist described in *The Words*, with the complication that while he sought the God he knew not to exist, he denied the truth he knew to be valid: 'The truth exists, I recognize it, I believe in it and I am *against* it' (*IF* 532). This is what (in part at least) drove him to the imaginary and hence to literature:

> Gustave justifies his mission simultaneously through Being and through Non-being: the imagination is prophetic, it catches the Truth, that is to say Being, *before* Science and *better* than Science; imagination is the Nothingness at the heart of being, it is Negation and Failure as futile testimony to an undiscoverable Elsewhere.
> (*IF* 592)

But the imagination, as we have seen, is not only a means of projecting a compensatory metaphysics on to a world that seems to be under attack from scientific reductionism – it may also be an escape-route from a subjectively intolerable situation. Gustave, like Lucien in 'The Childhood of a Leader', finds that he is constituted as 'an expectation of others'; the difference is that he is not equal to his expectation. He chooses, therefore, to be passive, apparently stupid, 'absent', to indulge in dreams rather than engage in rational action (*IF* 372), to become unreal. (Sartre uses two distinct terms for this denial of the real, '*déréalisation*' and '*irréalisation*', the former a process, the latter an achievement.) He gives himself over, in other words, to a life of the imagination; he 'desituates' himself, refusing to be localized anywhere (*IF 560-1*). But a curious thing happens when the imagination is exploited for the purposes of flight from reality; Sartre testifies to his own experience of it when France was overrun by the Germans in 1940: 'it was laughable, it wasn't true. In fact, I then understood, *it was I* who was becoming imaginary, for the lack of a response adapted to a specific and dangerous stimulus' (*IF 666*). Gustave, then, finds his own personality elusive; instead of recognizing an I he looks for the He of whom the others are making fun (*IF 776*). He comes to see (although, as Sartre points out, he himself would hardly have put it in these terms) 'that his objective being is that of a living centre of unrealization [*déréalisation*]' (*IF 792*). This remark of Sartre's comes at the end of a brief essay in aesthetics in which the art object is defined as a 'real and permanent centre of unrealization [*irréalisation*]' (*IF 786*); this definition is an extension of the notion of the *analogon*, and Sartre's treatment of it constitutes in my view an important contribution to the philosophy of art, the 'practico-inert of the imaginary', which deserves development by other philosophers in this domain.

Flaubert's relation to his own life is therefore anomalous. Very early on he grasped the principle of totalization in an extreme form, considering, according to Sartre, that his life was actually finished at every moment, that he had completed its course from youth to age. If anyone had asked the young Gustave what he thought of his life, Sartre is convinced that he would have replied ' "You've come at the right moment: it's just over, I who reply to you am old, am dead" ' (*IF 195*). But this meant that the for-itself as *project* had no sense; hence the passivity already referred to. The future was not something to be *made*, it could only be *suffered* (*IF 598*). Sartre draws attention to the undoubted fact that philosophical and psychological and literary studies of the emotions have tended to give a privileged place to those which are active;

> hardly any room is made, on the other hand, for grief, for panic, for rage: they happen nevertheless, cutting out our legs from under us, paralyzing our tongues, relaxing our sphincters; pushed to the extreme we lose our sense, and fall in a heap at the feet of the sworn enemy we would have wished to murder. (*IF 45*)

(This is exactly what happened to Flaubert in the 'crisis' at Pont-l'Évêque; the feet at which he fell were those of his elder brother Achille.) There are in fact two ways in which totalization can be undertaken, one a form of integration, the other a form of disintegration: either we build actively on the momentum of the lived (the *vécu*), on what the world has made of us (not 'rendering back completely what our conditioning has given us', to use a formulation from an earlier chapter), or we dissipate it in a kind of spiralling to earth like that of an aeroplane without power.

The existential problem is to find a way of grasping the arbitrariness of the given and making it into a project, of turning chance into necessity, to use a phrase that has become familiar in more recent years through the work of Monod: 'to take original contingency as the final end of constructive rigour' (IF 60). Flaubert finds such a way eventually, after his downward spiral and the literal fall at his brother's feet; he finds it neurotically, but in the process makes himself one of the world's great writers. Every person, says Sartre in effect, is the solution to such an equation, the equilibrium of a regressive movement and a progressive, and it has become a common-place that the neurotic solution may be more creative than the 'normal' one; in the third volume of the *Idiot* there is an implicit contrast between the cases of Leconte de Lisle and Flaubert in which the healthy art of the former fails completely to reach the level of the neurotic art of the latter.

In Sartre's example of 'unrealization' given above the arrival of the Germans was a matter of laughter. The role of laughter in Flaubert's formation is central; Sartre suggests that the comic is a masochistic form to the extent that it involves a kind of self-mockery and contributes to a division between the real and the unreal on the wrong side of which we may find ourselves ('it was I who was becoming imaginary'). His essay on the subject of laughter (IF 811-24) is one of the most brilliant of the philosophical asides in the *Idiot* and makes a contribution to the analysis of the concept of humour which stands easily alongside those of the major figures in this admittedly rather sparsely populated field – Bergson, Schopenhauer, Freud. Sartre's view is that laughter is essentially conser-vative (and when one thinks of it, the most damning feature of revolu-tionaries, as a rule, is their humourlessness), and that it is a phenomenon of seriality; essentially collective, it directs our joint attention to an exterior object and at the same time unites us, in Otherness to be sure, as belonging on the side of what is not laughed at. So laughter, instead of being an attack on the serious, as we might be tempted to think, is in fact a means of defending it. But if the object of laughter turns out to be ourselves then it contributes to our own expulsion from the seriality. Flaubert found himself immensely funny, and projected an *alter ego* in the form of the *Garçon*, a larger-than-life comic figure invented for the benefit of his school friends, whose exploits led to uncontrollable hilarity. But for Flaubert himself, as for many professionally comical people, Sartre suggests, there was a sharp edge to all this humour; it represented a form of self-refusal and contributed to his pre-neurotic unrealization.

After his crisis Flaubert takes on a new relation to the world – a neurotic one, but as we have seen a solution to the existential problem and the realization of a project which would eventually produce *Madame Bovary*. The question then becomes one of the objective conditions of his career as a writer, the historical setting which determines the point of insertion of this project into the world. In the third volume of the *Idiot*

- written some time after the first two and therefore opening, in characteristically Sartrian fashion, with a great deal of reflection that has little directly to do with Flaubert, which plays the role with respect to this last volume that the *Critique* played with respect to the first two, namely of relieving the philosophical pressure, as it were, getting rid of the incipient hernia – Sartre spends a great deal of time on the ideology of the eighteenth and nineteenth centuries and on the historical conditions in France before and after 1848. He pays special attention to the 'Art for Art' movement, which he explains in terms of a double alienation, of art from science and of art from society. We have seen the conflict between the 'two ideologies', science and religion; art was a way of grasping truth which was at once non-reductive and ahistorical, which transcended both ideologies and was misanthropic, disengaged, autonomous and imaginary (*IF 411-12*). Again his grasp of the situation is masterly, although critical commentary on it should properly come from historians of art rather than from philosophers. The philosophically important contributions of the third volume are in my view two: Sartre's treatment of the notion of the 'objective spirit' and his reconsideration at the end of the first half of the book of the nature of history.

The notion of the 'objective spirit', or what has sometimes been called in English the 'spirit of the age', is as Sartre rightly points out a highly suspect one, smacking of idealism; but it is one of his virtues to have insisted on the reality of concepts which have historical import, be they valid or invalid in themselves, and to have looked for an interpretation of them in other and more acceptable terms. In the case of the objective spirit he finds quite simply that it is nothing other than 'culture as practico-inert', that is to say the accepted formulations of the truth about man and the world that the inhabitants of the culture in question find at hand and operative in much the same way as the newspaper or the post office. (This notion of culture as practico-inert constitutes an alternative, and in my view far superior, solution to the nest of problems taken up by Popper in his *Objective Knowledge*; the hypothesis of a 'third world' which is 'superhuman' (Popper 1972: 159) makes heavy metaphysical weather of something which, construed in terms of our experience of traces left in the world of things by our predecessors, can be straightforwardly accounted for by his worlds 1 and 2. The apparently objective novelty of third-world problems is begotten upon the practico-inert by new praxis – but this argument belongs elsewhere.) The Art-Neurosis of Flaubert and others is a manifestation of the objective spirit. Literature, at about this time, becomes a dominant feature of the practico-inert; Sartre has penetrating insights into the social situation and role of readers and writers which deserve, again, serious consideration on the part of literary theorists (see especially *IF 3:50-107*). But what Sartre realizes here more clearly than ever, and what will lead us into the final reconsideration of the nature of history, is that the 'objective spirit . . . exists *in act* only through the activity of men and, more precisely, through that *of individuals*' (*IF 3:50*).

History means, it goes without saying, the history of humanity. This concept is familiar and it seems plausible; in its light the Marxist concept of historical materialism seems to make sense as an objective principle, presiding over the collective adventure of mankind, the 'totalization without a totalizer' to which Sartre had recourse at the end of the *Critique*. Not for nothing is the French Communist newspaper called *L'Humanité*. Unfortunately, as Sartre now admits (and as he has really known all along), there is no such thing as Humanity.

> In other words Humanity *is not* and corresponds diachronically to no concept; what exists is an infinite series whose principle is recurrence, defined precisely by these terms: man is the son of man. For this reason history is perpetually finished, that is to say composed of broken-off sequences each of which is the *divergent* continuation (not mechanically but dialectically) of the preceding one and also its transcendence towards *the same* and *different* ends (which assumes that it is at once *distorted* and *conserved*). (IF 3:436-7)

Now however there is only one candidate for the role of totalizer, namely anyone at all who takes upon himself the task of understanding the destiny of his epoch. 'The result of this is that an epoch can come to completion in an individual well before it comes to an end socially' (*IF 3:443*). Flaubert is such an individual (even if, in the preface to the first volume, Sartre could say that 'a man is never an individual' – one can perhaps forgive such inconsistencies of emphasis in a work of such magnitude), in whom nineteenth-century France finds, on more than one occasion, its epochal culmination. But individuals are multiple: 'the epoch *makes itself* as the totalization of a society in opposing itself to itself through thousands of particular incarnations which struggle among themselves for survival' (ibid.). History is never *one*, it is a matter of collective praxis which remains distributive; there cannot be a totalization without a totalizer. But it may be made one through the effort of such a totalizer, who succeeds in capturing it, perhaps in a single work, perhaps a work of literature, perhaps *Madame Bovary* itself.

It is appropriate to leave Sartre where *L'Idiot de la famille* breaks off: he is about to read *Madame Bovary*, the most complete expression not only of its epoch but of the writer who in his turn was the most complete expression, for Sartre at any rate, of what the writer is, and hence of what human beings are. The inscription at the end of the Sartrian corpus is, as was to be expected, 'to be continued'. But as Sartre himself has said of his last unfinished work, the fact that he will never finish it 'does not make me so unhappy, because I think I said the most important things in the first three volumes. Someone else could write the fourth on the basis of the three I have written' (L/S 20). Anyone, that is to say, can read *Madame Bovary* as well as Sartre could have read it, on condition of doing or at any rate following the kind of work that Sartre has done. This in the end is the hallmark not only of his reading but of his philosophy: it is accessible to everyone. By this I do not mean that what may be called 'the philosophy of Jean-Paul Sartre' is accessible to everyone or even anyone without effort; I mean that philosophy, for him, is accessible to everyone, it is not the province of a professional elite but an engagement with a condition which is common to all. Professional philosophy, for that matter, may in particular cases serve as just the kind of neurotic solution to an existential problem that literature and the imagination provided for Flaubert; there is a sense in which Sartre invites us to think this of his own philosophy, and indeed of his writing in general (see for example SBH 14), but it would be fair to do so only on condition that we considered the possibility equally in our own case. Sartre's own views, it is true, sometimes seems particularly vulnerable to such an interpretation; it would be easy to caricature him as the philosopher who maintained that men relate to the world through nausea, to one another through shame, to the social world through terror, and to work through neurosis. Yet those are ways, among others, in which we do relate to these things; in pointing them out Sartre does not belittle the human race. Nor does he ever exalt it. He realizes, as we have just seen, the radical plurality of the human, but it is a plurality of equals – at the end of *The Words* what remains is 'a whole man, made of all men and equal to them all and to whom anyone is equal (*que vaut n'importe qui*)' (MO 214). Sartre places himself, as he places Flaubert, as he would place every one of us, at the centre which is everywhere (to echo a much earlier tradition), the existential place of the universal singular.

Bibliography

Writers on Sartre, although they have an immense task of reading, have their work simplified for them in one important respect – they can dispense with bibliographies of the usual kind, because these have been prepared exhaustively by others. My own bibliography will therefore fall into two parts, both relatively brief: first the essential information about the standard bibliographies themselves, second the usual bibliographical details of works actually cited in the body of the book.

I *Bibliographical Sources*

A *for works by Sartre*

Michel Contat and Michel Rybalka, *Les Écrits de Sartre*, Paris, NRF/Gallimard, 1970. This volume includes a chronology, an annotated bibliography (of more than 500 items) up to 1969, and two appendices, one giving details of films made on the basis of Sartre's work, the other reproducing more than 200 pages of unpublished or out-of-print material. It has been translated as:

Michel Contat and Michel Rybalka, tr. Richard C. McCleary, *The Writings of Jean-Paul Sartre*, Evanston, Illinois, Northwestern University Press, 1974. Two volumes (vol. 1, *A bibliographical Life*; vol. 2, *Selected Prose*). For the English version the bibliography up to 1969 has been revised and new material added to bring the cut-off date to 1973.

B *for works about Sartre*

François Lapointe and Claire Lapointe, *Jean-Paul Sartre and His Critics: An International Bibliography (1938-1975)*, Bowling Green, Ohio, Philosophy Documentation Center, 1975. This is an unannotated bibliography of more than 5,000 items.

II *List of Works Cited*

de Beauvoir, Simone (EAM), tr. Bernard Frechtman, *The Ethics of Ambiguity*, Philosophical Library, New York, 1948.

de Beauvoir, Simone (*FA*), *La Force de l'âge*, Gallimard/NRF, 1960.

de Beauvoir, Simone (FC), *Force of Circumstance*, tr. Richard Howard, G. P. Putnam, New York, 1964.

de Beauvoir, Simone, (POL), tr. Peter Green, *The Prime of Life*, World Publishing, Cleveland and New York, 1962.

Cassirer, Ernst (1946), tr. Suzanne K. Langer, *Language and Myth*, Harper, New York.

Contat, Michel and Rybalka, Michel (*ES*), *Les Écrits de Sartre*. (See part I of bibliography.)

Contat, Michel and Rybalka, Michel (WS), tr. Richard C. McCleary, *The Writings of Jean-Paul Sartre*. (See part I of bibliography.)

Engels, Friedrich (1978), ed. Robert C. Tucker, *The Marx-Engels Reader*, 2nd ed., Norton, New York.

Foucault, Michel (1970), tr. anonymous, *The Order of Things*, Pantheon Books, New York.

Foucault, Michel (1972), tr. A. M. Sheridan Smith, *The Archaeology of Knowledge*, Pantheon Books, New York.

Hegel, G. W. F. (1952), tr. T. M. Knox, *Philosophy of Right*, Clarendon Press, Oxford.

Hegel, G. W. F. (1975), tr. William Wallace, *Logic* (part I of the *Encyclopedia of the Philosophical Sciences*), Clarendon Press, Oxford.

Hegel, G. W. F. (1977), tr. A. V. Miller, *Phenomenology of Spirit*, Clarendon Press, Oxford.

Heidegger, Martin (1964), tr. John Macquarrie and Edward Robinson, *Being and Time*, SCM Press, London.

Hempel, C. G. (1965), *Aspects of Scientific Explanation and Other Essays in the Philosophy of Science*, Free Press, New York (Collier-Macmillan, London).

Husserl, Edmund (1931), tr. W. R. Boyce Gibson, *Ideas*, Allen & Unwin, London.

Husserl, Edmund (1960), tr. Dorion Cairns, *Cartesian Meditations*, Martinus Nijhoff, The Hague.

Jeanson, Francis (1974), *Sartre dans sa vie*, Seuil, Paris.

Kant, Immanuel (1933), tr. Norman Kemp Smith, *Critique of Pure Reason*, Macmillan, London.

Kierkegaard, Søren (1944), tr. David F. Swenson and Walter Lowrie, *Concluding Unscientific Postscript*, Princeton University Press.

Kojève, Alexandre (1969), ed. Raymond Queneau, tr. James H. Nichols Jr, ed. Allan Bloom, *Introduction to the Reading of Hegel*, Basic Books, New York.

Kuhn, Thomas S. (1970), *The Structure of Scientific Revolutions*, 2nd ed., enlarged, University of Chicago Press.

Lacan, Jacques (1966), *Écrits*, Seuil, Paris.

Lévi-Strauss, Claude (1950), 'Introduction à l'oeuvre de Marcel Mauss', in Marcel Mauss, *Sociologie et anthropologie*, Presses Universitaires de France, Paris.

Lévi-Strauss, Claude (1966), tr. anonymous, *The Savage Mind*, University of Chicago Press (Weidenfeld & Nicholson, London).

Locke, John (1894), ed. Alexander Campbell Fraser, *An Essay Concerning Human Understanding*, 2 vols, Oxford University Press.

Marx, Karl (1930), tr. Eden and Cedar Paul, *Capital*, J. M. Dent & Sons (Everyman's Library), London.

Marx, Karl (1967), ed. and tr. Loyd D. Easton and Kurt H. Guddat, *Writings of the Young Marx on Philosophy and Society*, Doubleday Anchor Books, New York.

Marx, Karl (1978), ed. Robert E. Tucker, *The Marx-Engels Reader*, 2nd ed., Norton, New York.

Merleau-Ponty, Maurice (1973), tr. Joseph Bien, *Adventures of the Dialectic*, Northwestern University Press, Evanston, Illinois.

Popper, Karl R. (1972), *Objective Knowledge: An Evolutionary Approach*, Clarendon Press, Oxford.

Ryle, Gilbert (1949), *The Concept of Mind*, Hutchinson, London.

Sartre, Jean-Paul (ASJ), tr. George J. Becker, *Anti-Semite and Jew*, Schocken Books, New York, 1948.

Sartre, Jean-Paul (B), tr. Martin Turnell, *Baudelaire*, New Directions, New York, 1950.

Sartre, Jean-Paul (BN), tr. Hazel Barnes, *Being and Nothingness*, Philosophical Library, New York, 1956.

Sartre, Jean-Paul (BEM), tr. John Mathews, *Between Existentialism and Marxism*, Pantheon Books, New York, 1974 (New Left Books, London, 1974).

Sartre, Jean-Paul (CP), tr. Martha H. Fletcher with the assistance of John R. Kleinschmidt, *The Communists and Peace,* with 'A Reply to Claude Lefort', tr. Philip R. Berk, George Braziller, New York, 1968.

Sartre, Jean-Paul (CA), tr. Sylvia and George Leeson, *The Condemned of Altona*, Alfred A. Knopf, New York, 1964.

Sartre, Jean-Paul (CRD), *Critique de la raison dialectique (précédé de Questions de méthode)*, vol. I, *Théorie des ensembles pratiques*, NRF/Gallimard, Paris, 1960.

Sartre, Jean-Paul (CDR), tr. Alan Sheridan-Smith, *Critique of Dialectical Reason, vol. I: Theory of Practical Ensembles*, New Left Books, London, 1976.

Sartre, Jean-Paul (DGL), tr. Kitty Black, *The Devil and the Good Lord*, Alfred A. Knopf, New York, 1960.

Sartre, Jean-Paul (EMO), tr. Bernard Frechtman, *The Emotions*, Philosophical Library, New York, 1948.

Sartre, Jean-Paul (*ETE*), *Esquisse d'une théorie des emotions*, Hermann, Paris, 1960 (original ed. in *Actualités scientifiques et industrielles*, 1938).

Sartre, Jean-Paul (EA), tr. Wade Baskin, *Essays in Aesthetics*, Philosophical Library, New York, 1963.

Sartre, Jean-Paul (*EN*), *L'Être et le Néant: Essai d'ontologie phénoménologique*, NRF/Gallimard, Paris, 1943.

Sartre, Jean-Paul (E), tr. Bernard Frechtman, *Existentialism*, Philosophical Library, New York, 1947.

Sartre, Jean-Paul (*IF*), *L'Idiot de la famille: Gustave Flaubert de 1821 a 1857*, NRF/Gallimard, Paris, 1971 (vols 1 and 2), 1972 (vol. 3 appears as *IF 3*).

Sartre, Jean-Paul (*IN*), *L'Imagination*, Presses Universitaires de France, Paris, 1969 (7th ed.)

Sartre, Jean-Paul (IM), tr. Forrest Williams, *Imagination*, University of Michigan Press, Ann Arbor, 1962 (Cresset Press, London, 1962).

Sartre, Jean-Paul (INT), tr. Joseph P. Fell, 'Intentionality: a Fundamental Idea of Husserl's Phenomenology', *Journal of the British Society for Phenomenology*, vol. 1, no. 2, May 1970.

Sartre, Jean-Paul (L/S), tr. Paul Auster and Lydia Davis, *Life/Situations: Essays Written and Spoken*, Pantheon Books, New York, 1977.

Sartre, Jean-Paul (LPE), tr. Annette Michelson, *Literary and Philosophical Essays*, Collier Books, New York, 1962 (Criterion Books, New York, 1955).

Sartre, Jean-Paul *(MO), Les Mots*, Gallimard, Paris, 1964.

Sartre, Jean-Paul (N), tr. Lloyd Alexander, *Nausea*, New Directions, Norfolk, Connecticut, n.d.

Sartre, Jean-Paul (NYT), 'Sartre Accuses the Intellectuals of Bad Faith', interview with John Gerassi, *New York Times Magazine*, 17 October 1971, pp. 38 ff.

Sartre, Jean-Paul (PI) 'Playboy interview: Jean-Paul Sartre', *Playboy*, vol. 12, no. 5, May 1965, pp. 65 ff.

Sartre, Jean-Paul (PL), tr. J. A. Underwood and John Calder, *Politics and Literature*, Calder & Boyars, London, 1973.

Sartre, Jean-Paul (PSI), tr. anonymous, *The Psychology of Imagination*, Philosophical Library, New York, 1948.

Sartre, Jean-Paul *(RQJ), Reflexions sur la question juive*, NRF/Gallimard, Paris, 1954 (1st ed., 1946).

Sartre, Jean-Paul (RW), tr. Betty Askwith, 'The Responsibility of the Writer', in Haskell M. Block and Herman Salinger, eds, *Creative Vision*, Grove Press, New York, 1960.

Sartre, Jean-Paul (SG), tr. Bernard Frechtman, *Saint Genet: Actor and Martyr*, George Braziller, New York, 1963.

Sartre, Jean-Paul (SBH), tr. Richard Seaver, *Sartre by Himself* (interviews by Alexandre Astruc and Michel Contat), Urizen Books, New York, 1978.

Sartre, Jean-Paul (SM), tr. Hazel E. Barnes, *Search for a Method*, Alfred A. Knopf, New York, 1963.

Sartre, Jean-Paul (*S*), *Situations*, NRF/Gallimard, Paris, I: *Essais critiques*, 1947; II: *Qu'est-ce que la littérature?*, 1948; III: 1959; IV: *Portraits*, 1964; V: *Colonialisme et néo-colonialisme*, 1964; VI: *Problèmes du marxisme, 1*, 1964; VII: *Problèmes du marxisme, 2*, 1965; VIII: *Autour de 68*, 1972; IX: *Mélanges*, 1972; X: *Politique et autobiographie*, 1976.

Sartre, Jean-Paul (SIT), tr. Benita Eisler, *Situations*, George Braziller, New York, 1965.

Sartre, Jean-Paul (SS), tr. Irene Clephane, *The Spectre of Stalin*, Hamish Hamilton, London, 1969.

Sartre, Jean-Paul (*TE*), ed. Sylvie Le Bon, *La Transcendance de l'Ego: Esquisse d'une description phénoménologique*, J. Vrin, Paris, 1972 (copyright 1965; originally published in *Recherches philosophiques* in 1936).

Sartre, Jean-Paul (TE), tr. Forrest Williams and Robert Kirkpatrick, *The Transcendence of the Ego: An Existentialist Theory of Consciousness*, Noonday Press, New York, 1957.

Sartre, Jean-Paul (WA), tr. Lloyd Alexander, *The Wall and Other Stories*, New Directions, New York, 1948.

Sartre, Jean-Paul (WIL), tr. Bernard Frechtman, *What is Literature?*, Philosophical Library, New York, 1949.

Sartre, Jean-Paul (WO), tr. Bernard Frechtman, *The Words*, George Braziller, New York, 1964.

Spiegelberg, Herbert (1965), *The Phenomenological Movement*, 2 vols, Martinus Nijhoff, The Hague.

Wittgenstein, Ludwig (1961), tr. D. F. Pears and B. F. McGuinness, *Tractatus Logico-Philosophicus*, Routledge & Kegan Paul London.

Index

'Morals and Society' (colloquium), 15
Moscow, 138, 141
motion, 88-9
motivation, 115f
motive, 114ff

Napoleon, 186
nature, natural world, 5, 25, 96-7, 152; see also dialectics of nature
nausea, 9, 73-4, 95-7, 107, 198
Nausea, 10-11, 73, 77, 124
necessity, 14, 170
need, 161, 168-9
negation, 43, ch. V passim, 79, 86, 192; constitutive, 102, 162; external, 102, 104; internal, 98, 102-4
négatités, 67, 70, 91
neurosis, 195, 198
Newton, Issac, 105
Nietzsche, Friedrich, 131-2
nihilation, 42, 45, 62, 69, 82, 86, 102, 116
n'importe qui, 24, 97, 110, 121, 198
Nizan, Paul, 9-10
Nobel Prize, 17
No Exit, 12, 14, 98
Nothingness, 42, 66, 69-70, 81ff, 89, 91-2, 112, 116, 129, 193
notion, 133f, 191
nouveaux philosophes, 187
La Nouvelle Revue française (journal), 11

Objective Knowledge (Popper), 196
objective spirit, 196
Ockham, William of, 116
ontological proof, 64-5
oppression, 163, 183
The Order of Things (Foucault), 37
Organization, 177, 179
original sin, 109
Other, ch. VII passim, 155-6, 162-4, 172-4, 176, 181, 183-6
otherness, 97, 167, 172, 175, 181, 195

paradigm, 143
Parain, Brice, 20
Paris, 132
Partre, Jean-Sol, 12
Pascal, Blaise, 28, 149
passion, 115
peace, 137
perception, 32, 34, 44-6, 158
permanent revolution, 2
'Perspectives de sociologie rurale' (Lefebvre), 157

phenomenalism, 5, 61, 64
phenomenology, 5, 8, 11, 38, 41-2, 52-3, 60, 88-9, 95-6, 118, 157
The Phenomenology of Spirit (Hegel), 32
Philip II of Spain, 166
Philosophical Investigations (Wittgenstein), 19, 50
philosophy, domains of, 5-6, 118
The Philosophy of Right (Hegel), 144
Plato, 3, 106, 181
pluralism, 145
Poe, Edgar Allen, 30
poetry, poetic language, 27, 44, 123, 125
Poincaré, Henri, 88
police, 182
politics, political theory, 15, 28-9, 121, 129, 133, 142, 156, 159, 164, 179, 187
Popper, Sir Karl, 196
positivism, 96, 134, 150-1, 186
possibility, 76, 83, 100
practico-inert, 25, 110, 157, 165, 168, 171-2, 174-6, 182-4, 186, 194, 196
praxis, 127-9, 133, 137, 139, 146, 148-9, 155-6, 158, 161, 164-5, 168, 170, 172-3, 175-9, 182, 184, 186
pre-reflective cogito, 40, 89, 151
pride, 97
primitive accumulation, 169
'The Prisoner of Venice', 27
private property, 167
The Problem of Method, see Search for a Method
process, 173
progressive method, 41, 49, 158, 195
progressive-regressive method, 41, 157
project, 79, 112, 114, 116-17, 131, 153-5
proletariat, 132, 138-9, 167, 183-4
property, 156, 167
prose, 25, 27
The Provincial Letters (Pascal), 28
La Psyché (unpublished), 37
psychic body, 107
psychic temporality, 89
psychoanalysis, 38-9, 116, 123, 130, 148, 154, 159, 190
psychology, 11, 38, 106
The Psychology of Imagination, 11, 41ff
public opinion, 173, 183

quarks, 83
'Questions of Method', see Search for a Method